D0272340

JEWISH WRY

Jewish Literature and Culture
Series Editor, Alvin Rosenfeld

JEWISH WRY

Essays on Jewish Humor

EDITED WITH AN INTRODUCTION BY
SARAH BLACHER COHEN

INDIANA UNIVERSITY PRESS
BLOOMINGTON AND INDIANAPOLIS

"The Nature of Jewish Laughter," by Irving Howe, originally appeared in *American Mercury* 72(1951): 211–19. Reprinted by permission of the author.

"Jewish Humor and the Domestication of Myth," by Robert Alter, from Harvard English Studies, 3, *Veins of Humor,* ed. Harry Levin (Cambridge: Harvard University Press, 1972), pp. 255–68. Reprinted by permission of the author, the Harvard English Department, and Harvard University Press.

"On Sholom Aleichem's Humor," by Meyer Wiener, from *Prooftexts* 6(1) January 1986, 41–54. Reprinted by permission of *Prooftexts* and The Johns Hopkins University Press.

"Laughtermakers," by Albert Goldman, from *Next Year in Jerusalem,* ed. Douglas Villiers. Copyright © 1975, 1976 by Douglas Villiers Publisher Ltd. Reprinted by permission of Viking Penguin, Inc.

Manufactured in the United States of America

Library of Congress Cataloging-in-Publication Data

Jewish wry.

   (Jewish literature and culture)
   Bibliography: p.
   Includes index.
   1. Jewish wit and humor—History and criticism.
2. Jews in literature.   I. Cohen, Sarah Blacher.
II. Series.
PN6149.J4J48   1987   809.7'35203924   86-45045
ISBN 0-253-33185-4

1 2 3 4 5   91 90 89 88 87

TO THE MEMORY OF MY BROTHER, DAVE BLACHER

CONTENTS

ACKNOWLEDGMENTS

The comic gives us the strength to bear life's inevitable adversities. The completion of this book on Jewish humor helped keep my comic spirit aloft when it was in danger of sinking. I wish to thank the contributors of this volume whose essays buoyed me up and confirmed Nietzsche's view that "the most acutely suffering animal on earth invented laughter."

Let me also express my gratitude to the finders and facilitators who helped make this book a reality: Alvin Rosenfeld, the distinguished editor of the distinguished Indiana University Press series, *Jewish Literature and Culture;* Robert Mandel and John Gallman, press directors of wisdom and loyalty; Kathleen Ketterman, a promotions manager of ingenuity and imagination; Jo Burgess, a knowledgeable copy editor; Cheryl Reeves, a meticulous bibliographer; Barbara Day, an accurate typist; my sister, Bess Rosen, and Rose Rotenberg, generous retrievers of "dirty" Sophie Tucker and Belle Barth records; David Kaplan, insightful prober and whimsical prodder; John Caldwell, witty cartoonist and genial tolerator of perfectionists; and the beneficient State University of New York at Albany which helped pay for editorial costs.

A Yiddish proverb states, *"Leid macht auch lachen."* I am particularly indebted to my husband, Gary, who shared both the sorrow and laughter and helped me give birth to another book.

Finally, I wish to dedicate this book to the memory of my brother, Dave Blacher, a man of formidable courage and boundless love whose irrepressible humor kept his family laughing in the best and worst of times.

JEWISH WRY

INTRODUCTION

The Varieties of Jewish Humor

SARAH BLACHER COHEN

Jewish humor, born out of the vast discrepancy between what was to be the "chosen people's" glorious destiny and their desperate straits, is a relatively modern phenomenon. In the eighteenth century it scantly surfaced in the witty poetry of Heinrich Heine, who, caught in the emancipation, captured the comic irony of the German Jews straddling two worlds—the traditional one, dead, no longer serving their needs, and the enlightened one, alive, but restricting their entry. But in nineteenth century Eastern Europe that world was not dead, so Jewish humor became the plentiful emotional baggage which Jews from the West transported with them to their Russian and Polish villages. While they also carried their Torahs, Talmuds and rabbinic commentaries, they looked to them as repositories of sacred law, not profane laughter.

This is not to say these texts were devoid of any laughter. Despite Alfred North Whitehead's claim that the "total absence of humor from the Bible is one of the most singular things in all literature," or Salo Baron's equation of the biblical period with his "lachrymose conception of Jewish history,"[1] scholars have isolated comic fragments in the Bible. They have identified puns in the Tower of Babel section of Genesis and the Joseph story in Exodus; they have located trickster motifs in Abraham's passing Sarah off as his sister, in Laban's saddling Jacob with Leah rather than Rachel, and in Jacob's stealthily purchasing Esau's birthright with a mess of pottage. They have commented on the

1

miraculous jest played upon Sarah when at age ninety she bore a son, named Isaac, based on the Hebrew word "to laugh." They have singled out the satire and irony of the prophets, who chastised the stiff-necked Israelites for succumbing to pagan temptations, for defiling their God-given images.

The Talmud, too, has its remnants of humor. Though it contains the injunction, "All that is not Torah is levity," it still possesses its unique word play, the witty intricacies of *pilpul* (disputation), farcical animal fables, and various forms of ideological comedy. Similarly, the rabbis of the medieval period thought humor frivolous, yet they occasionally employed *sihat hullin,* light talk or banter, in their explication of the law. They permitted raucous Purim celebrations, the irreverence of *badchens* or wedding jesters, and mirthful stories told by traveling preachers. Yet humor was not the main component of their world view.

The Yiddish humor of the late nineteenth century principally defined the identity of the Jews of Eastern Europe. The butt of a cruel joke, they found that God had singled them out to be a light unto the nations, but had given them a benighted existence. Powerful in interpreting the vast complexities of sacred texts, they were powerless in their dealings with brainless peasants. Priding themselves on the cohesiveness of their private world, they felt isolated from the world at large. To cope with the anxiety produced by these incongruities, they created a humor in which laughter and trembling were inextricably mingled.

Moreover, this "folk community of garrulous intellectuals and hair-splitters cut off from nature and animal life, intrigued only by the oddities of the human and the divine, taking as its frame of reference the complex structure of ghetto society, ghetto life and Jewish tradition" created the "humor of an intelligence running amok . . .," a humor of "rebellious rationalism."[2] Theirs was a cerebral comedy of errors which showed the limitations of strained thinkers—the circularity of their reasoning, their faulty premises and absurd proofs. The caricatures they gave rise to were the Chelm Fools, those harebrained sages so consumed with their wrong-headed thought processes that they totally lost touch with mundane reality. The ghetto-dwellers also became the subject matter of a unique set of jokes which exposed their mental follies rather than their physical flaws.

The "characteristic strategy" of these jests was, according to

Irving Howe, "an irony which measured the distance between pretension and actuality, held it up for public inspection and then made of it the salt of self-ridicule." The following joke illustrates this point.

> Chernov, the *shnorrer* of Petrograd, had a very wealthy patron who, for some obscure reason, had taken a liking to the nervy little beggar. Each year he would give Chernov a handsome stipend—never less than 500 rubles.
>
> One year, however, the rich man gave him only 250 rubles.
>
> "What is the meaning of this?" demanded the insolent *shnorrer.* "This is only half of what you have been giving me!"
>
> "I'm sorry, Chernov, but I must cut my expenses this year," apologized the wealthy man. "My son married an actress and I am paying all the bills."
>
> "Well, of all the *chutzpah!*" roared Chernov, hopping mad. "If your son wants to support an actress, that's his business. But how dare he do it with my money!"[3]

The joke captures the comic reversal of roles whereby the destitute *shnorrer* pretends to be superior to his well-endowed benefactor. Not only is the *shnorrer* ungrateful, but he feels entitled to his rubles because he enables the wealthy man to perform the sacred duty of giving charity to the poor. So smugly accustomed is the *shnorrer* to receiving his fixed dole, that he is outraged at having his funds in any way reduced. The joke mocks his impudence for claiming absolute control over money that is not his.

A similar joke directs its barbs not at the Jew and his flawed relationships with his fellow Jews, but at the Jew and his God. It functions as a form of camouflaged blasphemy, permitting the Jew to give witty expression to his disappointment at divine promises not kept and to comically censure himself for his own hubris at challenging God:

> A traveler, arriving in a Galician town, orders a pair of trousers from a Jewish tailor. Three months later he leaves, without the trousers. After seven years he happens to pass through the same place again and, lo and behold, the tailor comes to deliver the trousers. "Well," the traveler exclaims, astounded, "God created the world in seven days—but you took seven years for a pair of trousers!" "True," the Jew agrees, quite unimpressed, "but look at the world—and look at my trousers."[4]

The joke disparages the reliability of the tailor for his failure to keep his word and for his ingenious way of deflecting criticism from himself. But above all, it castigates him for his impudence to see himself as the rival of God, as the better craftsman whose hand-sewn pair of pants is a better piece of handiwork than God's creation. But the joke also finds fault with God for his shoddy workmanship, for his creation of an imperfect world.

The fact that these *shtetl* Jews could so cleverly ridicule themselves and their God prompted Freud to claim that their self-mockery was the most distinguishing feature of Jewish humor. Drawing upon Yiddish wit for some of his examples, he wrote in *Jokes and Their Relation to the Unconscious:* "The occurrence of self-criticism as a determinant may explain how it is that a number of the most apt jokes . . . have grown up on the soil of Jewish popular life. They are stories created by Jews and directed against Jewish characteristics. . . . I do not know whether there are many other instances of a people making fun to such a degree of its own character."[5] Freud attributed the Jews' excessive ridicule of themselves to the excessive aggression they had to conceal to survive in such an inimical society. Their self-directed mirth was a camouflaged form of their masochism. It is as if they had to tell their oppressor, "You don't have to injure us. We'll take charge of our own persecution. And we'll do it more thoroughly than you ever could."

Jewish humor, however, is not only based on the masochistic characteristics of the Jews expressed in their self-critical jokes. It has also been a principal source of salvation. By laughing at their dire circumstances, Jews have been able to liberate themselves from them. Their humor has been a balance to counter external adversity and internal sadness.

The *shtetl* dwellers' attitude toward suffering is a case in point. Instead of valuing the tragic hero for his endurance of intense pain, they adopt as their model of heroism *dos kleine menschele,* the little man who takes suffering in his stride. He derives no ecstasy from agony but shrugs his shoulders at the inevitable misfortunes of life. Consequently, the Jewish comic vision, toughened by perennial troubles, punctures the inflated importance ascribed to suffering. According to Robert Alter, "Jewish humor typically drains the charge of cosmic significance from suffering by grounding it in a world of . . . practical realities." Recalling the Yiddish proverb, "If you want to forget all your troubles, put on a shoe that's too tight," he reminds us that "Weltschmerz begins to seem preposterous when one is wincing over crushed bunions."

This Yiddish proverb is perhaps best illuminated by the following Yiddish joke about painful shoes and the adept way to bear distress:

> Two woebegone talmudic students came to their rabbi and made a shamefaced confession. "Rabbi, we've committed a sin."
> "A sin? What kind of a sin?"
> "We looked with lust upon a woman."
> "May God forgive you!" cried the holy man. "That is indeed a serious transgression."
> "Rabbi," said the students, humbly, "what can we do to atone?"
> "Well, if you sincerely seek penance, I order you to put peas into your shoes and walk about that way for ten days. Perhaps that will teach you not to sin again."
> The two young men went home and did as the rabbi had ordered them. A few days later the penitents met on the street. One was hobbling painfully, but the other walked easily, his manner calm and contented.
> "Is this the way to obey the rabbi?" asked the first student reproachfully. "I see you ignored his injunction to put peas into your shoes."
> "I didn't ignore him at all," said the other cheerfully. "I just cooked them first."[6]

The joke, like the Yiddish proverb cited by Alter, refuses to ennoble suffering. It mocks the talmud student who strictly obeys the super-pious authority figure and willingly subjects himself to harsh punishment. His painful hobbling is seen not as a worthy act of penitence but as a senseless act of masochism. On the other hand, it applauds the ingenuity of the non-masochistic student who obeys the rabbi's directive but cleverly avoids the injurious consequences of it. He has the resource-fulness to crush obstacles and so make them more manageable to tolerate. He thus permits himself the pleasure of lusting after women and pays not too hurtful a price for it.

The joke tells us that in life we must inevitably step upon hard peas, but it also tells us we have the power to transform them or alter our response to them. This response is similar to "the humor of verbal retrieval, the word triumphant over the situation" found in Sholom Aleichem's work. "Not what happens to people is funny, but what they themselves say about it. There is

nothing funny about Tevyeh the dairyman as a character and
nothing funny ever happens to him. What Tevyeh does is to turn
the tables on tragedy by a verbal ingenuity: life gets the better of
him, but he gets the better of the argument."⁷ While more tears
than laughter predominate in the majority of Sholom Aleichem's
stories, he is able to create a comedy of affirmation grounded in
the harsh realities of Kasrilevke, the town of the poor, but cheerful, little people. When the Jews had no national homeland, he
created his own fictional territory fraught with plagues and pogroms. Yet the characters he created, the Tevyehs, the Menakhem-Mendls and the Motls, were able to survive there because
their comic spirit had not been subdued. It contains, writes
Meyer Wiener, "a sort of merriment that comes from having
overcome and tamed the fear of chaos, the fear of a maimed,
confused and falsely-ordered life."

Yet they could not remain in Kasrilevke. To escape persecution, their real life counterparts had to immigrate to America
where 1,300,000 came to the promised land between 1880 and
1915, to form a new beginning. Yet they still carried remnants of
their Yiddish humor with them: humor in which they wryly
deprecated their persecutors and bittersweetly mocked themselves; humor in which their adversaries were dimwitted and
besotted and they, themselves, were incorrigible *schlemiels,
schnorrers* and *luftmenschen* (beggars and men of the air). But
this time they were aliens in a larger, more uncertain world. Cut
off from *shtetl* solidarity, the enemy wasn't so easily identifiable
and friends were not readily available. Longing for the old country and baffled by the new, their marginal status, that is, the
psychological ambiguity of being on the outskirts, prompted
them to make comedy out of constraint. Initially, however, they,
like the Blacks, their fellow outsiders, were the butts of American society's aggressive humor. In pejorative tales and jokes the
dominant culture depicted Jews as avaricious, cunning Shylocks
and Blacks as genial, indolent Sambos. Such comic stereotyping
was designed to keep the minorities in their place, to keep the
"wretched refuse" from polluting the mainstream. But the
"wretched refuse" refused to be wittily swept out of sight. To
alter misconceptions, to sustain their pride and recoup their
powers, both Blacks and Jews retaliated with a hidden form of
protest humor, a response to subordination which Joe Boskin
characterizes as "inwardly masochistic and tragic and externally

aggressive and acrimonious." Just as Blacks employed covert trickster motifs to insult their white opponents, Jewish immigrant humor contained a similar veiled hostility. It was "defensive and private, a reserve for one's own bitter amusement in the homely curses muttered under the breath in Yiddish that the customer or employer couldn't possibly understand. 'Of course, Mrs. Morgan (You should bury your head in the earth like an onion). But naturally, you're absolutely right (You should only swell up like a mountain).' "[8] By concealing the sneer beneath the smile and the grimace beneath the grin, Jews, like Blacks, belittled the towering strengths of the giant majority and elevated their own status in the process.

But gradually as the Jews grew taller in their own eyes and their greenhorn identity was being washed away in the melting pot, their humor became less insular. In their transformation from *Yidn* to Yankees, they became more open and ebullient, more eager to embrace the unknown. In vaudeville and burlesque halls, owned and operated by Jews, the street-trained Eddie Cantor, Georgie Jessel, Sophie Tucker, Al Jolson and Fanny Brice mingled breezy Americanisms with racy Yiddishisms and capitalized on the rich humor of their hyphenated origins. As they sang "Yiddle on Your Fiddle, Play Some Ragtime," or "I'm an Indian" in a Jewish accent or "Mammy" in black-face with cantorial resonance, they became comic universe-changers, "importing into one sphere an entire universe of discourse with all sorts of associations from an entirely different sphere."[9] These Jewish entertainers were not ashamed of their Jewish identity. Fanny Brice's justification for her Jewish routines expressed their general attitude: "In anything Jewish I ever did, I wasn't standing apart, making fun of the race, and what happened to me on the stage is what could happen to them. They identified with me and then it was all right to get a laugh, because they were laughing at me as well as at themselves."[10] But in the later part of the thirties and forties, during the period of the de-Semitization of the arts, Jewish entertainers did not make their ethnic identity paramount. Jack Benny, for example, invented a grotesque stereotype called Schlepperman for his comic scapegoat. He, himself, was tight-fisted with money, but he passed that off as a personal idiosyncracy, not a Jewish trait. Though born Benny Kubelski, he was detached from his people and on occasion made fun of them. When, for example, General Motors recalled

72,000 Cadillacs on the eve of Yom Kippur, Benny quipped: "I've never seen so many Jews walking to the synagogue in my life."[11] The same secularization of self was true for Groucho Marx. Like Karl, another Marx brother, he waged his own comic class struggle against Margaret Dumont, that bastion of WASP respectability. But it was as the aSemitic scapegrace, not as the Jew who, resigning from the Friars, explained that he did not care to belong to a club that accepts people like himself as members.

During the fifties and sixties Jewish entertainers no longer kept a low ethnic profile. A belated pride in the founding of the state of Israel, combined with a profound grief for the loss of their fellow Jews in the Holocaust, prompted them to resurrect their buried Jewish identity and draw upon its wit for many of their routines. So contagious was their material that they infected their own people as well as the gentile public with fits of philo-Semitic laughter. So widespread was their impact that Wallace Markfield describes it as "The Yiddishization of American Humor" with the following results:

> Turn to any TV variety show, await the stand-up comic, and chances are good that he'll come on with accents and gestures and usages whose origins are directly traceable to the Borscht Belt by way of the East European *shtetl* and the corner candy store. His material is a million light years removed from the old-style Bob Hope-type monologue, with its heavy reliance upon a swift sputter of gags plucked from card indices, then updated and localized. It is involuted, curvilinear, ironic, more parable than patter.[12]

Though Zion seemed to have invaded Main Street, Zion was still ill at ease on Main Street. Granted, Sid Caesar, the celebrated TV funny-man of the fifties whose script writer was Mel Brooks, capitalized on the comedy of ethnic incongruity by inserting in his parodies of foreign films such antic Yiddish phrases as *gantze mishpochah* (the whole family), *gehakteh leber* (chopped liver) and *shmateh* (rag) as the stars of a Japanese film and *La Fligl* (the chicken wing) as the setting of a French film. Yet his main concern was producing travesties of Hollywood violence and churning out forms of low comedy. Like Buddy Hackett and Jack E. Leonard, he used Yiddish as the familiar deflater of the exotic, the vulgar leveler of the refined. But this occasional use of Yiddish in no way constituted substantial Jewish-American humor.

"Jewish humor in mid-twentieth-century America," according to Albert Goldman, "was not a gentle, ironic Sholom Aleichem folksiness; nor was it a sophisticated Heinesque intellectual wit; nor was it simply the one-two-three, laff pattern of the professional joke huckster. It was the plaint of a people who were highly successful in countless ways, yet who still felt inferior, tainted, outcast; a people who needed some magic device of self-assertion and self-aggrandizement."

The tainted, outcast spokesman of this people who most used humor as a form of plaint was Lenny Bruce. Though he incorporated some borscht belt routines in his jazz club performances and used Yiddish "like a wet towel in the hands of a locker room bully,"[13] he saw himself performing a higher function. With great flare, he ordained himself a preacher who sought to deliver non-sectarian sermons, to avoid the parochialism of any one religion. Despite his ecumenical pose, however, Bruce was still staunchly Jewish and saw the world divided between "us" and "them," Jews and Christians.

> To me, if you live in New York or any other big city, you are Jewish. It doesn't matter even if you're Catholic: if you live in New York you're Jewish. If you live in Butte, Montana, you're going to be *goyish* even if you're Jewish.
>   . . . Evaporated milk is *goyish* even if the Jews invented it. Chocolate is Jewish and fudge is *goyish*. Spam is *goyish* and rye bread is Jewish.[14]

His obsession with citing the differences between Jews and Gentiles did not blind Bruce to the flaws of each of them. He launched satiric jeremiads at them for their vindictiveness and venality, their racism and anti-Semitism, their prudery and lechery. Though Bruce, corrupted by what he ranted against, did not succeed as a moralist, he did succeed in producing a new kind of humor. "For Bruce," claims Sanford Pinsker, "the need to shock the Jews, to 'go public' with their secrets; the need to *shpritz the goyim,* to exorcise all their 'Southern-dummy-cheapo-drecky dumbbell shit,' all their white bread Protestantism, raised comedy-as-hostility and comedy as tragic catharsis to new levels, and to new expectations."

The title of Bruce's autobiography is *How to Talk Dirty and Influence People* and indeed he was the foulest Jewish stand-up comedian and had the largest repertoire of "tits and ass" jokes.

His audiences were shocked, but not too shocked because they expected such bawdiness to come from the Jewish male. Yet they were not prepared to issue the same sexual license to the Jewish female comic. Nonetheless, there were a group of unkosher comediennes—Sophie Tucker, Belle Barth, Totie Fields, and Joan Rivers—who, by being uproariously brazen, violated the code of gentility observed by respectable Jewish women. But they did not alienate audiences with their breaches of decency. Their Yiddish equivalents of foul language, their accented criticisms of anatomy, their caricatures of Jewish princesses and *yentas* amused rather than offended sensibilities. However, their humor was more than a form of ingratiation, more than a means of entry into a morally restrictive society. An act of camouflaged aggression, it enabled them to mask their hostility so they could mock judgmental society with impunity and improve it in the process. By being unkosher comediennes with a vengeance, they could infuse the bland with the off-color, the sterile with the racy, the staid with the forbidden.

Woody Allen, born Alan Stewart Konigsberg, is just the opposite of the tough, unkosher comediennes and the *macho-maggid* (preacher) Lenny Bruce. His film pose is that of the *schlemiel* figure who is the feckless son, the inept lover and the bungling urbanite. Like his *shtetl* ancestors, he unpacks his heart with whining words and contrasts his Jewish *angst* with gentile equanimity. He juxtaposes his imagination of disaster with their expectation of good fortune. A bundle of Freudian complexes and Kafkan insecurities, he flaunts his ineffectual self to win our pity, yet his inventive exposure of his weaknesses, his clever exaggeration of his vulnerabilities earn our sympathetic laughter. His other film pose is that of the caricature of the Jewish intellectual, replacing the stereotype of what Gerald Mast terms the "money-counting Jew" with the idea-generating one. Appearing in parodies, many of which are ludicrous imitations of conventional film genres and serious works of art, Allen is a master of half-knowledge and semi-enlightenment, the scrambled fragments of the world's great religious and intellectual thought. Yet he undercuts his high-toned philosophizing with the low-toned repartée of daily life as, for example, in *Play It Again, Sam* where Allen (as Allen Felix) attempts to meet a woman as they both admire a Jackson Pollock painting.

Allen: What does it say to you?
Woman: It restates the negativeness of the universe. The hideous lonely emptiness of existence. Nothingness. The predicament of Man forced to live in a barren, Godless, eternity like a tiny flame flickering in an immense void with nothing but waste, horror and degradation, forming a useless bleak straightjacket in a bleak absurd cosmos.
Allen: What're you doing Saturday night?
Woman: Committing suicide.
Allen: What about Friday night?

Here we have a representative sample of Allen's distinctive brand of humor: the juxtaposition of high-brow and low-brow, the sublime and the profane. Allen is, according to Mark Shechner, "the master of comic techniques based on those sudden collisions of perspective: the serious side of himself suddenly brought crashing to earth by the madman in him." This comic clashing of such disparate frames of reference within the individual self is characteristic of the funniest of the Jewish-American novelists, Philip Roth and Stanley Elkin, whose works most resemble those of the stand-up comedians. However, the amalgam of dualities within their writing contains the trivial and the tragic, the parodic and the painful. Alexander Portnoy best expresses these twin effects in his own life: "Spring me from this role I play of the smothered son in the Jewish joke: Because it's beginning to pall a little at thirty-three: And also it *hoits,* you know, there is *pain* involved, a little human suffering is being felt."[15] Jewish jests and Jewish agony are thus the stuff of Roth's fiction, or as he identifies the two influences present in *Portnoy's Complaint,* the stand-up comedy of a Henny Youngman and the "sit-down" comedy of a Franz Kafka. Alan Cooper enumerates the characteristics of these two comic modes as "on the one hand, comic *shtick,* set pieces, one liners, *shpritzes,* rapid changes and juxtapositions of a subject matter; on the other, the extended monologue, 'guilt as a comic idea,' the hero as the butt of some great cosmic joke, contention against some absurd authority."

These same characteristics are featured in Stanley Elkin's work, only his is a Jewish black humor. Many of his characters are physical grotesques who are disfigured, malformed excuses for human beings. In his novel, *The Franchiser* (1980), he calls

them "human lemons, Detroit could recall them." Others are
psychological grotesques whom he categorizes as "criers and
kibitzers," obsessive complainers of monumental griefs and
their opposite: compulsive gloaters of small-scale triumphs.
Alienated from each other, they are similarly alienated from a
God who is an indifferent, comic-strip being, a caricature of a
supreme authority. In his novel, *The Living End* (1979), God is
also a failed vaudeville entertainer who destroys the world because his audience doesn't appreciate him. Yet Elkin prevents us
from having any compassion for this doomed audience. Endow-
ing us with an extra dose of Bergson's "anesthesia of the heart,"
he makes us immune to their cartoon-like suffering, their hor-
rific, yet hilarious plights. Their language is extravagant, alternat-
ing between high-flown fantasy and low-grade fact, between the
grandiose and the insignificant. Yet these mock-heroic Jobs are
not conspicuously Jewish. Though they occasionally employ a
burlesque hall Yiddish, they are not practicing Jews. Even so,
Maurice Charney claims that Elkin creates "a world that is
convincingly Jewish . . . in its spontaneous assumptions, its
feeling that triumph is inexplicably mixed with catastrophe, its
manic urge for the small man through cunning, slyness and
whimsy to conquer the world, its protagonists who speak with
prophetic fervor tinged with neurotic insufficiency."

Though Elkin's humor is ironic and defensive, at times waver-
ing and tentative, it and the other Jewish-American humor we've
examined are firmly established, a highly admired and sought
after commodity by the whole country. This is not the case with
Mordecai Richler's Jewish-Canadian humor. As Canadian and
Jew, he is the doubly alienated minority writer who is forced to
be more caustic in his mockery of the majority. He must contend
with what Michael Greenstein terms a "double marginality." As
a Jew, he is barred from a rigidly stratified society of Canadian
Gentiles and as a Canadian, he is denied acceptance in the
Jewish-American mainstream, which he claims is a "veritable
Yeshiva." What Richler creates then is a Jewish-Canadian comedy of cultural revenge. The lineage of his characters does not go
back to *dos kleine menschele,* the little man of the *shtetl* who
cowered before hostile peasants but to the rogues of Isaac
Babel's *Odessa Tales,* whose vulgar physicality and bold de-
fiance of the law shocked the fastidious Jews and Gentiles alike.
Richler's urban comedy, with its unbuttoned candor, schoolboy

irreverence, and gutter literalness, ridicules the faithful and taunts the squeamish. Uncovering the venal within the venerable, it exposes the earthly fallibility of the seemingly virtuous.

The same bellicose comic vision of Richler's Canadian fiction is found in Israel's popular literature. Gone is the awkward syco-phantic smile of diaspora Jews, their use of self-deprecating humor as social lubricant to ease into the closed gentile society. In its place is an aggressive humor, confident of its muscle and vigor, which lashes out at condescension and bigotry. Yet it is also a humor which can laugh at its own pugnacity, as exemplified in the following joke by Israel's most celebrated humorist, Ephraim Kishon: "You are walking down the street and some-body kicks you from behind. 'Excuse me,' he says, 'I thought you were somebody else.' You say, 'Do you have to kick me?' 'Sir,' he says, 'are you telling me whom I am supposed to kick?' "[16] This joke mocks the Israelis' unchecked hostility, their supreme self-confidence, their stubborn resistance to change, their gleeful impudence. Other jokes by stand-up comedians ridicule Israelis' obsessive complaining about austere conditions while over-indulging in costly luxuries. In a skit called the "Ex-patriates" they take Israeli emigrants to task for their declaration of unswerving loyalty to the country, "promising to return soon—as soon as their three-year-old has graduated from col-lege." This humor thus reflects what Esther Fuchs describes as "the breakdown of the socialist Zionist value system and the growing consciousness of the incongruity between the ideal of the state and its actual reality." Yet this humor, despite its carp-ing criticism, its questioning of suspect values, ultimately is supportive of the state with all its flaws. It enables the state to persevere and survive.

So it is with all of Jewish humor. It has helped the Jewish people to survive, to confront the indifferent, often hostile uni-verse, to endure the painful ambiguities of life and to retain a sense of internal power despite their external impotence. The following anecdote illustrates the Jews' comic vision which en-ables them to cope with their impending doom:

> An Englishman, a Frenchman, an American and a Jew are in the midst of a philosophic discussion. The problem is posed how each would act when it became unmistakably clear that they had only a few hours to live. They hypothesize the situation in which a flood inundates the land, there is no means of escape and they are awaiting

the inevitable end. The Englishman speaks first: "I would open my best bottle of port. Sit and enjoy every sip. Think of the life I've lived, the experiences I've had and let the waters come and take me."

The Frenchman says, "I would drink a great Bordeaux, prepare a *coq au vin,* make love and let the waters overwhelm me thus."

The American is next: He would eat, drink, make love, try to improvise a raft and finally swim until his strength gave out, and he drowned, "fighting to the end."

The Jew says: "I would do all you have described and when the water got over my head, I guess I would have to learn how to live underwater."[17]

The Jews refuse to succumb to the dire circumstances. Abandoning the stance of tragic heroism, they create an alternative to an ennobling death. They learn to fashion their own reality. Though they are often gasping for air in their underwater existence, they somehow manage to survive, for humor is their life preserver.

NOTES

1. Berel Lang, "On the Biblical Comic," *Judaism* (Summer 1962): 249.

2. Irving Kirstol, "Is Jewish Humor Dead?" in *Mid-Century,* ed. Harold Ribalow (New York: The Beechhurst Press, 1955), p. 432.

3. Salicia Landmann, "On Jewish Humor," *Jewish Journal of Sociology* (Fall 1962): 204.

4. Henry D. Spalding, *Encyclopedia of Jewish Humor* (New York: Jonathan David Publishers, 1969), pp. 28–29.

5. Sigmund Freud, *Jokes and Their Relation to the Unconscious,* trans. James Strachey, in collaboration with Anna Freud (New York: W.W. Norton), pp. 111–112.

6. Spalding, *Encyclopedia of Jewish Humor,* pp. 2–3.

7. Maurice Samuel, *The World of Sholom Aleichem* (New York: Schocken Books, 1943), p. 186.

8. Earl Rovit, "Jewish Humor and American Life," *The American Scholar* 36 (Spring 1967): 240.

9. D. H. Monro, *Argument of Laughter* (South Bend: University of Notre Dame Press, 1963), pp. 45–46.

10. Quoted in Norman Katkov, *The Fabulous Fanny: The Story of Fanny Brice* (New York: Knopf, 1953), p. 205.

11. Mary Livingston Benny, *Jack Benny* (Garden City: Doubleday & Co., 1978), p. 235.

12. Wallace Markfield, "The Yiddishization of American Humor," *Esquire* (October 1965): 114.

13. *Ibid.*

14. John Cohen, ed., *The Essential Lenny Bruce* (New York: Ballantine Books, 1967), pp. 41–42.

15. Philip Roth, *Portnoy's Complaint* (New York: Random House, 1969), p. 39.

16. This joke was told by Kishon at the Fourth International Congress of Humor held in Tel Aviv on June 10–14, 1984.

17. Quoted in Kurt Schlesinger, "Jewish Humor as Jewish Identity," *International Review of Psycho-Analysis* (1979): 6.

THE NATURE OF JEWISH LAUGHTER

IRVING HOWE

At the heart of Yiddish literature, often in its most earnest works, one finds Jewish humor—the homely anecdote or joke. It is a remarkable fact that this people of tragic destiny insisted on making laughter a major strand of their folk expression. And their greatest writers—Sholom Aleichem, Peretz, Mendele— based their works on this laughter as a matter of course and without condescension. It bound folk and artist in a tight relationship such as can be found in no other modern culture.

It is not frivolous, therefore, to examine Jewish humor seriously, as art in the raw, as a unique distillation of the sorrows and insights of the race. The opportunity is provided by a recent compilation of Jewish wit called *Röyte Pomerantsen[1] (Red Oranges)*, "transliterated" from Yiddish—that is to say, printed in Latin letters reproducing Yiddish phonetically. The device was employed, the publishers say, to preserve the "untranslatable" flavor for Americans who understand but do not read Yiddish. The volume is a valid introduction to the tight little world of the Russian-Polish ghettoes that persisted for centuries, reached their cultural peak in the last half of the nineteenth century and came to an end in Hitler's slaughterhouses.

The very first joke in this collection shows how revealing folk humor can be:

> You tell a joke to a peasant and he laughs three times: when you tell it; when you explain it; and when he understands it.
> A landowner laughs only twice: when he hears the joke and when you explain it. For he can never understand it.

16

> An army officer laughs only once: when you tell the joke. He
> never lets you explain it—and that he is unable to understand it goes
> without saying.
> But when you start telling a joke to another Jew, he interrupts
> you: "Go on! That's an old one," and he shows you how much better
> he can tell it himself.

Now offhand this anecdote seems merely to express an unattractive sense of group superiority: the Jew is more clever than
anyone else. But take a second look at it and you see that it
contains something more subtle and complex. The anonymous
narrator is really poking fun at the weaknesses of his own people: their intellectual impatience and over-confidence. Though
usually subtle, this persistent self-criticism of Jewish humor
sometimes verges on self-denunciation. This ambivalent unity of
pride and criticism is classically expressed in the Jewish saying,
"We have a God in heaven, thank God; but has he got a people on
earth, God help him!"

The quoted anecdote is a concentrated expression of the relationships between the East European Jews and the social classes
of Tsarist Russia. Nearest to the Jews in social status is the
peasant; with him they have closest dealings and live peacefully
for stretches of time. So though you have to tell the peasant a
joke three times before he understands it, he at least can understand. But the landowner, scorned by the landless Jews even
though they often had to deal with him and seek his protection,
can never understand. And the army officer is most despised of
all: first because he is a professional soldier, a reprehensible
occupation for the Jews, and second because he represents the
Tsarist army which in not-too-distant times used to shanghai
Jewish boys for 25 years of military servitude. So we see that the
degree of comprehension the anecdote grants to the peasant, the
landowner and the officer reflects the attitudes of the Jews to the
social group each personifies.

Of course not all Jewish humor is so heavily laden with such
specific social relevance. Some jokes mock human folly and
vanity in general, as for example one which pits a Greek and a
Jew against each other. They boast of their ancient cultures.

> "Why," says the Greek, "the archaeologists were digging in the
> ruins of Athens and found wires—which shows that my ancestors
> had telegraph!" To which the Jew snorts back in reply: "Huh, that's
> nothing. They were digging in the ruins of Palestine and didn't find
> any wires—which shows that my ancestors had wireless!"

Or to quote another happy anecdote which seems universal in its application and relevance:

> Two Jews get into a furious argument and end up by agreeing to a duel. Next morning at six o'clock one of the Jews is waiting, pistol in hand. A half hour, an hour, an hour and a half go by. The other Jew is not to be seen. Finally, a messenger comes up to the Jew with the pistol and hands him a note from his opponent: "Listen, Joe, if I happen to be late, don't wait for me; go ahead and shoot!"

The majority of the East European Jews were descended from refugees who had fled from the anti-Semitic excesses of the Crusades. These wanderers of the middle ages brought with them a dialect which, though bred in German, was to borrow from many languages, give rise to numerous locutions of its own, and develop its own vocabulary, grammar, idiom and inflection. Between this tongue, Yiddish, and German there are only surface similarities. Where German is heavy and formal, Yiddish is breezy and conversational.

The position of the Jews in the Tsarist empire was always precarious and marginal; they usually lived in tiny villages where their economic function was to conduct petty trade between the peasantry and the towns. These villages were steeped in poverty.

The East European Jews clung tenaciously to their ways: religious customs frozen by centuries of use; isolation from western civilization and indifference to its affairs; condescension towards worldly knowledge and insistence that only in the Holy Books could truly useful knowledge be found. The East European Jews were the last to be attracted by the hope of assimilation.

In this isolated sub-world Hebrew was the language of prayer and study; men felt themselves the spiritual contemporaries of ancient prophets. But in the home and the marketplace Yiddish was the prevalent tongue; it thereby acquired a rich idiom drawn from daily life, which became one of the major ingredients of Yiddish humor.

Disintegrative tendencies often nibble away at a culture before it has reached its peak. When East European Jewry achieved its literary golden age in the nineteenth century, it was already under assault by alien influences: tempting dreams of wealth in America; contagious rationalistic doctrines from western capitals; works of science and literature to seduce youths weaned on the

Holy Books; disturbing doctrines of socialism and atheism. For though the Jews were often the victim of Tsarism, their way of life was inextricably bound up with it; neither could survive in the turbulent air of western capitalism.

This, then, is the world we meet in *Röyte Pomerantsen* and in the stories of Sholom Aleichem. It is a world of tension: half in the past and half in the future; a world of awareness: the self-consciousness of a transitional period; and a world of clashing values and intellectual excitement. And always evident at its base is economic primitivism and squalor.

Strictly speaking, Jewish humor is not humorous. It does not make you laugh uproariously nor does it provoke a carefree guffaw. The usual ingredients of current American humor—stylized insult, slapstick, horseplay, cruel practical jokes—are seldom present in Jewish humor. Rather is it disturbing and upsetting, its phrases dipped in tragedy.

For here was a people which clung to the myth of the Chosen People despite the most extreme adversity and persecution. Despite its pride it was much too realistic not to recognize how grandiose an anomaly was the contrast between its claim and its position. Hence the characteristic strategy of its humor was an irony which measured the distance between pretension and actuality, held it up for public inspection and then made of it the salt of self-ridicule.

Jewish humor is full of acute social observations. The group which struggles along on the margin of history is always in a better position to examine it realistically than the group which floats in mid-stream. But since Jewish humor was conceived as a means of *internal* criticism, it took for granted the poverty and misery which were the people's daily lot. These conditions were obliquely twisted into the materials of humor, but they are still observable in it. For instance:

> In the old days, you no doubt remember, they used to grab children off the streets and send them to the army. Just so long as they weren't married, they were taken at any age. So Jews—being Jews—found a way out. We used to marry off the children at the ages of six and seven. You'd walk along the street and see a husband, barefoot and in shorts, playing marbles. Once a Jew, seeing such a child, asked him why he wasn't at school. The child answered, "I don't go to school anymore, I was married yesterday." So the Jew asked him again, "If you got married yesterday and are now the head of a

family, why aren't you wearing long pants?" The child replied,
"Yesterday I got married, so I wore the pants; today my younger
brother is getting married, so he's wearing the pants."

This is not exactly a lighthearted joke; yet one cannot but feel a
certain admiration for a people which can laugh at these tragic
facts of its own life. We find the same unrelenting realism in
another anecdote which centers around a fabulous character,
Hershl Osstropoler, who does all sorts of hare-brained things and
then offers justifications which make one wonder if his oddities
are not more relevant to life than our common sense.

> Hershl is working as an assistant to a rabbi when a distraught
> woman comes for advice. In the rabbi's absence, he hears her out.
> She complains that her daughter has been in labor for three days and
> still can't give birth. Never at a loss, Hershl tells her to place a
> copper penny on her daughter's navel in order to hasten the birth. A
> few days later the woman comes back and this time the real rabbi is
> present. She throws herself at the rabbi's knees and thanks him for
> the wonderful advice. The copper penny on the navel did the trick:
> the baby came out immediately. Guessing that this was another of
> Hershl's tricks, the rabbi turns to him and sternly asks, "Are you
> crazy unto death? Why a copper penny on the navel?" To which
> Hershl replies, "Listen, rabbi, I figured that if the little pauper saw
> the penny he'd jump right out to grab it."

Beneath Hershl's wisecrack there is an intimate sense of history, of helplessness before its inexorable sequences and yet of
ultimate scorn for its workings. A classical expression of this
attitude is found in another anecdote, one of the many
"Rothschild jokes" which counterpose the fabulously wealthy
Rothschild to clever beggars.

> Two Jewish beggars once went to Rothschild's house for alms. Said
> the first to the second: "You know what? You go inside and I'll wait
> here."
> The second beggar went in and told one of Rothschild's secre-
> taries that he had come for alms. The poor beggar was passed along
> from secretary to secretary; slips of paper were filled out about his
> request; and finally after an hour of being shunted from office to
> office, the bewildered beggar reached the chief secretary. But when
> he got to the chief secretary's office, the beggar was brusquely told
> to beat it: no alms today.
> As the beggar stepped out of Rothschild's house, he was asked by
> his companion, "Well, what did you get?"
> "Get?" replied the beggar, "I got nothing, of course. But I must

say that never in my whole life have I seen such a system as they have at Rothschild's."

Implicit in this joke is a sly scorn for wealth and its bureaucratic apparatus together with a recognition of the need to concern oneself with them. A similar attitude is expressed in another Rothschild joke:

> A Jew once came to Paris where a friend took him to the Jewish cemetery. There he saw Rothschild's grave over which looked a large and beautiful tombstone. So the Jew looks at it and looks and looks—and then he turns to his friend and says, "You see, Yankl, you see that tombstone Rothschild has; that's what I call living!"

Here the knife is being twisted several ways. Obviously the Jew who makes the ironic remark is aware that, come what may, it is better to be poor and alive than rich and dead. Yet he also notices that the dead Rothschild is in a position to "live" better in his grave than we poor people who are really alive.

The same acute social perception can be found in the humor the East European Jews developed about those threats of external aggression from which their life was never free. That the Jews should be skeptical about wars and inclined to pacifism is understandable. One is reminded of the joke about the Albanian in the first world war who, when asked his opinion about the war, replied, "Two dogs are fighting over a bone and you ask the bone how it feels!" As the bone in the squabbles between dogs, the Jews ridiculed the idea of war *per se* and gently noted their lack of passion for things military. What is perhaps the most famous of all war jokes is of Jewish origin.

> A Jewish soldier in the Russo-Japanese war shoots up in the air instead of at the enemy. He is brought before a Russian court martial and asked why he fired upwards. In apparent innocence he replies, "What do you mean? In front of me there were people; if I'd shot at them I might have killed someone!"

Through the wit and satire of these folk anecdotes we also see an even greater danger to the life of the East European Jews: the pogrom. One of the most poignant and magnificent anecdotes of *Röyte Pomerantsen* is a subtle comment on this danger.

> In a Jewish village there once appeared a circus with many animals. One evening a bear escaped. How and why, don't ask; he escaped

and that's all there is to it. So the chief of police ordered that
whoever saw the bear should kill him. When one Jew heard of this
he decided to leave town immediately. "Why are you running
away?" asked a friend. "You're not a bear." The Jew replied, "Listen to me. Before you know what has happened they'll kill a Jew—
and then go prove he's not a bear!"

Though a joke usually involves a thrust at someone else,
Jewish humor is often a thrust at the Jews themselves. The plight
that is ridiculed is often that of the narrator, with whom the
audience can easily identify itself. But the Jewish joke is not
merely self-criticism; it is at the same time self-justification. Or
more accurately, it is in a state of constant tension between
criticism and justification. For the narrator is a sly fellow. If you
extend his remark just a bit, it becomes a sardonic comment, not
merely on the plight of the Jews, but also on the plight of all
humanity:

In the midst of a ship's voyage, a severe storm broke out which
endangered the lives of all aboard. The ship swayed from side to
side; women fainted all over the place; people bewailed their fate.
One Jew aboard the ship kept shrieking: "Help, Oh Lord! The ship
is sinking, the ship is being smashed; help, help, the ship!"
    Annoyed with the shrieking, another passenger went over and
calmly asked him, "Why are you making such an uproar? What are
you screaming about? Is it *your* ship?"

If we understand the word in its original Latin sense, Jewish
humor is genuinely *vulgar*. It is not earthy, for the Jews lacked
roots in the land and paid scant attention to nature. It is seldom
obscene, for Jewish humor is too fascinated with the
ridiculousness of man's total condition to be interested in his
quickly decaying physical parts. But it is vulgar, common, ordinary, full of the affairs of common life; its scenes are kitchens,
marketplaces, railroad stations and streets; its characters,
housewives, mothers-in-law, children, merchants and beggars. In
Jewish humor we move along the social ladder from top to
bottom, and often savor those delicious contrasts of manners
between social strata which the Jews so enjoyed noticing.

A basic situation in Jewish humor is the counterposition of
Rothschild, the archetypical millionaire, against the *schnorrer,* a
sort of high-class beggar. Though the *schnorrer* is poor, he is also
proud and will brook no humiliation. In one anecdote the *schnor-*

rer insists on seeing Rothschild personally and when he finally gains an interview, he asks for alms.

> "Couldn't you see my secretary if that's all you want?" asks Rothschild in anger. "See here, Mr. Rothschild," replied the *schnorrer,* "you may be very competent in your field, but don't tell me how to run *my* business."

If *schnorrers* have wit—what else can they live on?—then the *shadchen,* or matchmaker, is something of a philosopher. Faced with the task of pairing off doubtful human material, he becomes a bit skeptical about human nature. When he extolls the virtues of a bride-to-be, he quietly remarks, "Well, so what if she is a little pregnant?" Such things happen in this world and no one knows it better than the *shadchen.* But sometimes even he forgets himself. One joke tells of a *shadchen* who tries to convince a bachelor to marry. But what are the advantages of marriage? asks the bachelor.

> "Ah," answers the *shadchen,* "your wife cooks for you, she takes care of you, she mends your clothes, she blesses you with children, and she talks to you . . . and she talks to you . . . and she talks . . . the devil take her the way she talks!"

But the most perennial and beloved character of Jewish humor is the *schlemiel.* How can one define a *schlemiel?* That he is completely poverty-stricken goes without saying; that is the least of it. Let us rather say that he has a positive gift for getting into trouble, for doing things the wrong way, for saying the inept word at the inappropriate moment—and always with the best of intentions. He is the eternal innocent, and yet one is never sure if he is merely a good-natured fool or if there is a reservoir of hidden wisdom beneath his foolishness.

A typical *schlemiel* joke tells of the not-too-bright young man who before going to meet his bride-to-be is instructed by his father to talk about love and family affairs and then to wind up with a bit of philosophy. That should be safe enough. The young man dutifully begins his conversation with his betrothed by asking her—

> "Tell me, my love, do you love noodles?"
> "Why of course I love noodles."
> "Tell me, darling, do you have a brother?"
> "No, I have no brother."

> Well, at this point the young man has exhausted two of his three
> subjects and that leaves only philosophy.
> So he asks her, "But suppose you did have a brother, would *he*
> love noodles?"

The special bitter-sweet taste of this humor is largely dissipated in translation; language and content are too intimately wedded. It is the same flavor that marks off the major figures of Yiddish literature from any other European literary group, and binds them to the masses for whom they wrote. When Sholom Aleichem died in New York, when Peretz died in Warsaw, crowds of 150,000 attended their funerals. They were mourned even as members of one's own family.

Though there was a Yiddish cultural movement of some proportions in America during the early part of the century, it has recently been restricted to an increasingly narrow circle. What has percolated into American life is a sad subsitute—the dialect joke, often vicious and always cheap; the Broadway clowns who can only vulgarize Jewish humor; and the supercilious dialect writers for "sophisticated" magazines who exploit Jewish humor but fancy it proper to hold their noses while doing so. These vulgarizations have less genuine connection with Jewish humor than did, say, Will Rogers, with the American folk humor of Mark Twain. But in the pages of *Röyte Pomerantsen* and the stories of Sholom Aleichem, one may see the true and splendid expression of both a folk and its greatest artist in humor which mocks pomp and wealth, which shatters pretension and which upholds the poor and the suffering. (1951)

NOTE

1. Immanuel Olsvarger, ed., *Röyte Pomerantsen* (New York: Schocken Books Inc., 1947).

JEWISH HUMOR AND THE DOMESTICATION OF MYTH

ROBERT ALTER

It is an instructive paradox that one of the grimmest stretches in Jewish history—the recent centuries of Yiddish-speaking culture in Eastern Europe—should also prove to be the period in Jewish history that produced the most richly distinctive humor. Especially since popular stereotypes of diaspora Jewish history tend to represent it wholly in the image of the ghettos of Central and Eastern Europe and the townlets of the Pale of Settlement, it is worth stressing that rarely before had Jews been so physically constricted, so continuously depressed economically; and perhaps not since the Crusades and the Black Plague did they feel so repeatedly threatened by physical havoc as in Russia during the last decades under the czars. In such circumstances, it has been suggested, a shrewdly ironic humor became a source of necessary inner strength, a mode of survival. Maurice Samuel, the eloquent expositor of East-European Jewish culture, states the case pointedly:

> There was nothing jolly and hilarious about the destitution that lay like a curse on millions of Jews in the Yiddish-speaking world; and it would be grotesque to speak of Sholom Aleichem's and Mendele's *kaptsonim* [paupers] and *evyonim* [indigents] as 'poor and happy'. They were miserable, and knew it; but the question that haunts us historically is, why did they not disintegrate intellectually and morally? How were they able, under hideous oppression and corroding privation, under continuous starvation—the tail of a herring was a dish—to keep alive against a better day the spirit originally breathed into man? The answer lies in the self-mockery by which they rose above their condition to see afar off the hope of the future.[1]

This is beautifully apt, but the implications of "self-mockery," and its relation to a sense of the future, deserve exploration. The European cultural tradition, I would suggest, characteristically conceives suffering as a mystery, beginning with and drawing on the cultic or literary formulation of the mystery of suffering in Greek tragedy and in Christ's passion. Affliction is the medium through which man must realize his humanity, or more-than-humanity; accordingly he must view both himself and his suffering with the utmost seriousness, defining his time, which is the time of human fulfillment, by the internal rhythm of his suffering. Hamlet, Werther, Dmitri Karamazov, Camus's Stranger are paradigmatic figures of this European tradition. Against them, one might usefully set Sholom Aleichem's Tevye, who acts upon the wisdom of the Yiddish proverb "burdens are from God, shoulders, too," never for a moment imagining that it would be appropriate to seek fulfillment through suffering, to create a mythology out of suffering; and who uses his shoulders as much to shrug at adversity as to bear it.

Jewish humor typically drains the charge of cosmic significance from suffering by grounding it in a world of homey practical realities. "If you want to forget all your troubles," runs another Yiddish proverb, "put on a shoe that's too tight." The point is not only in the "message" of the saying, that a present pain puts others out of mind, but also in its formulation: *Weltschmerz* begins to seem preposterous when one is wincing over crushed bunions. If in the tradition of Jewish humor suffering is understandably imagined as inevitable, it is also conceived as incongruous with dignity—thus the sufferer is at least faintly ridiculous, his complementary comic embodiments of *schlemiel* and *shlimazel* become central in the folk tradition and the literature deriving from it. The perception of incongruity implies the perception of alternate possibilities, humor peeking beyond the beleaguered present toward another kind of man and another kind of time; for the very aura of ridicule suggests that it is not, after all, fitting for a man to be this pitiful creature with a blade of anguish in his heart and both feet entangled in a clanking chain of calamities.

As the sense of inner crisis has deepened in modern literature, one important direction taken by writers beginning with Conrad, Mann, and Eliot has been a conscious re-mythologizing of literature, usually in order to make it sound the full cultural resonance of our collective disorders. Against this general drift of literary modernism, writers significantly touched by the Yiddish heritage have often been de-mythologizers, using the wryness and homey realism of Jewish humor to suggest that a less melo-dramatic, less apocalyptic, perspective than that of myth might be appropriate for viewing even the disquieting state of affairs of the modern world. I would like to begin with an extreme exam-ple—a novel peopled entirely by WASPs and black Africans, set in the heart of the dark continent, with not a hint of an *oi* or a *veh* amidst the native ululations—precisely because it may illustrate the persistence of a Jewish modality of imagination even in the total absence of Jewish realia. The book I have in mind is of course *Henderson the Rain King,* a novel that remains one of the most engaging of Saul Bellow's fictions, despite the flaws of its conclusion. Bellow, it should be observed, is one of the very few American Jewish writers who has more than nostalgic misinfor-mation about the Yiddish-speaking ancestral world: from his ghetto childhood in Montreal he retains enough Hebrew to make proper use of biblical and liturgical motifs in his fiction, enough genuinely literate Yiddish to have produced admirable transla-tions of stories by Sholom Aleichem and I. B. Singer. *Henderson* would seem to be a conscious attempt on the part of a writer who generally uses Jewish milieux and characters to write for once a thoroughly American novel. (In this, and little else, it resembles Malamud's *The Natural* and Philip Roth's *When She Was Good.*) The hero is a strapping Westchester county millionaire of Protes-tant descent, first seen wallowing among pigs on his farm. The plot consists of a spiritual safari to Africa—Henderson's initials, Leslie Fiedler has observed, are the same as Ernest Heming-way's—in which the hero eventually tries to prove his manhood and discover wisdom by staring down a lion in an underground cell.

Henderson's irrepressible innocence suggests a kind of aging Huck Finn of the Eisenhower years, yet for all his exuberant Americanism, one is also strongly tempted to apply to him some of the rubrics of Yiddish characterology. An inveterate misad-venturer, there is a good deal of the self-perceiving *schlemiel* in Henderson, tinctured with an admixture of the *klots* (clumsy oaf) or the eternal *grober yung* (slob, boorish young man). Following parodistically on the trail of Conrad's Marlow, Lawrence's Kate Leslie, and other modern questers into dark regions, Henderson clearly carries along a very different apparatus of imagination, and it is worth observing precisely how his mind copes with the unspeakable mysteries of the jungle. His version of a native ceremonial procession is characteristic: "amazons, wives, children carrying long sheaves of Indian corn, warriors holding idols and fetishes in their arms which were freshly smeared with ochre and calcimine and were as ugly as human conception could make them." So far, this seems a factual enough evocation of a primitive rite, and might easily fit into a narrative by Conrad except for its avoidance of those Conradian adjectives of looming immensity and ominous things impending. Immediately, however, something peculiar begins to happen to the exotic scene: "Some were all teeth, and others all nostrils, while several had tools bigger than their bodies." The conversational hyperbole ("all teeth," "all nostrils") of course heightens the grotesqueness of the idols while suggesting a quality of ironic observation or perhaps even wondering amusement which separates the speaker from the savage rite, and that quality is reinforced by the use of the familiar-colloquial (but not obscene) "tool" to describe the carved phalluses. Henderson, who has excruciating difficulties with a broken dental bridge, who feels the world's beauty through a tingling in the gums, to whom even the African mountains look "as though they might have bad teeth," is struck first by the apparition of toothy gods: as with the pinched feet in the proverb, the novel as a whole tends to shrink suffering and sensitivity to the realistic dimension of a homey physical detail. Henderson goes on to render his response to the African scene through a rhetorical device that he uses repeatedly elsewhere: "The yard suddenly became very crowded. The sun blasted and blazed. Acetylene does not peel paint more than this sun did the doors of my heart. Foolishly, I told myself that I was feeling faint. (It was owing to my size and strength that this appeared foolish.) And I thought that this was like a summer's day in New York. I had taken the wrong subway and instead of reaching upper Broadway I had gone to Lenox Avenue and 125th Street, struggling up to the sidewalk."[2]

The energy of the style makes Henderson's experience seem very "real," but in a way that violently assimilates Africa to an American metropolitan landscape. Henderson's narrative is a continual farce of deliberately gross similes: acetylene torches and peeling paint, bubbling percolators, baseball stadiums, limousines to La Guardia Field, the smokestacks of Gary, Indiana, cover the African vistas of the novel. The technique effectively destroys any possibility of using exotic climes as a vehicle for myth. Henderson is in his own way open to new experience, as his friendship with King Dahfu demonstrates, but he remains imaginatively anchored in a world of familiar places, objects, and implements; and he cannot be drawn into a yawning abyss of the unknown because his first mental reflex is to domesticate the unknown with a comparison. (The deflation of mysteries through an attachment to the familiar also operates in his sense of who he is. In whatever bizarre roles circumstances cast him, he knows that Henderson the clumsy clown is no mythic Fisher King. Here, he maintains the comic self-consciousness of a knowing *schlemiel,* which enables him in the midst of his account of a wild ceremony to note how absurd it is that such a hulk of a man as he is should think himself on the point of fainting.) Many a newcomer to New York has undergone the inadvertent *rite de passage* of neglecting to change trains at 96th Street and thus discovering himself in the heart of Harlem instead of at Morningside Heights. Henderson's invocation of that experience at this point vividly conveys a sense of sudden disorientation in an unfamiliar crowd of Negroes, but there is an underlying congruity in the comic incongruity of the comparison that might best be paraphrased with a Jewish verbal shrug: "Natives, shmatives, there are people everywhere. So maybe someone can tell me where I should go?"

The point of the comedy of similes throughout *Henderson* is to banish from the protagonist's world the possibility of a primordial Other Side of human life. We deceive ourselves, the novel suggests, with the drama of a return to archaic origins. Through Henderson we are led to acknowledge the home-truth that we have only our civilized selves to work with. Appropriately, Dahfu, Henderson's spiritual guide, turns out to be a former medical student with looney theories about the road to inner transformation—more or less, a black cousin germane to the New York Jewish intellectuals (like Bellow's friend Isaac Rosenfeld) who, for example, plunged into Wilhelm Reich and built themselves orgone boxes to hasten a personal redemption.

A similar process of ironic or playful domestication of myth is often observable when Jewish writers deal with heaven, hell, and the realm of fantastic creatures in between. Though it is customary to think of Judaism as a this-worldly faith, Jews in fact have often believed fervently in reward and punishment after death, in ministering angels (invoked by name in the bedtime prayer) and lurking demons. Nevertheless, all these other-worldly paraphernalia never quite attained what would be canonical status in another religion, a fact that has given the folk imagination and writers inspired by it considerable freedom in treating these materials. Thus, the charm of Itzik Manger's *Book of Paradise* (1939) depends upon the completely uninhibited way in which the celestial Eden is recast in the image of the Rumanian *shtetl* that Manger knew as a boy. The first glimpse of the streets of Eden at nightfall is of a piece with everything that follows: "Bearded angels were bent over yellowed holy books. Fat lady angels with triple chins were patching shirts; young mother angels were rocking cradles, lulling the first-born little ones with song," while at the local tavern—named after Noah, the proverbial biblical drunkard—angels of the coarser sort "were sitting at small tables, drinking spirits, smoking cheap tobacco, and continually spitting at the floor through their teeth."[3]

Manger's translation of a spit-covered tavern floor into the fields of paradise has an imaginative affinity with Bellow's conjuring up Lenox Avenue and 125th Street in the supposed heart of darkness, though the emotional effect is rather different: Bellow transports a zest for things familiar into the scary realm of the unknown, while Manger, equally moved by affection for the familiar, introduces into the True World *(di emese velt)* the grossness, the poignancy, and the sadness of things flawed in the world below. In both cases, humor is generated by the disparity between our expectations of an ideal type (the primordial African, the paradisiac soul) and what the writer actually invents for us; but Manger's comedy is tinged with wistfulness, for if indeed we have only our familiar world to imagine with, then whenever there is life, schoolboys are whipped, poor tailors starve, parents and children bicker, and the spiritual magnates *(tsadikim)* lord it over the common people.

Something of this mood of soberly realistic humor touched with sadness is present in Bernard Malamud's naturalization of fantasy to the American Jewish immigrant milieu. Malamud has his own vividly humanized angels—the black Jew from Harlem in "Angel Levine" who, trying to earn his wings, comes to the aid of a poor Jewish tailor; and Ginzburg, the ominous Yiddish-accented figure in "Idiots First" who turns out to be the *malekh-hamoves,* the Angel of Death. At the penultimate moment of "Idiots First," Mendel, the distraught father, seizes Ginzburg in anger, crying, "You bastard, don't you understand what it means human?"[4] and a moment later Ginzburg is actually shocked into relenting, despite himself allowing Mendel's idiot son to depart for California. This final turn of the plot could serve as an emblem of how the whole mode of imagination works, wresting a kind of concession from the ultimate powers by the very act of humanizing them, conceiving them in such a way that they will understand what it means human.

A related translation of the fantastic into the familiar is effected, perhaps with more artistic success, in another Malamud story, "The Jewbird." It becomes evident very soon in the story that this remarkable talking bird—"Gevalt, a pogrom" are its first words when the Jewish paterfamilias takes a swipe at it — is virtually an allegorical figure of the wandering old-world Jew. Its name, after its color, is Schwartz, and in the eyes of its unwilling host it is clearly what is known in the vernacular as a *shvartser yid,* a Jew who is "black" not in the racial sense but in the foul oppressiveness of his crude manner and his religious obscurantism. "The Jewbird," in fact, deals in its peculiar way with essentially the same predicament of identity as Philip Roth's "Eli the Fanatic"—the ambivalence, guilt, and impulse to rejection aroused in an American Jew by the confrontation with a black-garbed survivor of the ancestral world. Without the fantasy of the talking bird, and the muted comedy generated by that incongruity, this would be merely a sour story. As it is, the conclusion is bleak enough, Schwartz finally being cast out and ending in the snow with a twisted neck. Without the grubby realism in which the fantasy is embodied, the bird would be only a contrived symbol and the story would lack conviction. Malamud's invention engages the imagination precisely because the black bird of exile is able to assume so persuasively the habits and accents of a familiar milieu and a familiar type. He has a fondness for herring and schnapps, his breath stinks of garlic, his speech is a chain of wry Yiddish twists only minimally conforming to the prevalent syntactical and lexical requirements of spoken English.

Now, one might be tempted to dismiss all this as a compound of anecdotal affectation passed off as fictional invention were it

not for its necessary function in the Jewbird's relation to his host,
Harry Cohen. For Cohen, the "Americanized" frozen-food salesman, the bird must embody in all its details the stigmatized
stereotype of a kind of Jew that he emphatically wants to leave
behind. Cohen is really attacking a part of himself in his hostility
toward Schwartz; this becomes clear at the end of the story
when, swinging the bird around his head, he enacts a parody of
the ceremony of *shlogen kapores,* in which a rooster was whirled
in the air before being slaughtered on the eve of the Day of
Atonement, while the person holding the bird recited the formula
"this is my surrogate, this is my atonement." What the reader
quickly realizes is that Cohen is by far the grosser of the two
figures, and that by contrast Schwartz, in the very pungency of
his garlic-redolent Yiddishisms, possesses a certain quality of
nobility.

He is a creature who lives meagerly, but lives nevertheless, by
his wit, and even though this resource finally fails him, the
impression he makes is of a shrewd, engagingly stubborn survivor. He knows too much of the hardships of surviving to have
any grand expectations of future circumstances, but his mental
shrugs help him maintain some sort of inner equilibrium through
his difficulties by ceding their inevitability while contracting their
ruinous nature to imaginable dimensions. The very first words of
the story, where the narrator seems to move immediately to a
rendering of Schwartz's interior speech, briskly define the use of
a kind of acerbic stoicism as a means of coping with adversity:
"The window was open so the skinny bird flew in. Flappity-flap
with its frazzled black wings. That's how it goes. It's open, you're
in. Closed, you're out and that's your fate."[5] As we perceive from
the grief to which the Jewbird finally comes, this is hardly a way
of overcoming disaster, but it does provide a strength of resolution to go on.

The procedure of amiable domestication to which Manger and
Malamud subject their angels is happily applied by Isaac
Bashevis Singer to the multitude of demons who variously
prance, slink, and amble through his stories. One of the most
memorable of all these is the nameless narrator of "The Last
Demon," a story in which the immense sadness of matter and the
delightfulness of matter constitute a paradigm for the use of
comedy as a last defense of the imagination against grim fate.
This story is one of the rare attempts anywhere in Singer's work

to respond to the horror of the Holocaust, and it is effective precisely because of the brilliant obliquity of its method. The demon briefly alludes to the Holocaust in the opening words of his tale but then promptly drops the subject and seems to forget about it until the last three paragraphs of the story: "I, a demon, bear witness that there are no more demons left. Why demons, when man himself is a demon? Why persuade to evil someone who is already convinced? . . . I board in an attic in Tishevitz and draw my sustenance from a Yiddish storybook, a left-over from the days before the great catastrophe."[6] The original is less ambiguous, since *khurben,* the word rendered as "catastrophe," is the accepted term for the Holocaust. In any case, our immediate attention is caught less by the magnitude of the catastrophe than by the amusing, cool-headed logicality of the speaker— "after all, should I go convince someone who's already convinced?"—who at once proceeds to affirm by statement and demonstrate by tone his authenticity as a familiar folk figure: "I don't have to tell you that I'm a Jew. What else, a Gentile? I've heard that there are Gentile demons, but I don't know any, nor do I wish to know them. Jacob and Esau don't become in-laws." Tone, of course, is tied up with language, and so "What else, a Gentile?" catches only part of the homely nuance of *"vos den bin ikh, a goy?"*—while the humor of Jacob and Esau as in-laws is largely lost because there is no English equivalent for the Yiddish *mekhutonim,* which implies an elaborate and dignified sense of social alliance and extended kinship, and is sometimes also used jocularly or sardonically to suggest a dubious or presumptuous relationship.

The demon-narrator is thoroughly engaging not only in his easy command of the comic inflections of the folk, sharpened in the Yiddish by his talmudist's fondness for Hebraisms and Aramaicisms, but also in the way he maintains the jaunty posture of a city slicker (from Lubin) condemned by the infernal powers-that-be to cool his heels among the hayseeds. He has a worldling's contempt for Tishevitz, a one-horse, mud-choked town so small, he claims, that "in the tailors' synagogue a billy goat is the tenth in the quorum."[7] He can only condescend to the resident imp of Tishevitz, a hopeless yokel who "cracks jokes that didn't amuse Enoch" and "drops names from the Haggadah," to whom he charitably proposes the possibility of a devil's position elsewhere: "We have an opening for a mixer of bitter herbs. You only work Passovers."[8] Alongside the breezy urbanity of the demon, the virtuous young rabbi whom he chooses as his target seems a pale figure. The minimal plot of the story consists of the demon's futile effort to tempt the rabbi. The implicit point of that action is its very humanity: this is a world where good and evil are still struggled over and the rules of the game are familiar to both sides, where the rabbi is truly saintly and the demon one of the old school, the sort that can quote Bible and Talmud with the best of them and conjure up for his victim visions of sex and power and even a chance at messiahship, who preens himself on his abilities but is smart enough to know when he has met his match. Then, in a few swift sentences, with no transition and without the hint of an appeal for pathos, this whole world is wiped away:

> The rabbi was martyred on a Friday in the month of Nisan. The community was slaughtered, the holy books burned, the cemetery desecrated. The *Book of Creation* has been returned to the Creator. . . . The generation is already guilty seven times over, but Messiah does not come. To whom should he come? Messiah did not come for the Jews, so the Jews went to Messiah. There is no further need for demons. We have also been annihilated. I am the last, a refugee. I can go anywhere I please, but where should a demon like me go? To the murderers?[9]

Tempting though it may be to read the last word of the passage as it appears in English with a throat flooded with outrage, it seems to me that what the whole content of the story calls for is another sardonic shrug, closing the circle of those with which the story began—"what do you think, a self-respecting demon like me should go mix with murderers?" The consideration of tone is essential because the tone suggests that even after genocide—and the entire story, we must recall, is told retrospectively after that ghastly fact—the demon maintains his humanity (what else, devilishness?) by preserving his knowing, ironic sense of things, though tinged now with bitterness.

Significantly, the story ends with the narrator's attention wholly absorbed in the Yiddish storybook he alluded to at the beginning. The book is an old-fashioned compilation in the best demonic manner, filled with blasphemies, denials of God's justice, invitations to transgression and despair. "But nevertheless the letters are Jewish," the last demon affirms, and he lingers over them, torturing each one with the traditional *pilpul* of interpretation, drawing nurture from them. In cabalistic lore, the twenty-two letters of the Hebrew alphabet, the letters through which God created the world, remain ontological constituents of reality. Through their combinations and permutations man can tap sources of cosmic power, establish connections with the ultimate ground of being. The Yiddish black book over which the demon pores represents merely a reversed mirror-image of that cabalistic tradition: the narrator concludes with the recitation of a demon's alphabet, from *aleph* to *yod,* in which each sacred letter is made to spell disaster but nevertheless remains a sign in a system of cosmic orthography, a key of meaning, though the meaning is dismal. Humor collapses in the face of utter chaos, and the characteristic Jewish humor of shrewd observation especially needs to assume a realm of meaning accessible to intelligence, even if it suspects that whatever meaning it unearths will be perverse, unconsoling.

Something of the general function of the comic domestication of myth may be revealed by the fact that in Singer's story the surviving demon proves in the end to be a surrogate for the writer—a wry teller of tales in the old way, steeped in the values and traditions of a vanished world, conjuring with the letters of the lost in the sickening vacuum left by their destruction. My description, of course, of the narrator's final predicament is a little misleading because it neglects his engaging buoyancy of tone in all but the three concluding paragraphs of the story: the last demon is not a self-dramatizing Survivor[10] but, almost eerily, an enlivening voice from the old world, demonstrating the peculiar vitality of its values through his own person.

Instructively, writers who draw on this whole mode of folk imagination tend to create fictional events that are not impersonally conveyed but manifestly *narrated,* as though the act of narration and the presence of a narrator sane enough to be funny in a mad world were a way of hanging on to lucidity. If much modern writing, from Rimbaud's attempted *dereglement de tous les sens* to the jumbled hallucinations of William Burroughs, has conceived radical disorientation as the necessary path to reality, the legacy of Jewish humor, by contrast, seems to encourage a kind of traditionalism in writers, leading them to draw even the realms of the ultimate unknown into a comfortable human space warmed and worn by long usage. This imaginative at-homeness with the experience of a personal and collective past generally implies a stubborn if cautious hopefulness about the future, or perhaps simply the ability to imagine a human future. Thus Singer's demon draws "sustenance" from the letters, knowing that when the letters are gone he will be gone too, and the imaginable world at an end. If disaster, whatever the scale, seems to be our general fate, the persistence of the comic reflex is itself evidence of the perdurability of the stuff of humanity: a shrug is a small and subtle gesture, but, in the face of the harshest history, it may take a world of strength to make.

NOTES

1. Samuel, *In Praise of Yiddish* (New York: Cowles, 1971), pp. 210–11.

2. Bellow, *Henderson the Rain King* (New York: Viking, 1959), p. 166.

3. Manger, *The Book of Paradise,* trans. from the Yiddish by Leonard Wolf (New York: Hill and Wang, 1965), p. 8.

4. Malamud, *Idiots First* (New York: Farrar, Straus, 1963), p. 14.

5. *Ibid.,* p. 101.

6. Singer, *Short Friday* (New York: Farrar, Straus & Giroux, 1964), p. 119. The original appears in *Gimpel tam un andere dertseylungen* (New York: Central Yiddish Culture Organization, 1963), pp. 237–47.

7. *Ibid.,* p. 120.

8. *Ibid.,* p. 125. The translation here, though in the jaunty spirit of the original, is a free improvisation on the Yiddish, in which "mixer of bitter herbs" is literally "salad-chef."

9. *Ibid.,* pp. 129–130.

10. The hint of melodramatic tremulo in the title is absent from the Yiddish, in which the story is simply called "A Tale of Tishevitz."

ON SHOLOM ALEICHEM'S HUMOR

MEYER WIENER

The Victory over Human Fear

Brave children, when fearful upon entering a dark room at night, sing cheerful songs to themselves. Like most metaphors, this one is only partially applicable, but there is a kind of humor that depends, in part, on this sort of spunky singing in the dark. So too, in Sholom Aleichem's humor we find not only laughter and tears, but the sort of merriment that comes from having overcome and tamed the fear of chaos, the fear of a maimed, confused and falsely-ordered life. This conquest of fear of the tragic in life ennobles and deepens humor, lending it an aspect of nobility.

Sholom Aleichem presented the poverty of the great masses of Jews in the *shtetl* and the city during the period of imperialistic capitalism, but without yielding to the spirit of depression and lament. When Motl Peysi's impoverished family reached the point of having to sell all of its possessions, Sholom Aleichem had Motl describe this in the following way: "Of all the household things we sold, none gave me more pleasure than the glass cupboard." After the cupboard was sold, there were some "technical problems" in removing it from the house. Motl says: "For a moment I was afraid for the cupboard"—he is actually afraid that it may remain in the house!

Motl describes his mother crying because everything was being sold. His sick, dying father calls from the next room to ask what is going on. " 'Nothing,' mother answers, wiping her red eyes, and the way her lower lip and her whole face quiver you'd

37

have to be made of stone not to burst out laughing." When
everything is sold, and they are down to their last possessions,
Motl [looking forward to rolling about on the floor] says, "the joy
of joys was when they got to my brother Elye's sofa and to my
cot."

The tsarist pogroms were the culmination of horror and dread
in the lives of the Jewish masses. Sholom Aleichem was very
shaken by these occurrences; it is, therefore, remarkable to note
how he handled this subject in his work. The tragedy of the
pogroms is frequently dealt with, yet in his literary works he
avoided direct descriptions as much as possible, and rendered
them, when he did, in an oddly "lighthearted," almost humorous
manner.[1]

There were not a few writers who relished and lingered over
the horror of pogrom descriptions. Certain passages of Bialik's
work set the tone for this; its end-product was Lamed Shapiro's
pogrom story "The Cross." But at whom was their rage directed?
On close consideration, it is clear that to a large degree, it was
directed at the victims of the pogroms themselves. This sort of
Bialikian "Pain and Outrage" emphasizes the national contradictions. Sholom Aleichem's art, on the other hand, stirs the conscience, because it is addressed to that which is most human in
our humanity, and is imbued with faith in man and his future. It
diverts us from a fruitless, misanthropic fear and guides us
towards a purer vital spirit, toward that crucial striving for a
better sort of life. Here, too, Sholom Aleichem's humor is ennobling and purifying.

Motl says: "At first when I heard people talking about 'a
pogrom' I was all ears. Now when I hear the word 'pogrom,' I
run! I prefer happy stories." Sholom Aleichem says "I dislike
sad stories. My muse does not wear a black veil; she is poor but
happy." There is so much love for the oppressed in this "hatred
of the black veil," and so much sadness in this "happiness in
poverty."

Sholom Aleichem reports a conversation between two children emigrating to America with their parents after a pogrom:

> I ask him, what's a pogrom? I hear all the emigrants talking about
> 'pogrom' but I have no idea what it is. Kopl gloats over me:
> "You don't know what a pogrom is? Gee, are you dumb! Pogroms
> are everywhere these days. They start from nothing, but once they
> start, they go on for three days."

"But what is it," I ask, "a fair?"

"Some fair! They break windows, smash furniture, tear up pillows—feathers fly like snow."

"What for?"

"What for? For nothing ! A pogrom isn't only against houses, it's against stores too. They smash all the stores, throw everything out into the streets or steal it, push things around, douse everything with kerosene, strike a match, and burn it up."

"Don't be funny."

"What do you mean, y'think I'm kidding? Then, when there's nothing left to steal, they go from house to house with axes and sticks, followed by the police. They sing and whistle and shout 'Hey, guys, kill the dirty Jews!' They smash, kill, stab with spears . . ."

"Who?"

"What do you mean who? Jews!"

"What for?"

"What for? 'Cause it's a pogrom!"

"So it's a pogrom, so what?"

"Get away, you're an ass. I don't want to talk to you," Kopl says to me, pushes me away, and puts his hands in his pockets like a grownup.

These are supposedly children talking like children, but the words are pure Sholom Aleichem. And the proof of this is his treatment of the subject of the pogroms in other works, for example in his study *Di groyse behole fun di kleyne mentshelekh* ("The Great Hulabaloo of the Small Folk"). The story's bitter irony borders on the grotesque: the inhabitants of Kasrilevke escape from a pogrom to Kozodoyevke, and those of Kozodoyevke to Kasrilevke, because where else should they run? (It is interesting to note, that in his final version of this story Sholom Aleichem omitted or softened those parts that had provided a more detailed realistic treatment of the pogroms.)

The same motif reappears some years later (1906) in the chapter "Shprintse" of *Tevye*. "It seems that the 'Constitution' [an ironic euphemism for the pogroms—MW] must be more powerful there than here in Yehupetz, because they are on the run, they are all on the run. You may ask: why are they running to us? But then, why do we run to them? It has become a local custom, praise God, that at the first rumor of pogroms, Jews start running from one place to another, as it says in the Scriptures: And they set forth, and they encamped, and they encamped and they set forth—which means, 'you come to me, I'll go to you.' "

And then, years later, we find the same tone in the cited

pogrom passage of *Motl, Son of Peysi, the Cantor*, where the seemingly naive, childish conversation exposes the senseless brutality of the murderous Black Hundreds with much greater bitterness than in the "prophetic" ranting of Bialik. There is also more anguish in these words, more love for the folk and more attachment to it.

The assumption behind Bialik's censure is a belief in a "Black-Hundred"-quality of mankind, a belief that the reactionary forces constitute an eternal law of nature. Bialik's censure-and-insult pathos leads ultimately to petty nationalism, to a gloomy, pessimistic view of the world.

Sholom Aleichem's comical-ironic pathos is immeasurably more realistic and more humane. Its deepest assumption is a faith in the progress of the human race, a hope for a better, more intelligent social order. He exhorted his readers to strive hopefully, not to submit to the obstacles before them, but to grasp hold of life, to work and demand their due.

Remarks about Tevye

At first glance, the subject of *Tevye the Dairyman* is a homey Jewish one, "the problem of child-rearing." Actually, this cycle of "portraits from private life" depicts not simply the misfortunes of one family, and the conflicts between generations, but also the very way in which the foundations of society are eroded in a period of transition from one historical age to another.

The family here is simply a microcosm of the basic characteristics of contemporary society as a whole. Family feelings play a large part in this work, "because the curse of children is the worst of the biblical litany of curses" ("Shprintse"), but the ideals of the family do not stem from the normal bourgeois tendency toward individualization and atomization of society; they are the historic consequences of persecutions and oppression which have persisted through the generations and have resulted in a withdrawal to the family as the sole source of consolation. Tevye's life, which forces him out of his family and back into the real world in violent and tragic fashion, reflects the fundamental social forces of that period.

The plot of *Tevye* is simple enough, even transparent. Collisions and catastrophes occur, but never any complicated events or actions: great humor cannot support oversubtlety. The end of each chapter is fairly predictable from the beginning; there are no great surprises. After the first half of this unique poem there is no doubt about how it will end, and yet there is so much innovation, so much of the unexpected. The great classical outline of the work is discernible in the simplicity of its construction.

The basic plots, from the chapter "Modern Children," to the end, are not new. A daughter chooses a husband against the wishes of her parents (the obstacles are social or ideological); the conflict with her parents ensues with tragic results. This subject is varied five times.

The narrative core of these variations is also not new: mis-alliance (Tseytl, Shrpintse, Beylke); difference in background and even religion, between parents and the daughters' beloved (Hodel and Khave). By the time Sholom Aleichem wrote these chapters, all these subjects had already been treated by others. Even the motif of wandering, *"Lekh-lekho"* ("Go Forth"), written in 1914, was familiar in Yiddish literature.

This did not bother Sholom Aleichem: his purpose was not to invent new plots. Certain plots are almost unavoidable and self-evident if one wants to depict the primary characteristics of an age, and not its secondary features. They are so typical, that simply finding them is no accomplishment; they are, as it were, the natural plots of the time. The challenge is to treat these plots in a lively and profound manner. Otherwise, the result is banal, although in real life these issues are far from banal. Raising these run-of-the-mill stories to such a magnificent level, risking five variations on the same theme in a single work—this required Sholom Aleichem's plain genius.

Tevye is a solemn work, yet it exudes a high degree of lyricism. Amazing how Sholom Aleichem leads Tevye into the woods, against a background of "nature," a forest landscape, hardly a typical setting for the Jewish man of the soil. This poor shred of an idyll is indispensable to the characters of Tevye and his daughters.

Sholom Aleichem treated the old subject of the ignorant, hard-working hick in an extremely novel manner. What Sholom Aleichem saw in him! Who else could see these things? Incidentally, it often appears to me that Tevye's proverbs and biblical quotations are not as ignorant as he pretends, that his "translations" are purposefully contorted, in a sort of spirited wittiness. It often seems as if Sholom Aleichem himself was stylizing the matter here.

Description

Dickens and Mendele had a great influence on Sholom Aleichem's style, but when we compare their work, certain differences are obvious. Dickens loved description and portraiture; Mendele indulged in it willingly, occasion permitting; Sholom Aleichem rarely paints or describes and then only in hasty strokes.

Details interested Sholom Aleichem too, but from an acoustic rather than an optic point of view: how does a character respond verbally to a private or social event.

It is widely acknowledged that Sholom Aleichem in two or three strokes can sketch a character with complete accuracy. It used to be said that he could do portraits, but not landscapes. That is not so:

> And the wagon, as if out of spite, crept slowly along. Before you can reach the Dnieper you have to cross one sand dune and then another, thick yellow sand, kneedeep; slowly, step by step, the horses drag themselves forward, barely able to pull their legs out of the sand. The wheels sink and the wagon groans, as the Dnieper appears closer and closer, in all its breadth and beauty.
>
> On the banks of the river tall green rushes, speckled with yellow, spread their long, sharp leaves, which are reflected in the water, lending the old river a special charm. All is still.
>
> The river spreads far and wide, like the sea, in all directions: the waters flow quietly by. Where to? It's a secret. The blue sky looks down from above and catches its reflection in the water along with the sun, which is not about to set. The sky is clear. The water clear. The sand clear, and the air. And a divine stillness reigns, reminiscent of the Psalms. "The expanse is the Lord's." Suddenly, a bird streaks from the rushes with a cry, cuts like an arrow through the pure still air, soaring away in a zigzag. But then, apparently, thinking better of it, the bird zigzags back and disappears once more into the yellow-green rushes. (*From the Fair,* chap. 37)

This is a very delicate and beautiful landscape, a sort of Japanese graphic. Sholom Aleichem could paint and describe nature as well, but did so seldom; it was not his style. Sholom Aleichem shared Dickens' passion for description only with regard to speech; his artistic attention concentrated for the most part on the nuances of emotions as expressed in words.

The Garrulousness of Sholom Aleichem's Characters

Sholom Aleichem's humor constitutes a unique category in world literature: it is possible to locate the various influences on the development of his style of humor, but with Sholom Aleichem, a new division of the poetics of comedy begins, a category known as "Sholom Aleichemian humor" to go alongside Aristophenian laughter, Dickensian humor, Heinesque irony, Gogolesque satire, and so on.

If the reflection of reality in art is connected in some way with imitating and reproducing reality, then Sholom Aleichem's style, both directly and indirectly, is extremely mimetic in all its details, even to the gesticulations which are hinted at by the words themselves.[2] In every successful story of Sholom Aleichem, an actor is there, playing his part, even when the story is read silently.

Sholom Aleichem has a special sort of "comic" prose style. All the usual poetic devices are transformed into elements of verbality: the comedy derives not so much from the stories as from the style in which they are recounted—from the various styles of garrulousness of the characters. These are, so to speak, his metaphors, tropes, stylizations, and so forth.

His sentences are directed in the first place not to the eye, but to the ear; dialogues or monologues are his favorite forms. His stories are comedies in prose, and can be easily transformed into stage comedies.

In "If I Were Rothschild" (1902), Sholom Aleichem even inserted two bits of stage directions, "comes to a halt," and "reflects for a moment," which are aimed at the reader as well as the recitateur. These stage directions are vestigial remnants of the umbilical cord which links Sholom Aleichem's prose style to comedy itself.

No Yiddish writer has a style as close to the language and narrative manner of the "ordinary Jew" as Sholom Aleichem. No one so accurately reproduced the language of the toiler, the common man, the artisan, coachman, pauper, maid, all the varied inhabitants of Kasrilevke, the bohemian *luftmentsh* and the ordinary *luftmentsh:* the speech of the Menakhem-Mendlian maniac, the happy pauper, the bitter, oppressed housewife, the feverish, nervous talk of the market women and the sedate, tranquil talk of intelligence and experience: Tevye's language; the language of little children, unhappy mothers, actors, pious Jews, card-players, the talk of all sorts of professions, districts, dialects; tremendous treasures of language, reflecting the enormous diversity of life.

This is one side of the issue. It is quite wrong to assume, however, that Sholom Aleichem actually reproduced the language of "real life" in its raw form. His language so closely resembles colloquial speech that the "experts" were led to conclude that this was not literature at all, but something simultaneously greater and less than literature, something "snatched" from life and, therefore, life itself. Because of this claim, naive people think that there is nothing simpler than writing like Sholom Aleichem—record what you hear, and there you have it. The results of such limitations are well known.

Actually, the transformation of language in Sholom Aleichem's works occurred by means of an extension of the idiosyncracies in the styles of the real Menakhem-Mendl, the real Tevye, the actual prototypes of various groups and regions, etc. to their logical conclusions, the point at which they assume the form which they would have taken had they existed in the exact same circumstances for many more generations. In this sharpened state, their speech is transmuted by the author's affectionate and poetic personality until they assume a lyrical smoothness, an artistic polish, charm and beauty, and became Sholom Aleichem's own style.

The characters and events described in Sholom Aleichem's *From the Fair* are in effect, prototypes of characters and events in many of his other depictions of Kasrilevke and Mazepevke. But although this fictional autobiography is very far from historical accuracy, there is nonetheless a very definite difference between these characters and events and those in his other works. This same difference applies between actual, colloquial speech and Sholom Aleichem's style.

Wordplays

Sholom Aleichem's humor is linked with "speech" to a greater degree than that sort of humor which emphasizes the comedy of antics or events. The essence and meaning of Sholom Aleichem's characters also emerges, of course, from the facts and situations in which they operate, but these are for the most part more tragic than comic. The comic situation is less compelling than the words in which it is related. Sholom Aleichem humorized mostly through speech, or more precisely by allowing his characters to speak. The funniest situations in his works achieve their comic appeal mostly through the way in which they are related by his characters, by their verbal reaction to events.

The social and economic rootedness of Sholom Aleichem's characters is illusory, the entire milieu, its behavior, psychology, its modes of thinking and of feeling are affected by this illusoriness. Thus the verbosity, the talkativeness of his characters—as opposed to their actual deeds—assumes a special significance (as a substitute) for their actions.

This verbosity, with all the by-products of such intense speech, repetition, and digression—gesticulation, voice modulation, facial expression—has no effect in actual life and is rather "unreal" or "fantastic." These elements, which Sholom Aleichem noted and absorbed, were singularly important in the formation of his style. When he attempted to exceed the limits of this style—especially in his novels—he fell short of mastery; only when he himself adopted the tone of one of his characters did he make even the most "imaginary" facts, events and situations become compelling and realistic.

It is not paradoxical, therefore, to claim that the reality which Sholom Aleichem portrayed was "imaginary": his realism consisted of discovering the "imaginary" aspects of the life he describes, as well as its objective bases and ideas.

This explains Sholom Aleichem's proclivity for dialogue, monologue and for the verbal, essentially comic form. It also accounts for his attraction to the would-be feuilletons, in which the conversations of his characters are supposedly overheard by the author. Even his true feuilletons, where he takes a direct stand on contemporary problems, were generally not written in a direct, fully personal manner, but were stylized, composed of various narrative mannerisms of his different characters. Style is not simply a means, but an integral part of the subject matter itself: it reflects the subtleties of life.

The modulation and intonation of words is therefore as crucial to his style as their meaning: the words must themselves indicate how to reproduce the entire illusorily-expressive, artful wordplay of busy self-importance. Correctly understood, the words of the text signal the intonation and gesticulations that should accom-

pany them. Sholom Aleichem constructed his sentences so that
the naked words would project how everything should look and
sound.

This Sholom Aleichem did *consciously*. As early as 1884 he
wrote: "Our jargon has more scope for satire than other languages: with a small shrug, an aside, a nickname, the slightest
stroke of emphasis, a sentence turns satirical and evokes a spontaneous smile from the reader. Not to mention imitations of the
individual speaker (practically every Jew has his own language
with all his varied gesticulations)."[3]

Here Sholom Aleichem attributes to the language his own
artistic skill, and substitutes the speaking-style of his major
characters for that of the Yiddish language itself. But these
words clearly show that even at this early stage Sholom Aleichem realized the possibility of transmitting with the word,
through the word, the entire range of accompanying gestures to
suggest the emotional impulse that called the word forth.

Sholom Aleichem wanted to present speech in its full dramatic
scope, in order to communicate its illusory sources. The act of
speaking, after all, plays such a major role in this life, where a
Menakhem-Mendl can do and accomplish so little. The comedy
of Sholom Aleichem's stories derives not only from the meaning
of the words, but also from the gesticulations with which the
reader associates them.

For this reason Sholom Aleichem's masterpieces do not have
their greatest impact when read, but rather when declaimed:
Sholom Aleichem's works are directed, in fact, not only to the
factual imagination but to the verbal "imagination," if such imprecise terminology may be used. (It is imprecise because both
forms of imagination proceed from a concrete, essentially similar
basis in the "facts of reality.")

Speech, as such, can only be appreciated aurally, just as dramatic works must be staged, so Sholom Aleichem's stories must
be declaimed, acted out. Sholom Aleichem himself made a habit
of reading his stories publicly, and it is no coincidence that of all
the Yiddish writers (and certainly most of the non-Yiddish writers), his works are most often publicly recited and read.

Sholom Aleichem's works, even the smallest of his master-
stories are therefore a sort of wordplay, depicting an illusory,
playacting, world. This is a new genre in world literature. On the

surface it appears to be prose, but in essence, it resembles high comedy.

The Tragedy of Illusions

"What is there about Jewish singing and playing, that always evokes only sad thoughts?" It embodies the life of the people.

Sholom Aleichem's "happy stories" are one large satirical elegy on the oppressed nature of man, his abasement through hunger, through the hatred of one people for another, the backwardness of life and thought, and the disablement of his creative powers, all of which results from the cruel order of things which condemns one man to be exploited by another. The free creative spirit thrives only from plenty; when subject to exploitation, people sink into pettiness; they become "little people with little notions."

Even the bodily movements of such "little people" are funny; they seek and strive and bustle about, show the most strenuous exertions, work themselves to death—over a trivial, joyless shred of "bliss" which is either fabricated or worthless. These figures are far from heroic, but they proceed along their quixotic adventures with unusual, almost heroic courage.

The pettiness of their ideas is tragic in itself, but more tragic is the fact that their superhuman energies are expended in vain. The comedy lies in their external appearance, in the movements, words, the details of their predicaments; the tragedy lies in the content, in the conclusion which in the works of Sholom Aleichem is almost always tragic.

In Sholom Aleichem's major characters there is always a bit of the *shlimazl:* sometimes the character is good-hearted, charming, decent and sometimes simply sad and foolish, but he is always a *shlimazl.* Sholom Aleichem almost never depicts happiness, fulfilled goals.

Tevye's nobility raises him qualitatively above anything laughable: certain deliberately humorous aspects of his garrulousness are only meant to intensify the tragic essence of the story. Here, too, the laughter does not derive from plenty, because there is not the smallest measure of joy, of happiness.

No one evoked as much laughter as Sholom Aleichem, and yet

no one so exclusively chose the joylessness of Jewish life as the subject of his work. Perhaps this is why Peretz disliked Sholom Aleichem, while admitting his artistic power. Peretz praised Sholom Aleichem for this ability to "scrape off the mould," that is, educate through satire, or more specifically, to destroy illusions.

Sholom Aleichem was constantly demonstrating to the masses that their happiness in their social condition was illusory, that this sort of life was itself almost illusory. In his works he always asked the seemingly "happiest people" of all, the "Kodnis": What are you so happy about? The illusoriness of their entire *luftlife,* of their crippled and damaged existence, is the main theme of his work.

Sholom Aleichem disliked "happy endings"; they would be a distortion, contradicting the essence of his work; they would trivialize his humor.

The story of the bewitched tailor, which is constructed like a sunny joke, and suffused with a lyrical, idyllic tone, is actually a melancholic, marvelous poem with an infinitely tragic ending, or more precisely, with no ending at all, for the tragedy is limitless. It ends with the poet's shrug.

> The reader will ask, "And the fate of the tailor? the moral? The purpose of the story?" Don't make me continue, children! The ending was not a happy one. The story began well enough, but ended, as most happy stories do, alas, very sadly . . . and because you know that the author of this story is not given to bouts of sadness—in fact you know how he hates to "point a moral" and prefers jolly tales to gloomy plaints, he therefore bids you farewell with a smile, and blesses both Jews and people at large with more of laughter than tears. Laughter is healthy; doctors prescribe laughter.

The bitter irony of this last, famous dictum of Sholom Aleichem must be evident from its context, even to the most thick-skinned reader.

The history of the ending of the novel *Wandering Stars* is characteristic of the author's intentions. The book was first written for serial publication in a newspaper. At that time the great writer was living in very dire circumstances, forcing himself to accommodate the wishes of the subscribers as much as possible.

The novel described the colorful local atmosphere of the contemporary Yiddish stage, a cross between chaos and folk theater. Sholom Aleichem portrays a whole gallery of full-blooded characters: actors, comedians, directors. This work is in the typical tradition of the theater novel, which extends from Scarron's *Comic Novel* to George Sand's *The Handsome* and beyond. Though it contains some excellent passages, the novel as a whole does not count among his masterpieces.

In the version published serially in an American newspaper, the novel concludes with a "happy end" [Wiener's phrase in the original], as the taste of the audience dictated. But during his last revision of the novel, Sholom Aleichem threw out this ending and concluded with these words: "It seems that there is no happiness in this world, only the striving for happiness. Happiness itself is no more than a dream, a fantasy." This was Sholom Aleichem's conclusion about that period in human history, "as long as people still exploited one another, as long as men still showed traces of bestiality in their nature."

Sholom Aleichem's critics have made intelligent but also some foolish observations about him. Once I wrote that Sholom Aleichem was a "consoler." What nonsense! How simple it would have been for him to round out at least some of his works with happy endings, instead of with misery, and often crude misery to boot. This would not have detracted from the comedy of the works, and would have soothed and comforted the spirits of his readers. But it would have banalized his work, being more suitable for the role of a great jester, which several of his critics have attempted to apply to him, but which is as completely foreign and contrary to his tragic consciousness. It would have been more genial, but not realistic—it would have undermined the truth about the life of the masses at that time, that their desires, lusts, dreams, had to remain unfulfilled and unrealized in those given social conditions. The oppressed classes *were* always abused, aggrieved, deceived; so it was and so Sholom Aleichem depicted it.

Characters and Passions

Comic genres generally deal with fools, *shlimazls*, dreamers, maniacs: with miserable, unsuccessful, false, or evil people and deeds. As soon as the characters or their deeds cease to exhibit such qualities, they also cease being comical. One might therefore assume that there is nothing much to seek in the satiric-comic genres, no meaningful figures, no heroic passions, and of course, no problems. The truth is very different of course: in Aristophanes' comedy even philosophical themes were broached; Don Quixote is a fool, a *shlimazl*, a dreamer, a maniac, but it cannot be denied that apart from these comic elements of his character, there are qualities that command respect. In his crazy actions we catch glimpses of "heroic" passions, and in his striving we can see, as in a crooked mirror, something approaching lofty goals and spiritual concerns.

Our Mendele's Benjamin III is an unfortunate fool, a *shlimazl*, a dreamer and maniac: his behavior is clumsy, his goal is delusional, but one cannot dispute the nobility of his intention, and the existence of distinct—though convoluted and comical—elements of the "heroic" in his quixotic striving. All these and similar comic-satiric characters are more or less broken and crippled, but they nonetheless possess significant qualities of character and something oddly heroic in their passions and quests.

A character normally attains significance through *passions* which exhibit something of greatness, albeit in a comical-distorted, contradictory form. Tevye is a character of significance,[4] but we see in him more pathos than passion—the pathos of a bitter, wise, passive resistance to raging forces of life.

Sholom Aleichem's artistic heroes, Stempenyu, Yosele Solovey, Rafalesko, all possess some sublime qualities, but they are not Sholom Aleichem's master characters, nor are they developed comically.

In general, Sholom Aleichem did not encourage the contradictory play of loftiness and worthlessness in his *characters:* the situation, the event rather than the individual stands at the center of Sholom Aleichem's stories. His characters—usually some variation of the Menakhem-Mendl type—are individualized only as much as is necessary to vary his eternal theme.

Whether it is a fault or not, Sholom Aleichem did not imbue his characters with sublime passions, which echo—accurately or distortedly—ideological battles of the time; he did not give us characters who could be spokesmen for the contemporary worldviews.

Sholom Aleichem's humor is based on a profoundly accurate idea: that the prevailing social conditions oppressed and crippled man until he became not only miserable but ridiculous. The comedy inherent in the senseless and passive suffering during the period of imperialism is depicted through characters who, with the exception of Tevye, are so crushed by the old and new economic, social and national oppression and so removed from normal consciousness that the roar of the struggle for the liberation of the world does not even reach them.

The tragedy of the Menakhem-Mendl type lies also in the absence of noble—be they illusory or convoluted—strivings: the mad hustling and get-rich scheming is not a passion in the true sense of the word. Menakhem-Mendl is actually a slight though fanatic competitor, and if by some chance he were to meet with success, we know from the monologue, "If I were Rothschild," what he would be likely to do. Nervous zest is not the same thing as passion.

Passions must somewhat be rooted in real life: they may be mistaken, confused or confounded, but unless they have some basis in reality, they are simply madness. Don Quixote's fantasies are *no longer* realistic, at least they were once so, in part: a hundred or two hundred years earlier he would have been much less comical. The distance between Don Quixote's fantasies and reality is much smaller than in the case of Menakhem-Mendl; Don Quixote's mistaken judgment in his ideals is considerably less than that of Menakhem-Mendl.

From the very outset, Menakhem-Mendl's goal lacked even a grain of realism. But beyond that, the goal itself was so very pitiful. The fate of all of the Menakhem-Mendls evokes in the reader, among other responses, a gnawing dissatisfaction with the immensity of the effort, the fervency of the enthusiasm, that have been expended in the pursuit of such a negligible goal, one which is not even achieved as the character loses everything he has. The reader, too, feels somewhat cheated in his expectations.

At first glance, there is nothing to be regretted in the frustration of such a goal, nor anything tragic in itself. Even the comedy remains superficial until we grasp its essence, the conditions which condemned people to such fates. Only at that point can we be moved by the wretched sort of life which turns people into Menakhem-Mendls, and only at that point can we discern the writer's full intent, the comic tragedy of his characters.

The presence of sublime qualities in his comic figures would have destroyed the uniqueness of Sholom Aleichem's humor. The tragedy of Menakhem-Mendl would not emerge as graphically were he imbued with "tragic" (heroic) qualities. In humor, every minor sin against realism is much more serious, and is punished much more swiftly, than in any other genre: it loses its humor. An essential feature of Menakhem-Mendl's comedy is the fact that both his ambition and his goal are so dismal and trivial, that he lacks any lofty goals. Sholom Aleichem told things as they were, and this gives no joy to a poet. The misfortunes of the groups which Sholom Aleichem depicted extended to some extent to his own creation: we detect in them something of the petit-bourgeois outlook on life.

NOTES

First published in 1941, *Vegn Sholom-Aleykhems humor* was reprinted in vol. 2 of Wiener's *Tsu der geshikhte fun der yidisher literatur in 19tn yorhundert* [On the History of Nineteenth-Century Yiddish Literature] (New York, 1946), pp. 281–378. The translation is from chaps. 5–10, 12, and was done by Ruth R. Wisse.

1. He did write publicistic "letters" with detailed descriptions, but refused to lecture about the pogroms. See *Dos Sholom-Aleykhem-bukh,* ed. Y.D. Berkovitsh (New York, 1926), p. 213.

2. The words "mime," "mimical," etc. come from the Greek "mimesis," i.e., imitation, and relate to any artistic reproduction, but most particularly to that of the actor.

3. "In the Junkheap—Among the Rags" [Yiddish], an unpublished review, in *Dos Sholom-Aleykhem-bukh,* p. 326.

4. Sholom Aleichem tried to create a sort of scholarly variation of Tevye in the character of Reb Yuzifl. This poor, oppressed, hurt and deeply wounded creature crawls into a deep lair—the "other world"—no longer wants to see the sunshine, and exhibits much senseless courage, extraordinary stubbornness and quiet but wild determination in his withdrawal from life. "There is nothing funny about us," says Reb Yuzifl. "My God, one must cry and learn our lesson about what we are and what we have become."

BEYOND *KVETCHING* AND *JIVING*

The Thrust of Jewish and Black Folkhumor

JOSEPH BOSKIN

> The greatest height of heroism to which an individual, like a people, can attain is to know how to face ridicule: better still, to know how to make oneself ridiculous and not shrink from the ridicule.
>
> MIGUEL DE UNAMUNO, *Tragic Sense of Life* (1926)

1.

Humor's peculiarity lies in its polar elasticity: it can operate for and against, reject and elevate, oppress and liberate. On the one hand, it enables the creation of pejorative images; yet, on the other, it makes possible the reversal of such stereotypes. Its power extends to severe humiliation but its ability to liberate is equally potent. Just as it has been utilized as a weapon of insult and persecution, so, too, has it been employed as a device of mockery and masochism. Nowhere in the history of humor has this duality, this range of expressive opposites, been more sharply illustrated than in the experiences of America's most discriminated minorities: Jewish and African-Americans, the ultimate odd-couple in American popular culture, as Joseph Dorinson has aptly dubbed them.[1]

Even prior to their contemporary coupling, Blacks and Jews were fused together, at times in rather peculiar fashion. Biblical

53

references connected the two groups, English games and drama linked them, and early America conjoined them, as for example in the curious identification of the "mulata Jue" in Massachusetts in 1668. Their individual trek over time has led to various parallel designations. The community term for the European Jew was legally termed the ghetto, the same expression now derisively sociologically pinned on the Black community. Jewish and Black males have been derided, respectively, as "Jew boys" and "boys"—their sexual and physical prowess regarded as a constant threat. In more recent decades their political power has been equally viewed as a menace to the social fabric. A 1930s valentine rhyme pointed the finger at the New Deal for bringing together the Jews and Blacks into an unwholesome alliance:

> Eleanor wrote to Franklin:
>   Dear Frank, how are you?
>
> Franklin wrote to Eleanor:
>   Dear Eleanor:
>   Roses are red
>   Violets are blue
>   You court the niggers
>   And I'll court the Jews
>   And we'll stay in the White House
>   As long as we choose.[2]

This coupling has even extended to the desperate strains of their respective stereotypes, Black work-habits with Jewish money-grubbing:

> What do you get when you cross a Negro with a Jew?
>
> You still get a janitor, but he owns the building.[3]

Not only have Blacks and Jews shared in various similarities of oppression, they have been, more specifically, the butt of aggressive laughter. This is hardly surprising. As Sigmund Freud has made us painfully aware, there is a direct connection between humor and aggression, between joking and subordination. In his seminal work, *Jokes and their Relation to the Unconscious* and "Humor" in his *Collected Papers,* Freud posited that all humor serves an aggressive intent, that all joking is tendentious. Humor is employed, he observed, as a means of circumventing civilization's obstacles in its thrust toward "making our enemy small, inferior, despicable or comic." In this manner, "we achieve in a roundabout way the enjoyment of overcoming him."[4]

Whether Freud is correct in asserting the aggressive ends of humor—it should be particularly noted that several theorists in recent years have argued that humor strives toward a form of psychic liberation as well—other scientists have echoed him in a chorus of hostile chant. Konrad Lorenz, in his brilliant study *On Aggression,* noted that laughter in geese resembles "militant enthusiasm"; psychologist David Singer declared that the "mask of humor's subtlety and its seeming innocuous character are used by the humorist to conceal his destructive motives and thus to bypass inhibitions in his audience and himself"; and centuries ago the philosopher Thomas Hobbes took cognizance of the "sudden glory" which emanates from the realization of "some eminency in ourselves by comparison with the infirmity of others."[5]

In American society, the forms of aggressive humor directed toward Jews and Blacks were institutionalized in stereotyped roles. Economic circumstances dictated the shape of the image which entrapped Blacks, whereas historical forces had consigned an image which fused Jews. To rationalize slavery, whites developed the figure of Sambo: childish, inept, indolent, and comical. To control Jews, Christians fixed on the machinations of Shylock: industrious, sly, grasping, and smart. To maintain and perpetuate these stereotypes, the dominant culture concertedly devised a lexicon of comic tales, jokes, and variations of the essential pejorative form.

The repertoire of aggressive humor, indicating the degree of hostility to which both groups have been subjected over the centuries, is testament to the power of stereotypes, indeed to their ability to withstand evidence reflecting contrary behavior. All this fury has not been lost on either Jews or Blacks who have countered their situations by developing a special body of humor extraordinarily creative, vibrant, devious, and flexible. Folklorists have identified this type as a prime example of "protest humor."[6] By protest is meant a highly complex approach to the problem of subordination. At its basic level there is belief that personal salvation is to be found strictly within the group and that acceptance of the customs of the majority inevitably lead to a heavy personal loss. A second characteristic utilizes a favorite form of retaliation, the trickster motif, whereby a minority member scores by countering a specific insult offered by one's enemy. Third, a parody is devised against an alleged somatic or cultural image. The fourth approach logically accepts or follows the majority's thinking but twists the conclusion to allow for an ultimate escape. A fifth technique carries the action into role reversal: it derides the majority group by either deprecating its high status, pinpointing its weaknesses, or miming its behavior. Finally, the entire scene is reversed so that the images appear topsy-turvy, and the minority group emerges triumphant.

These techniques are crucial if the minority group is to maintain an elevated morale, a sense of dignity, and a feeling of power. To counter the thrust of humor stereotyping, it is essential that the denigrated group employ as many means as possible to fend off the worst effects and to retaliate. The objectives here are not the adaptation of the majority's prejudices but rather a different perspective. The desired end of humor for the out-group is not only the development of techniques to ward off stereotyping but the creation of an internal fulcrum that helps it maintain a sense of historical space and direction. The end of their laugh is actually the beginning of liberation.

In certain crucial ways, Jews and Blacks share most deeply the humor of the oppressed. Thus, much of their laughter emanates from a history of intense discrimination. Similarities in their backgrounds and experiences have produced a complex humor largely characterized as inwardly masochistic and tragic and externally aggressive and acrimonious. Until quite recently, both groups regaled themselves with tales and anecdotes that reflected prejudices turned partially inward and generated forceful hostilities directed toward a virtually unassailable oppressor. Yet, throughout the Jewish experience, there has been a growing intuitive notion—buttressed by an accumulating storehouse of jokes—that the laughter was leading to a sort of humorous promised land, a place impervious to insults, and more, a Shangri-la where laughter replaces all pain. It would appear that a similar characteristic has been developing within the Afro-American community recently as well. One major cultural consequence of these struggles has been its impact upon the parameters and content of American humor itself. It should be noted that from the early decades of the twentieth century, with the rise of mass media—specifically vaudeville, radio and film and later extended in television—the national form of humor has been radically altered by the laughter of these two groups. It could be argued that the humor of the present century is mainly that of urban, alienated masses, whose relationship to the dominant culture has been and continues to be that of the outsider. It is protest humor honed into an art form.

Outsider history has clearly resulted in specific humor responses. One identical reaction originating from trapped circumstances is what Freud has termed "gallows humor." This type of humor perches on the edge of personal destruction. Essentially, it confronts a hopeless and unavoidable situation and recognizes its inevitability by figuratively and literally depicting oneself as being hanged. Gallows humor enables the individual to not give in without recognizing the scene and insulting it at the same time. It is an awareness which causes the individual to "hang in" regardless of how terrifying or hopeless it might be.

Gallows humor is an unmistakable index of the morale and spirit of resistance of the oppressed, the absence of which reveals either resigned indifference or a serious breakdown in the will to resist tyrannization.[7] Victor E. Frankl, a psychiatrist who spent three years at Auschwitz and other Nazi prisons during World War II, wrote that a stranger would be surprised to find forms of art in concentration camps but "even more astonished to hear that one could find a sense of humor there as well." Frankl quickly added, however, that the humor was "only the faint trace of one" and "then only for a few seconds or minutes." Gallows humor has built-in limitations. Frankl further added, though, that humor was one of the "soul's weapons" in the struggle for self-preservation. "It is well known that humor, more than anything else in the human makeup, can afford an aloofness and an ability to rise above any situation, even if only for a few seconds."[8]

Jews and Blacks have created many tales of a gallows nature. "Well, what's news today?" asked Simon to a friend during the Nazi-dominated 1930s. "At last," replied Nathan, "I do have something new. I have just heard a brand new Nazi joke. What do I get to tell it?" "Don't you know by this time?" Simon quickly shot back. "Six months in a concentration camp." The Afro-American version is similar. Having just arrived in town, a Black man asks a policeman, "Can you tell me where the Negroes hang out in this town?" "Yes," said the officer, "Do you see that tall tree over there!?"[9]

A whimsical fatalism often attaches to the gallows style making it more palatable:

> Three Jews were about to be executed. They were lined up in front of a firing squad, and the captain addressed each in turn. "Do you want a blindfold?" he asked the first. "Okay," replied the Jew, with an air of resignation. "Do you want a blindfold?" he asked the second. "All right," came the equally resigned response. "Do you want a blindfold?" he asked the third. "No," said the man, with a show of defiance. At that, the second Jew leaned over to the third and whispered, "Take the blindfold. Don't make trouble."[10]

A comparable Black story touches on Jewish terrain though it overarches white society as well:

> Two black men were visited by a fairy who told them that she would grant their fondest wishes.
> The first man turned to his friend and said, "I'm going to buy me a white suit, white shirt, white shoes, white Cadillac and drive to Miami Beach and lay in the white sand."
> He then asked his friend what wishes he desired most. He quickly replied: "I'm going to buy me a black suit, black shoes, black Cadillac, and drive to Miami Beach, and watch them hang your Black ass."[11]

Various tales focus on the absurdity of the oppressor in his drive to eliminate subordinate groups. Several such stories utilize law enforcement personnel since they obviously represent the ruling classes. This Jewish joke is set in nineteenth-century Czarist Russia:

> A man was drowning in the Dneiper River. He cried out for help. Two Czarist policemen ran up. When they saw it was a Jew, they said, "Let the Jew drown!"
> When the man observed that his strength was ebbing, he shouted with all his might, "Down with the Czar!" Whereupon hearing such seditious words, the policemen plunged in, rescued him and proceeded to arrest him.[12]

The corresponding Black joke is set in the South in the pre-World War II period:

> Late one evening, the two Carter brothers decided to steal a pig from a nearby white farmer. They drove their raggedy truck to his farm, grabbed the pig and took off down the road. The farmer saw the event and telephoned the sheriff. In a short while, the sheriff overtook the two brothers on a lonely road. As the truck pulled over,

the brothers quickly propped up the pig and put a hat on his head.

The sheriff shined a flashlight into the cab and asked the driver, "What's your name, boy!" "Willie Carter, Suh," he answered. The sheriff turned the light on the other brother. "What's your name, boy!" "Mah name is Billie Carter," he replied. "And," the sheriff said to the other figure, "what Carter are you?" "Oink," grunted the pig. "O.K.," said the sheriff, "drive on. I don't see no pig here."

The sheriff went to the farmer's house and reported that he couldn't locate the pig. "Couldn't find the pig!" declared the farmer. "Ah was sure them two Carter brothers stole him." "Two brothers?" said the sheriff. "Ah saw three brothers. And let me tell you, that Oink Carter is the ugliest nigger ah evah saw."[13]

Other parallels have been equally operative. Both groups have devised techniques of disguise for addressing their adversaries. Each has accented body movements and/or voice inflections to offset suspicion of improper thought or action. The ironic curse, an intent concealed by a statement meaning its opposite, pervades Jewish folklore, whereas the African-American community prefers the double entendre. In dealing with his detractors, the Jew obliquely refers to their welfare: "My enemies, they should live so long!" "They should live and be well!" Speaking of a leader's illness: "It couldn't happen to a nicer fellow." Blacks refer to whites as "The Man," shake their heads in amusement as they talk about caucasians, declaring that "whites sure are funny," "whites sure have rhythm," "The Man got it All." Both groups have special names and nick-names for their oppressors. Blacks especially have devised a substantial number of words over the centuries to undercut and demean whites: ofay, Mr. Charlie, Miss Ann, pig, grey, honkey, splib, vanilla. Such descriptions can be traced back to the plantation when slaves dubbed their masters after animals, "hogeye" and "hogjaw," to suggest just some of the more familiar ones. For Jews, the term *"goy"* has generally served to relate to all Christians but the word "WASP" has been in heavy use since the 1960s.

Different types of trickster motifs have been employed by minorities to undermine the most insulting aspects of prejudice ascribed to them. Mexican-Americans, for example, have totally reversed the degrading term "Chicano"—Anglo for lazy, indolent, sluggish—by adapting and elevating it to describe group power. Similarly, Blacks have almost completely rendered the

slur words "nigger" and "ugly" impotent through constant use
and by refashioning them in their own meaning. Comedian
Richard Pryor titled his book *Nigger, Nigger.* Comedian Redd
Foxx, to the bewilderment of about four hundred whites but the
uproarious approval of approximately thirteen thousand Blacks
at a benefit held at the Long Beach Sports Arena in 1966, silently
peered over the audience for a short moment and then slowly
said, "Ugly, Ugly. You are the ugliest Negroes I have ever seen. I
thought Negroes in Los Angeles were ugly. But you Long Beach
Negroes are even uglier." The whites in the audience looked at
each other very cautiously.[14] Likewise, Jews laugh at the declaration of not being able to tell one Jew—paralleling Afro-American
sentiments—from another. The phrase "funny but you don't look
Jewish" has become a punchline without need of a story. An
example tells of an orthodox Jewish businessman who was in
China on Yom Kippur and desired to attend services. He inquired about and learned of an Orthodox synagogue. It took him
hours to locate it but once there he was amazed to find Chinese
worshippers and a Chinese rabbi. After the service he went over
to the rabbi and exclaimed that it was one of the finest he had
ever attended. The rabbi looked him over and asked, "Ah so, are
you Jewish?" "Of course I'm Jewish," the man said in a pained
way. "Funny," said the rabbi, "you don't look Jewish."[15]

Finally, both communities have relied heavily on retaliatory
humor as a means of counteraggression. Unable to reply physically to discriminatory practices, these groups have been forced
to resort to the magic and majesty of language. In this respect,
both Blacks and Jews have fashioned powerful, subtle, intricate,
biting expressions to identify and excoriate their detractors. Over
the centuries, the oppressor has been carefully analyzed and
dissected in the quest to emerge from the denigration with self-
esteem and inner control. Moreover, they have created a niche
within the popular culture from which they managed constant
guerrilla humor raids.

2.

Within these comparative dimensions of humor, however, the
two groups have responded differently to the continuous stress
they confront. The unique qualities of Jewish humor have been

its self-criticism, reliance on rationality and realism, its cautious yet positive assessment of the next moment and its high degree of historical perspective. "Jewish humor is more than a comedy of affirmation," surmised Sharon Weinstein. "It is more accurately a comedy of continuity. To be Jewish is to remember what Jews *have been* as well as what they are." As Weinstein observed of the significant element of religious celebrations, the key word is *remember*. But the emphasis goes beyond the past, it connects to what is coming. "Jewish humor, their sense of triumph even, emerges from a fluid connection with their history and with the prevailing optimism that this too, no matter how horrible, shall pass, and that Jews as a people will endure." [16]

A profound consequence of this continuum has been a humor which operates at virtually every level and represents diverse modes of laughter. Not at all easy to define, Jewish humor provides such a challenge that virtually everyone tries to wrestle with it. For Joseph Dorinson, there is at the very least one profoundly simple cause: "The humor in the main was derived from the pain." As support, he turns to a marvelous statement by Mel Brooks who has had a profound impact on the parameters of American humor from the late 1960s to the 1980s: "If your enemy is laughing, how can he bludgeon you to death?" [17] In a similar vein, Robert Alter has declared that "Jewish humor typically drains the charge of cosmic significance from suffering by grounding it in a world of practical realities: 'If you want to forget all your troubles put on a shoe that's too tight!' " [18] At the other end of the spectrum is Larry Mintz's paradigm which defines the boundaries of Jewish humor by first ironically observing that the continuum moves from right to left. It begins with laughter about Jews by non-Jews and proceeds through self-deprecating humor, "realistic" or self-analytical humor, on to aggressive and re-taliatory laughter. These categories are not necessarily mutually exclusive. However, its variety and complexity, Mintz observed, demands a recognition that Jewish humor cannot be described or explained with any amount of ease or assuredness. [19]

An understanding of Jewish humor in America begins with a telescopic view into distant historical reaches. It is over-whelmingly a history of marginality and of endurance. Isaac Deutcher illuminated a salient feature of Jewish existence when he stated that it has often been on the borderlines of different civilizations, religions and national cultures. "They lived on the margins or the nooks and crannies of their respective nations. Each of them was in society, yet not in it, of it yet not of it. It was this that enabled them to rise in thought . . . and to strike out mentally into wide horizons, and far into the future."[20]

Purpose and endurance, twin characteristics of elevation and survival, led to an internalization of discrimination and oppressive insults. This quality of perseverance, noted by various thinkers, has rooted in the humor of self-ridicule. Freud was the first to recognize self-mockery as essential to in-group stability. The process he described fulfills an important ingredient in humoring oneself:

> A particularly favorable occasion for tendentious jokes is presented when the intended rebellious criticism is directed against the subject himself, or, to put it more cautiously, against someone in whom the subject has a share—a collective person, that is (the subject's own nation, for instance). The occurrence of self-criticism as a determinate may explain how it is that a number of the most apt jokes . . . have grown up on the soil of Jewish popular life. They are stories created by Jews against Jewish characteristics.[21]

The circuitousness of Jewish humor—an ability to fend off the attacker's arguments by redirecting the insult inwardly—has received considerable attention because of its delightful economy. Even a joke aimed at someone else might well be thrust at the Jews themselves. Such humor has a masochistic component and uses features of the stereotype as the basic material for joking. Against the image of the Jew as a grasping businessman is the story of a merchant who, on his deathbed in the small room behind the store he owned, with eyes closed, asked for his family:

> "Sarah, my wife, are you here at my bedside?"
> "Yes, Sam, I'm here as usual."
> "My oldest son, Benjamin, are you here?"
> "Yes, Dad, I'm standing right here."
> "My daughter, Rachel, are you present?"
> "Father, I'm at the head of the bed."
> "And my youngest son, David, are you here also?"
> "Yes, Dad, I'm right beside you."
> "Then," said the merchant, "if all of you are here, who's minding the store?"[22]

A similar story parodying the Shylock image contrasts other religious groups:

A Priest, Rabbi and Minister converse. The Minister informed his companions that he had hit on a good way to make converts; that yesterday he had a famous Protestant singer sing "Rock of Ages" and obtained 10,000 converts. On meeting again in one week, the Priest told them he had a famous Catholic singer sing "Ave Maria" and obtained 15,000 converts. At a still later meeting, the Rabbi informed them he had a famous Jewish singer sing "Gold Mine in the Sky." "How many converts did you make?" asked the Minister. "None," replied the Rabbi, "but 50,000 Jews joined the airforce."[23]

And a more recent quip which appeared after the Arab-Israeli Six Day War:

Why did the Israelis win the war?
Because everytime the Egyptians charged, the Israelis over-charged.[24]

The intellectual tradition of Jewish culture added a special dimension to its humor, a quality connected to self-analysis, one labeled "rebellious rationalism" by Irving Kristol. A colloquial example reflecting this tradition is the rejoinder to the question, "Why does a Jew answer a question with a question?" The answer of course is "Why not?" Kristol has incisively noted that "Jewish humor dances along a knife-edge that separates religious faith from sheer nihilism. It 'knows' that the material world is the only true reality, but it also finds that this world makes no sense in its own terms and is impossible to live in."[25]

Thus the humor has been extraordinarily cerebral, creating a distance between the reality and the individual, enabling the person to confirm a mental loftiness while at the same time keeping a cautious skepticism. "How are things?" is a folk expression which can be found at every level of Jewish culture. "How should things be?" is the wary reply. Since images have a way of being deviously manipulated, trust resides in the literal:

My son has just lost his wife, who left him with three small children; his house has burned down, and his business gone bank-rupt—but he writes a Hebrew that's a pleasure to read.[26]

Similar to all other minority groups but central to Jewish humor, the overcoming of adversity has been partially accomplished by protesting cosmic relationships. Simmons observed that one protest technique is to draw a close connection to symbolic majority religious figures. Several stories portray the

troubling situation in which Christianity cannot be ignored albeit
it certainly can be piqued. The first deals with Jews and Catholics:

> An old Jewish man was admitted to a Catholic hospital for an
> operation. A nun asked him what relative would be responsible for
> his bill. The old Jew replied, "My only living relative is my sister, but
> she cannot be responsible as she is an old maid, a convert to
> Catholicism and a nun." The nun immediately said, "I'll have you
> know we are not old maids—we are married to Jesus Christ."
> Whereupon the Jew exclaimed, "Oh, in that case, send the bill to my
> brother-in-law!"[27]

A second relates the conversation between an anguished father
and the local rabbi, who represents wisdom and sound judgment.
On its surface level, the tale examines the problem of being
Jewish in a Christian world. A closer look, however, reveals a
subtle twist so that the joke is turned inward and becomes an
example of masochistic ordering:

> "Rabbi," cried the little Jew, "a terrible thing has happened. My
> son wants to marry a Gentile girl."
> "Your son!" replied the Rabbi. "Look at me and my son. Here I
> am, the leader of the community. Everyone looks up to me as an
> example, and looks to my family, and my son wants to marry a
> Gentile girl and wants to be baptized."
> After a silence, the little Jew said, "Everyone comes to you with
> their problems, but what do you do when you have such a terrible
> problem? To whom do you turn?"
> "What can I do? I turn to God."
> "And? What did God tell you?"
> "God said to me. 'Your son! . . . Look at mine.'"[28]

Yet it should not be assumed that this humor is primarily one
of deprecation. Similar to other oppressed groups, Jewish energies are galvanized to retaliate. Almost all downgraded groups
have resorted to putting down their adversaries by utilizing virtually the identical stereotypes employed against them. As in the
humor of oppression, the main insult by the majority group has
been its insistence on minority dumbness. Because of their accent on intellectual attainment, Jews have avoided this particular
aspersion. Nevertheless, they have constantly harped about the
intellectual inferiority, if not stupidity, of their oppressors. In
contrast to "The Man," coined by African-Americans, Jews
have employed the term *they* and the much harsher *goy* although

on many occasions they have turned to other Yiddish slang terms such as *schlemiels* and the anatomical *schmucks*. Hence, the majority is regarded as unworthy because *they* are slovenly, *they* eat like *chazars* (pigs), *they* drink liquor, *they* possess *goyishe*— meaning dumb—minds. Especially, *they* just don't *think*. Consider the story of the Jew who converted to Christianity:

> A Jewish man decided to convert to Christianity and entered a program of conversion. After months of religious training he was baptized into the church.
>
> On the morning following this symbolic act, his wife found him praying in the traditional manner, with a skull cap and a shawl wrapped around his shoulders.
>
> "Harry," his wife cried out, "what are you doing? You're praying in the traditional Jewish way." Harry looked up, slapped his forehead, and shouted, "Oh, my *goyishe* mind."[29]

Not only against their oppressors, but on other ethnic and racial groups have Jews cast their insults. Similar to other minorities, Jews have learned the American pecking order and adopted the national style. So there are aggressive jokes and anecdotes directed toward Blacks, Poles, Mexicans, Puerto Ricans and others. These jokes exemplify the immigrant movement itself in that the newcomer's role is often identical to the one held by those who arrived earlier. These antitales have been passed down from one minority group to another as it rises significantly in social standing and a lower group fills the position previously held, a characteristic of the numbskull or idiot jokes. An instructive tale of the mid-1960s, which also struck the "chord of absurdity" of contemporary life as writer Bruce Jay Friedman acutely phrased it, is set in New York City following the ruling by the Vatican Council in 1964 exonerating the Jews as the executors of Jesus Christ:

> Two elderly Jewish ladies meet on the street after a long separation. "How are you, Sadie?" asked her friend. "How should I be?" replied Sadie. "I'm fine, thank goodness. I've been watching television."
>
> "Television?" remarked her friend.
>
> "Yes. I've got lots of time, so I watch all the programs."
>
> "What have you watched lately?" asked her friend.
>
> "Well, I recently saw a news program which came from the Vatican. It said that we Jews are no longer responsible for killing Christ."

"Is that right?" said her friend. "Well, if we didn't kill Christ, who did?"

"I don't know," replied Sadie. "Probably the Puerto Ricans."[30]

Despite such outward jibes, however, the quintessence of Jewish humor remains its resourceful inner mechanisms. As Martin Grotjahn has cleverly perceived, the self-deprecating joke can disguise the mask. "It is by no means a sign of masochistic perversion. The Jewish joke constitutes victory by defeat, an ancient device of pride. The persecuted Jew who makes himself the butt of the joke deflects his dangerous hostility away from the persecutors onto himself. The result is not defeat or surrender, but victory and greatness."[31] Thus Mel Brooks's article of faith in guiding him through a hostile environment is that "every small Jew should have a tall *goy* for a friend, to walk with him and protect him against assault."[32]

Whatever triumph occurs emanates also from a type of realism or self-analytic assessment that, as Mintz has pointed out, is more related to incongruity theory than to tendentious notions.[33] That is, the humor seeks the truth in experience rather than operating mainly as a weapon. An illustration of realism is a proletarian tale set in a clothing factory. It is a story of seeming futility and resignation, yet also suggests realism through a combination of oral and motion energies; and, finally, it demonstrates eventual triumph in an entrapped situation:

> Two workers in a clothing factory in New York were back together after the weekend and conversed as they worked: one folded the material and passed it to the other who in turn folded again and passed it on to an imaginary worker next to him; and so on.
>
> "So, Harry, how was your weekend?" asked Sam as he passed the material. "Fine, fine," replied Harry as he folded the material. "I went hunting."
>
> "Hunting!" exclaimed Harry, as he folded the material.
>
> "What did you hunt?" asked Sam, as he passed the material.
>
> "Moose," as he folded the material.
>
> "Moose?" as he passed the material.
>
> "Moose!" as he folded the material.
>
> "So what happened?" asked Sam, as he passed the material.
>
> "What happened?" answered Harry, as he folded the material. "I took my rifle and my toot and I tooted for the moose. Pretty soon, a huge moose came over the hill and I tooted some more. He finally saw me, lowered his head and charged."
>
> "So?" as he passed the material.

"So," as Harry folded the material, "I raised my rifle and pulled the trigger."

"So?" as he passed the material.

"So, nothing," as he folded the material. "The gun didn't go off."

"So, so?" as he passed the material.

"So," as he folded the material, "I shot again but nothing happened. The moose kept charging at me and pretty soon it was right on top of me."

"Now wait a minute, Harry," as he passed the material. "You mean to say that you shot at this big moose twice and nothing happened, that he was right on top of you and you're here right now. How come you're not dead?"

"You call this living?!" answered Harry, as he folded the material.[34]

A counterinterpretation to this idea was advanced by Dan Ben-Amos who has argued that joking in Jewish culture does not involve mocking of the self directly or obliquely, but rather manifests social differentiation. "The fact that Jews tells jokes about each other demonstrates not so much self-hatred as perhaps the internal segmentation of their society. The recurrent themes of these anecdotes are indicative of areas of tension within Jewish society itself, rather than the relations with outside groups."[35] This would explain the rise of the *JAP*, "Jewish-American-Princess," joke cycle of the late 1970s which clearly mirrored strains within the larger fabric of the Jewish family as well as conflict between men and women.

Regardless of interpretation, what emerges from the thrust of Jewish humor are several major themes, one being the ability to ward off oppression through a complexity of humorous defenses, and the other being the uses of humor to achieve a sense of liberation. "We are two thousand years of history, and significantly, the history of an unrelieved oppression," appears to be the folk message, "Nothing could be more cosmically hilarious." It is, therefore, beyond *kvetching*.

3.

Prior to the 1960s, little was known of African-American humor. Before the Civil Rights and Black Nationalist movements had reached deep into the inner sensitivities of the white world, few caucasians had heard the tales, jokes and expressions of

Blacks. Certainly jazz musicians, and occasionally folklorists, writers and others were privy to the lore and language of the African-American community, but they were a small number capable of reaching only a limited audience. Sometimes caucasian writers or entertainers utilized Black materials and inflections—Joel Chandler Harris and Al Jolson and a host of minstrel composers and performers share this dubious distinction—but they came to Black society more often with an outsider's presumptuousness. Yet by the time Stokley Carmichael uttered those thunderclapping and rallying words before Mississippi sharecroppers on the Meredith March in 1966—"We Want Black Power!"—whites were being hauled into the arena of the struggle by acts of verbal abuse, spontaneous outbursts, printed denunciations, and most significantly, humorous stories and satirical jibes. Ralph Ellison's incisive and symbolic *Invisible Man* was immediately cast into a historic hue, no longer applicable to the generation of the post-1960s.

The drive in the past several decades to confront the white majority was made possible not only by the Black sense of rejection but by a folk tradition of incredible power and latitude. Distinguished by its literary quality, imaginative expressiveness, breadth of experience, psychological flexibility, and unique historical perspective, African-American folklore extends deep into the past. Although its roots can be traced back to African culture, the slave era reinforced its function while altering its patterns. The concerted attempt by slave owners to obliterate African culture forced slaves to develop devious means of communicating in order to transmit values, attitudes, religious connections and existential affirmation to other slaves and succeeding generations. Ralph Ellison conveyed this essence in a dialogue with Robert Penn Warren in the mid-1960s:

> When the country was not looking at Negroes, when we were restrained in certain of our activities by the interpretation of the law of the land, something was present in our lives to sustain us. This is evident when we look at the folklore in a truly questioning way, when we scrutinize and listen before passing judgment. Listen to those tales which are told by Negroes themselves.[36]

As with most areas of African-American life, the expression of laughter was hidden until the protest period of the 1950s and

1960s. Part of the obscurity resulted from the stereotype whites developed to maintain and perpetuate the slave and caste systems. Particularly, Blacks were denied a range of social and intellectual capacities, among them the ability to translate life experiences into creative humor of their own reflection and not a humor copied from white society. That Blacks had indeed devised a humor language with unique qualities and complexity throughout the centuries was overlooked by whites, conveniently and purposely, in order to sustain their initial stereotype. *Sambo* was regarded as a natural buffoon whose comic base was essentially childlike.

Accommodative humor, therefore, was frequently the only form of humor heard by whites, because for Blacks to laugh at their oppressors, regardless of socioeconomic position, was to invite certain punishment. Like other subordinate groups, African-Americans learned to laugh out of earshot of whites, in a sort of permanently arranged box. A Southern Black described a special laughing box in his town:

> In my hometown there was a laughing box. Any time a Negro wanted to laugh he had to run to the box, stick his head into it, laugh and proceed home. If you lived too far away from the box, you could put the laugh into an envelope and mail it in, or put it into a bag and take it to the box.[37]

Segregation in almost all areas of life, but especially in the fields of entertainment and mass communication, compounded the situation by preventing the emergence of humorists who could have corrected the picture. African-American storytellers and comedians of the past played mainly to Black audiences on the "Chitlin" circuit or T.O.B.A. network. Few persons outside the community prior to the contemporary period could have identified such humorists as "Moms" Mabley, "Slapsey" White, Pigmeat Markham, Redd Foxx, George Kirby, Nipsey Russell and a host of lesser-known figures such as Timmy Rogers. Even the knowledgeable poet-humorist Ogden Nash expressed astonishment about the reach of Black humor. In a review of Langston Hughes's work, *The Book of Negro Humor*, Nash wrote in 1966:

> The range of humor here collected is a surprise. One would not have expected so many kinds, from so many sources. There are the

contemporary comics. . . . There are jokes having to do with jive
and the blues. There are anecdotes from the pulpit. There are stories
from Orleans and Harlem.[38]

Since that time, however, many anthologies of African-American
humor and folklore have been published along with many outstanding scholarly works by Blacks and whites treating the im-
port of humor in the community.

One of the most vital rearrangements in American culture in
the 1960s was the rise to national prominence of Black comedians and humorists. The emergence of "Moms" Mabley, Dick
Gregory, Godfrey Cambridge, Bill Cosby, Richard Pryor, Flip
Wilson, Redd Foxx, Eddie Murphy, and others reflects the
Blacks' insistent challenge to the social structure. The routines
seen and heard on television, in night clubs, films and college
auditoriums, on records and in books—in short, the dissemina-
tion of the humor through the interlacing levels of the mass
media—have made whites aware of Black attitudes and feelings
for the first time in centuries of slavery and segregation. Although many of the comedians' acts reflected idiosyncratic
nuances, they drew much of their material from a vast body of
folk humor.

Because of their rejective situation, Blacks turned to laughter
as one road to salvation. And that laughter, always noted but
never quite understood by whites, was there from the beginning.
"The remarkable thing about this gift of ours," wrote Jesse
Faucet in the 1920s, "is that it has its rise, I am convinced, in the
very woes which beset us. . . . It is our emotional salvation."[39]

Black-American humor arose, then, from compensatory and
accommodative sources, imprinting what W. E. B. Du Bois so
profoundly defined as the dual consciousness of Blackness. To
cope with a society that constantly and over-poweringly employed its imagination to oppress, Blacks adopted a gaming
stance. From this position they developed an ingenious mask
that, while presenting a stoic demeanor, allowed inner feelings to
range more freely. An anonymous early nineteenth-century slave
rhyme declared,

> Got one mind for white folks to see,
> 'Nother for what I know is me;
> He don't know, he don't know my mind,
> When he sees me laughing
> Just laughing to keep from crying.

The mask enabled not only an inner play but a means of "puttin'
on ole massa," of "just plain foolin' *The Man.*" From a slave
song,

> I fooled Old Master seven years,
> Fooled the overseer three.
> Hand me down my banjo,
> And I'll tickle your bel - lee.[40]

Survival necessitated the mask, the fooling, the contrived
smile, not only as a way of creating an inner world of dignity and
expressiveness but also as a means of sheer physical durability.
To combine both the psychic and the stomach and mix it with
laughter was to achieve a high degree of resourcefulness, if not
triumph. And survival necessitated the telling of funny stories. In
this way one's adversary is dissected and the triumph smacks
sweeter. This tale about a group of hungry slaves and how they
managed to scrounge extra food on the plantation from the
master makes the point quite sharply:

> I remember Mammy told me about one master who almost
> starved his slaves. Mighty stingy, I reckon he was.
> Some of them slaves was so poorly thin they ribs would kinda
> rustle against each other like corn stalks a-drying in the hot winds.
> But they gets even one hog-killing time, and it was funny, too,
> Mammy said.
> They was seven hogs, fat and ready for fall hog-killing time. Just
> the day before Old Master told them they was to be killed, something
> happened to all them porkers. One of the field boys found them and
> come a-telling the master: "The hogs is all died, now they won't be
> any meats for the winter."
> When the master gets to where the hogs is laying, they's a lot of
> Negroes standing round looking sorrow-eyed at the wasted meat.
> The master asks: "What's the illness with 'em?"
> "Malitis," they tells him, and they acts like they don't want to
> touch the hogs. Master says to dress them anyway for they ain't no
> more meat on the place.
> He says to keep all the meat for the slave families, but that's
> because he's afraid to eat it hisself account of the hogs' got malitis.
> "Don't you all know what is malitis?" Mammy would ask the
> children when she was telling of the seven fat hogs and seventy lean
> slaves. And she would laugh, remembering how they fooled Old
> Master so's to get all them good meats.
> "One of the strongest Negroes got up early in the morning,"
> Mammy would explain, "long 'fore the rising horn called the slaves
> from their cabins. He skitted to the hog pen with a heavy mallet in
> his hand. When he tapped Mister Hog 'tween the eyes with that

mallet, 'malitis' set in mighty quick, but it was an uncommon 'disease,' even with hungry Negroes around all the time."[41]

The poetry of the tale partly obscures the bitterness undergirding its origins, a bitterness that flows through much of Black humor. A sense of superiority, though, also emanates from the portrayal of the master as being not only foolish and vicious but, more significantly, also quite ignorant of Black culture.

Nor should the tale obscure the humor which developed within the inner reaches of the community. The outstanding characteristics of the humor that flourished over the centuries encompass its play qualities, which ward off punishment, a style that permits quick retaliation, a deep scrutiny, which enables important time lapse for assessment purposes, and a type of control humor vital for the maintenance, especially among the young, of a highly attuned and carefully sensitized community. Much of this has involved the play of words, which is extraordinarily elastic and elegiac and is buttressed by body gestures. "Playing the Dozens" is an example of control humor that relies upon a quick rhyming response within a stressful situation. The dozens are a verbal contest between several males and are usually fused with sexual bravado:

> I saw your Moma walking down the railroad track,
> She had a Pullman mattress under her back.
>
> Man, don't let it make you nervous,
> I saw your Moma yelling curb service.

There are conflicting interpretations regarding the origins and purposes of the dozens. Thomas Pettigrew offered the idea that the repartées are endurance tests that provide training for a lifetime of insult, while John Dollard suggested that the function of this form is to operate as a release mechanism for the anxieties of Black children. Finally, Roger Abrahams, in a fascinating and extensive investigation of the Afro-American community of Philadelphia, disputed Dollard's contention that the dozens are displaced aggression and argued instead that they are a folk method used "to develop one of the devices . . . which the nascent man will have to defend himself—the verbal contest."[42]

Despite the different opinions, it is the style by which the humor is transmitted that has become highly prized in the community. Black style, said one observer, "is more self-conscious, more expressive, more colorful, more intense, more assertive, more aggressive, and more focused on the individual than is the style of the larger society of which Blacks are part."[43] How a person did it is as important as what was actually said. The style is "full of drama," and plays out an entire culture. "Much of the humor, particularly in the toasts and the dozens, is characterized by a musical rhythmical quality, a love of verbal play and a delight in rhyme and pure sound."[44]

Even more than Jews, who themselves have developed an array of biting terms to counter the enemy, African-Americans have savored language as a means of conflict and control. For humor purposes, words are a means of cleverly and wittingly denigrating whites. Invectives are continually invented to demean "The Man" and nicknames are often used to highlight his uncivilized behavior. Thus the city of Birmingham, Alabama, which was the scene of at least eighteen bombings during the civil rights movement, one of which killed five little girls in a church, was renamed "Bombingham" by Black residents. Sheriff Jim Clark and his deputies who unleashed dogs and heavy streams of water on civil rights demonstrators were called—in the tradition of the white western—"Jim and the Clark boys." The ludicrous is often employed as a way of conveying perspective to the majority; in fact, historical and existential perspective has been a primary objective of Black humor. A student jailed in 1962 for sitting at a lunch counter that refused to serve coffee to Blacks, for example, retorted to the white waitress's statement, "We don't serve Negroes here," "That's good because I don't eat them."[45]

The acrimonious quality of the quips has consistently poured through as Blacks have assessed and reassessed white behavior. A mythical sign at the outskirts of a Southern town from which Blacks were barred delineated this sharp edge:

> If you can read this sign, run—
> If you can't read this sign, run anyway![46]

And despite denials of prejudice from whites, tales from the community have indicated a deep cynicism. One anecdote was about a politician, a U. S. senator, who told reporters that he was completely without bias against Negroes, and, in fact, had many as friends and was even writing a book about his famous Negro friends. In his book, he further explained, there was a chapter on a baseball player and another on a singer, and so on. A reporter inquired, "Senator, what is the title of your book?" The senator replied, "Famous Niggers I Have Known."[47]

Compensation against discrimination, however, has also been achieved through the process of inversion, whereby the superior/inferior roles are rearranged. On the crucial subject of intelligence, a story which reverses the image:

> A colored maid and her white employer became pregnant at the same time and gave birth on the same day. A few months later the white woman came running into the kitchen and exclaimed to the maid: "My baby said his first word today!" In the crib the colored baby sat up and said, "He did? He did? What did he say?"[48]

On the topic of stealing, to which Blacks are allegedly addicted:

> A white minister arrived in Africa and was met by an African chief and his party. The chief indicated to the minister that his bags would be picked up by his men and transported to the interior. But first he wanted to show him around the village. The minister demurred, pointing to his belongings. The chief smiled and allayed his fears: "You don't have to worry about your bags. There isn't a white man within a hundred miles of here."[49]

External and aggressive joking has always been complemented by internal jiving. As Langston Hughes once remarked, "Certain aspects of the humor of minority groups are often so inbred that they are not palatable for outside consumption."[50] Blacks have regaled and manipulated each other, as other groups assuredly do, with quips, barbs and anecdotes. Once limited strictly to the Black community, the laughter of retaliation and mockery, of control and defensiveness, has become an integral part of the popular culture. Exulting in a sense of mission and triumph because of the protest and revolt of the past several decades—fortified by the emergence of Black performers in the electronic media—the public air has been filled with Black humor. Dr. Martin Luther King, Jr., summed up this marked change in his intensely passionate "I have a dream" speech at the march on Washington in 1963, which he ended with an old slave witticism: "We ain't what we ought to be and we ain't what we're going to be but thank God we ain't what we was."

Open challenge and chiding admonishment quickly became major parts of the humor in the decades after the 1960s. Amiri

Baraka and several friends mocked the watermelon stereotype on a busy Washington, D. C. thoroughfare during the rush hour in full view of passing motorists; Black laundry workers refused to clean Ku Klux Klan robes in North Carolina; Dick Gregory playfully threatened to picket the U. S. Weather Bureau until it names a hurricane after a Black woman called "Beulah" (which, in fact, it eventually did); and Black students mimicked whites at college dances who were trying to dance in the Black style. And folk expressions criss-crossed the country:

> One Black to another: "I'm not prejudiced. I have lots of white friends. When I see them I treat them just like people."

> President Johnson to Dr. Martin Luther King, Jr., in a telephone conversation: "But look here Reverend King. It's been called the White House for over a hundred years."

> On the KKK practice of burning crosses on Black front lawns: "A white couple moved into a Negro neighborhood. That night a watermelon was burned on their front lawn."[51]

Multiplied across the country, these actions have echoed as a chorus of militancy in humor. Blacks openly defied, indeed taunted, whites, particularly those who had been at one time inviolate. Before he was the victim of an assassination attempt which left him paralyzed, Governor George Wallace of Alabama—who had stood in the doorway to block a Black student from entering the University of Alabama in the mid-1960s—became a target of Black humor.

> Governor Wallace goes for his annual medical checkup. The doctor examines him thoroughly and tells him to return for the results in a week.
> A week passes and Wallace comes in for the doctor's report. "Well, Doc, how'm ah doin?" The doctor looks at him carefully and says, "Gov'ner, I got good news for you and bad news."
> "Good news and bad news?" repeats Wallace. "All right, give me the good news first."
> "The good news, Gov'ner, is that you got cancer." Wallace blanched. "That's the good news, that ah got cancer?" "That's right." "Well, if that's the good news, what the hell is the bad news?"
> "The bad news is that it's sickle cell anemia," says the doctor.[52]

In addition to gaining a sense of power over detractors and events, the humor of militancy also reflects a high degree of self-acceptance. An intriguing change in the humor of the contemporary period is the increasing open evaluation of African-Americans by themselves. Mocking features ascribed to them by outsiders has been one of the most prominent infusions into the national humor. By so doing, Blacks have effectively undercut many of the stereotypes advanced by the majority. Consequently, the image of *Sambo* no longer dances or wears blackface or grins his watermelon smile. A dialogue between a Black man in Chicago, unemployed, down, and seated on a curb, and God who suddenly hears his plight, gives a clue to the direction of Black humor:

> "Tell me, Lord, how come I'm so black?"
> "You're black so that you could withstand the hot rays of the sun in Africa."
> "Tell me, Lord, how come my hair is so nappy?"
> "Your hair is nappy so that you would not sweat under the hot rays of the sun in Africa."
> "Tell me, Lord, how come my legs are so long?"
> "Your legs are long so that you could escape from the wild beasts in Africa."
> "Tell me, then, Lord, what the hell am I doing in Chicago?"[53]

The jive is gone and in its place is acceptance.

4.

Afro-American laughter, then, in common with Jewish laughter is aimed at the foibles of those who have come to the place Pogo finally came to accept. Pogo and his friends spent the better part of the day seeking the enemy. Tired, they eventually sat down in the swamp, ruing their ineffectuality. Pogo looked at them and exclaimed, "Friends, we have met the enemy and they is us." The liberation of the self, as Jews and Blacks have redeemingly found, begins with that observation: it is essential to go beyond *kvetching* and *jiving* to achieve oneness.[54]

NOTES

1. Joseph Dorinson, "The Gold Dust Twins of Marginal Humor: Blacks and Jews," *Maledicta* (Winter 1984): 163–92.

2. Nathan Hurvitz, "Blacks and Jews in American Folklore," *Western Folklore* 33 (October 1974): 302–6; Dorinson, "The Gold Dust Twins," p. 163 indicated he heard the rhyme in his neighborhood in 1944.

3. Alan Dundes, "A Study of Ethnic Slurs: The Jew and the Polack in the United States," *Journal of American Folklore* 84 (1971): 202.

4. Sigmund Freud, *Jokes and Their Relation to the Unconscious,* VIII (London: Hogarth Press and the Institute of Psycho-Analysis, 1905), pp. 97–104.

5. Konrad Lorenz, *On Aggression* (New York: Bantam Books, 1963), p. 284; David I. Singer, "Aggression Aroused: Hostile Humor, Catharsis," in *Motivation in Humor,* ed. Jacob Levine (New York: Atherton, 1969), p. 104; Thomas Hobbes, "Human Nature, or the Fundamental Elements of Policy," in *The English Works of Thomas Hobbes,* ed. Sir William Moleworth (London, 1840), p. 47.

6. Donald C. Simmons, "Protest Humor: Folklorist Re-Action to Prejudice," *American Journal of Psychiatry* 120 (1963): 567.

7. Antonin J. Obrdlik, "Gallows Humor—A Sociological Phenomenon," *American Journal of Sociology* 47 (March 1942): 709–12.

8. Victor E. Frankl, *Man's Search for Meaning: An Introduction to Logotherapy* (New York: Pocket Books, 1963), pp. 68–69.

9. S. Felix Mendelsohn, *Let Laughter Ring* (Philadelphia: Jewish Publication Society of America, 1941), p. 109; Author's notes, Los Angeles, 9/66.

10. Harvey Mindess, *Laughter and Liberation* (Los Angeles: Nash Publishing Co., 1971), p. 132.

11. Author's notes, Los Angeles, 4/68.

12. Nathan Ausubel, *A Treasury of Jewish Folklore* (New York: Crown Publishing Co., 1948). p. 442.

13. Author's notes, Los Angeles, 4/68.

14. Author's notes, 4/66.

15. Author's notes, 6/65.

16. Sharon Weinstein, "Jewish Humor: Comedy and Continuity," *American Humor: An Interdisciplinary Newsletter* 3 (Fall 1976): 1.

17. Kenneth Tynan, *Show People* (New York: Simon and Schuster, 1979), p. 213.

18. Robert Alter, "Jewish Humor and the Domestication of Myth," in *Veins of Humor,* ed. Harry Levin (Cambridge: Harvard University Press, 1972), p. 256.

19. Larry E. Mintz, "Jewish Humor: A Continuum of Sources, Motives and Functions," *American Humor: An Interdisciplinary Newsletter* 4 (Spring 1977): 4.

20. Isaac Deutcher, "The Non-Jewish Jew," in *The Jew in the Modern World,* ed. Paul Mendes-Flor (New York: Oxford University Press, 1980). p. 231.

21. Freud, *Jokes and Their Relationship to the Unconscious* in Standard Edition, 8 (London, 1960), pp. 111–12.

22. Author's notes, 11/65.

23. Simmons, "Protest Humor," p. 568.

24. Howard J. Ehrich, "Observations on Ethnic and Intergroup Humor," *Ethnicity* 6 (December 1979): 385.

25. Irving Kristol, "Is Jewish Humor Dead?" in *Mid-Century: An Anthology of Jewish Life and Culture in Our Time,* ed. Harold U. Ribalow (New York: Beechurst, 1955), p. 436.

26. Irving Howe and Eliezer Greenberg, eds. *A Treasury of Yiddish Stories* (New York: The Viking Press, 1954), p. 26.

27. Simmons, "Protest Humor," p. 669.

28. Martin Grotjahn, "Jewish Jokes and Their Relationship to Masochism," in *A Celebration of Laughter,* ed. Werner M. Mendel (Los Angeles: Mara Books, 1970), p. 139.

29. Author's notes, 6/66.

30. Recounted by Arnold Pasternak, 6/66.

31. Grotjahn, "Jewish Jokes," in *A Celebration of Laughter,* p. 137.

32. Tynan, *Show People,* p. 213.

33. Mintz, "Jewish Humor," *American Humor Newsletter,* p. 4.

34. Recounted by Arnold Pasternak, 6/66.

35. Dan Ben-Amos, "The 'Myth' of Jewish Humor," *Western Folklore* 32 (April 1973): 112–31.

36. Robert Penn Warren and Ralph Ellison, "A Dialogue," *Reporter* (March 25, 1965), p. 43.

37. Author's notes, recounted by Solomon Jones, 4/70.

38. *Los Angeles Times, Calendar Section* (March 13, 1966), p. 33.

39. Jesse Faucet, "The Gift of Laughter," in *The New Negro,* ed. Alain Locke (New York: Albert and Charles Boni, 1925), p. 166.

40. B. A. Botkin, ed., *Lay My Burden Down* (Chicago: University of Chicago Press, 1945), p. 3.

41. Botkin, *Lay My Burden Down,* pp. 4–5.

42. Thomas Pettigrew, *Profile of the Negro American* (New York: Van Nostrand, 1964), p. 40; John Dollard, "The Dozens: The Dialect of Insult," *American Imago* I (1939): 3–24; Roger Abrahams, *Deep Down in the Jungle* (Hatboro, Pa,: Folklore Associates, 1964), pp. 57–58, but see entire chapter.

43. Thomas Kochman, *Black and White Styles in Conflict* (Chicago: University of Chicago Press, 1981), p. 130.

44. Daryl C. Dance, "Black American Humor," *American Humor: An Interdisciplinary Newsletter* 4 (Spring 1977): 3–4.

45. Joseph Boskin, "Humor in the Civil Rights Movement: Laughter in the Outer Sanctuaries," *Boston University Journal* XVIII (Spring 1970): 2–7.

46. Author's notes, 6/67.

47. Langston Hughes, "Jokes Negroes Tell on Themselves," *Negro Digest* 9 (June 1951): 25.

48. Author's notes, 4/67.

49. Author's notes, 7/71.

50. Hughes, "Jokes Negroes Tell on Themselves," *Negro Digest,* p. 25.

51. Author's notes, 7/65.

52. Author's notes, 8/72.

53. Author's notes, 8/72.

54. Joseph Boskin, "Goodbye, Mr. Bones," *New York Times Magazine* (May 1, 1966): 31, 84–92; Norine Dresser, "The Metamorphosis of the Humor of the Black Man," *New York Folklore Quarterly* 26 (September 1970): 216–28; Robert Brake, "The Lion Act is Over: Passive/Aggressive Patterns of Communication in American Negro Humor," *Journal of Popular Culture* 9 (Winter 1975): 549–60.

LAUGHTERMAKERS

ALBERT GOLDMAN

"Jewish" and "comic" are words that slot together like "Irish" and "cop," "Chinese" and "laundry," "Italian" and "tenor." From the earliest years of vaudeville—Weber and Fields, Dutch jokes, slapstick; to silent movies, Ben Blue, Charlie Chaplin; to early radio, Ed Wynn the Fire Chief, Eddie Cantor, Jack Benny; to talkies, the Brothers Marx and Ritz; to burlesque, Phil Silvers, Red Buttons; to Broadway revues, Bert Lahr, Willie Howard, Phil Silvers, Zero Mostel; to night clubs, Joe E. Lewis, Henny Youngman, Buddy Hackett; to the great days of television, Milton Berle, Sid Caesar; to the cabaret theater, Nichols and May; to the sick comics, Lenny Bruce, Mort Sahl, Shelly Berman, Woody Allen—they've all been Jews.

Yet until the 1950s there was never any Jewish humor in the American media. So many Jewish comics and never a Jewish joke! Far from exploiting their identity as Jews, most comics did everything in their power to disguise the fact that they were Jewish. They changed their names from David Kaminski to Danny Kaye, from Joey Gottlieb to Joey Bishop, from Jerome Levitch to Jerry Lewis, from Murray Janofsky to Jan Murray. They tacked cute little pigtails on their names: Joe-y, Dan-ny, Sand-y, Len-ny, Hen-ny. They studied radio announcers' diction so they shouldn't nasalize, dentalize, glottal stop, and fall into the yeshiva student singsong. Nose jobs they got because people wanted to see a nice gentile face—no more beaks and popeyes. Quiet "tasty" clothes; cigarettes instead of cigars; flat-finished tuxedos instead of shiny mohair—why, some of those Jewish comics studied so hard to be *goyim,* rubbed out so many Jewish features from their faces, cosmeticized their voices and speech so drastically, they wound up looking as if they had been molded in the same factory that makes Barbie dolls. "Ladies and gentlemen, the networks are proud to present Bob Blank! He isn't Jewish—but then he isn't human either."

Some comics might let down and do some Jewish material at a meeting of the Friars or Lambs (show-biz organizations) or at a big B'nai B'rith dinner or UJA banquet—not much, just enough to say *"Ich bin ech a Yid"*—"I'm a Jew too." Or if they were working the "mountains," the Catskill resort and outside New York, they would adjust to audiences most comfortable in Yiddish. Apart from such old-fashioned ethnic enclaves, there was no room in America for Jewish humor, which was regarded as a dangerous and embarrassing commodity: something the *goyim* could never understand; something the Jews themselves—the successful, highly assimilated Jews—would be embarrassed to acknowledge. So your typical Jewish comedian, like Jack Benny, would pretend to be a typical American, a small-town skinflint from Waukegan, Illinois. Just in case you missed the point, he would bring on a caricatured old Jew out of vaudeville—a Schlepperman or Meester Kitzel—to play opposite him and bleach his already immaculate face a whiter shade of pale.

Jack Benny's comedy—and that of most of his radio contemporaries—was emasculated comedy, comedy that insisted on being beyond reproach: a humor that would shock nobody, offend nobody, challenge nobody's tastes or prejudices. Perhaps it was radio, the first mass medium, or perhaps it was the Great Depression, that forced American humor in the thirties to enter a phase of white-on-white neutrality, that made it impossible for a Jewish comedian—or, for that matter, any comedian—to stand forth and speak his mind with the force and clarity of comic genius.

Back in the days when Chaplin ruled the screen, American comedy had been the unfettered expression of the comic artist. Chaplin was an English Jew who was at pains always to deny or minimize his Jewish origins. At the same time his comedy was an abstract of Jewish humor, with the essential Jewish properties operating in their traditional Jewish manner, the only difference being that the Yiddish tags were removed so as to achieve a "universal" effect. The Little Fellow was the apotheosis of the *schlemiel*. His vulnerability and helplessness, his quick wit and

ingenuity in self-preservation, his absurd affectation of dan-
dyism, his infatuation with blond-haired, fair-skinned, volup-
tuously innocent maidens, whom he courted with eyes brimming
with Jewish soul and sentiment, were the classic notes and signs
of the Jewish comic hero.

The comedy of the Marx brothers was also Jewish farce *man-
qué*. If Chaplin distilled the self-pitying comedy of the *schlemiel,*
the Marx Brothers brought to intense focus the other great mode
of Jewish humor: the anarchic mockery of conventions and
values, which crumble to dust at the touch of a rudely irreverent
jest. "Subversive" was the word for the Marx Brothers, as it has
been the word often since employed both as condemnation of and
tribute to the work of Jewish humorists who refuse to be tram-
meled by the conventional pieties, delighting instead in demonstrating the fragility and preposterousness of much that passes as
social law and order. (The Jew is not only exceptionally adroit at
assimilating the values of other cultures but stubbornly skeptical
about the value of many of these values.) So the essential dy-
namic or working power of Jewish comedy operated powerfully
in America without declaring itself as such—until it was throttled
by the age of the corporation-sponsored, family-entertainment
gag. *Gag* indeed!

Meanwhile, in the American ghetto, pure, uncut Jewish humor
continued to play the vital role it has always played in Jewish life
wherever Jews have lived or however they have fared. Surely no
other people in history has made greater use of humor to assuage
its pain, assert its pride, exhibit its wit, consolidate its sense of
identity, buoy up its spirits, intensify its sexual attractiveness—
even blaspheme against its god!—without taking any more responsibility than a man who makes an innocent joke! To tabulate
all the ways in which humor functions in the Jewish community
would be virtually the same as tabulating all the ways in which
Jews are Jews.

When I first moved to Jewish Brooklyn in the early fifties
(having been reared in a wholly gentile community in western
Pennsylvania and consequently viewing Jewish society in the
same way as a *goy* who has for some odd reason been accepted as
a fellow-Jew), I was stunned by the audacity, the ferocity, the
originality, the sheer abundance and ubiquity of humor among
the young people of the neighborhood. Getting together in ritual
staging sessions at the backs of candy stores, in parked cars or in

some well-barred bedroom, they would perform for hours, much like professional stand-up comics but with vastly greater freedom in the use of obscene language and references, in Yiddish and English, pouring ridicule equally on the feared, admired, and despised *goyim* and on the Jewish family and society that surrounded them and infected them with the disgusting taint of Jewishness. The Jewishness of their humor lay precisely in its obsessional concern with the fact of Jewishness, a fact as ineluctable and irritating as the piece of grit inside the oyster, and just as productive of the pearl-like luster of gleaming wit.

What these laughtermakers were doing was exorcising the Jewish evil spirit, the *dybbuk,* from their souls by screaming out the curses of a particularly hysterical and obscene self-mockery. They were all *schlemiels* puffed up with a great sense of their own importance, but at the same time painfully deflated by the endless discovery of weaknesses, failures, and stupidities in themselves that militated against the cherished self-image. Eager to purge themselves before suffering another's criticism, they made endless verbal confessions of weakness, folly, and depravity, not only forestalling criticism but distancing their true "good" selves from the selfish, mean, stupid little beings they had been in the past. Theirs was the Jewish psychological predicament in America, the exaggerated demand upon the child by his parents that he attain some wonder of achievement, undermined at the same time by a rearing so fondly indulgent and devoid of frustration that the child never developed the discipline and self-control necessary for great accomplishments. Hence the solution provided by humor, that marvelous device of fantasy that enables us to fail and be forgiven, to attack and not be resented, to assert ourselves to the height of our bent and never have to deliver anything more substantial than a laugh to a receptive and sympathetic clique.

Jewish humor in mid-twentieth-century America, I soon discovered, was not a gentle, ironic, Sholom Aleichem folksiness; nor was it a sophisticated Heinesque intellectual wit; nor was it simply the one-two-three, laff! pattern of the professional joke huckster. It was the plaint of a people who were highly successful in countless ways, yet who still felt inferior, tainted, outcast; a people who needed some magic device of self-assertion and self-aggrandizement. Humor was for modern urban American Jews as basic and necessary as food and drink. It was their stimulant, their narcotic, their secret weapon. It was also the only channel through which their imaginative and creative energies seemed to flow with fable-like fluency in countless "bits" and "shticks" and uproariously funny narratives of the *schlemiel* and his endless discomfitures.

Inevitably, as the generation to which these young people belonged made their way into the entertainment industry, some of this potent, explosive but hitherto unacknowledged Jewish humor began to leak out through the media. One of the first manifestations was the comedy of Sid Caesar, the great television comic of the fifties. Caesar was a master of travesty, taking off from some typical Hollywood film type or some familiar social situation to soar into vastly exaggerated burlesques that substituted for the object of satire a grotesque satiric myth of the sort in which a cruder and half-illiterate Swift might have rejoiced. Caesar blew up the hoodlums and cowboys and ethnic stereotypes of American folk consciousness to monstrous dimensions and produced a cathartic laughter that was the comic counterpart to the catharsis of terror and violence triggered by his Hollywood originals. Though there was nothing decisively Jewish about his paranoid imaginings, there was often a sly insertion of Jewishness in his skits. The characters in his Japanese movies bore names like Takah Mishiggah or Prince Shmatah (literally, "Really Crazy," "Prince Rag"). The barrister in his British court scene would complain, "Your honor, the defendant *opened such a mouth to me!*" Sid himself bore plainly the stamp of the urban Jewish scene in his accent, gestures, and facial grimaces. He was the newly assimilated American Jew: no longer a shuffling, stoop-shouldered character epitomized by the Yiddish actor Menasha Skulnik, but a young man of prodigious size and power. Mel Brooks, Caesar's principal writer, quipped: "Sid was the strongest comic in history. He could punch a Buick in the grill—and kill it!" The last great Jewish comic of the old tradition, the tradition of infusing Jewish fantasy and soul into the universal forms of low comedy, Sid Caesar provided at the same time the direct inspiration for the first great Jewish comedian of the new style, the explicit comedy of the Jew as Everyman.

Lenny Bruce was a comic genius who revolutionized his art by insisting that the tightly impacted humor of the New York ghetto be made the common property of the American people. Driven

by the twin screws of talent and chutzpah, Lenny blasted into the
open the golden veins of comedy that for many years had lain
hidden behind tons of shame and self-consciousness and fear of
self-assertion. Reared in a totally gentile environment on Long
Island, Lenny discovered Jewishness when already a grown man.
Fascinated by the difference between Jew and Gentile, he was
fond of ticking off—like God with a wet pencil stub in his
mouth—the entire creation into Js and Gs:

> All Drake's cakes are *goyish*. Instant potatoes are *goyish,* TV din-
> ners are *goyish*. Fruit salad is Jewish. Black cherry soda's very
> Jewish. Macaroons are very, very Jewish! Lime jello is *goyish*. Lime
> soda is very *goyish*. Titties are Jewish. Trailer parks are so *goyish*
> that Jews won't even go near them. Chicks that iron your shirt for
> you are *goyish*. Body and fender men are *goyish*. Cat boxes are
> *goyish*. Ray Charles is Jewish. Al Jolson is Jewish. Eddie Cantor's
> *goyish*.

Lenny's obsession with Jewishness proved prophetic of the
whole period of the sixties: the Jewish Decade. Overnight, the
Jew was raised from his traditional role of underdog or invisible
man to the glory of being the most fascinating authority in
America. Benefiting from universal guilt over the murders by the
Nazis, stiffening into fresh pride over the achievements of the
State, Israel, reaping the harvest in America of generations of
hard work and sacrifice for the sake of the "children," the Jews
burst suddenly into prominence in a dozen different areas of
national life. They became the new heroes of commerce, art, and
intellect. They scaled the social heights. Characteristically, they
celebrated their triumph in a rash of Jewish jokes that ran the
gamut from advertising slogans to masterpieces of oral and written humor.

At the high point of the Jewish Decade, you could walk into a
bookstore and find it stacked with such entertainments as: *How
to Be a Jewish Mother, Kosher Kaptions, Oy Oy Seven;* Jewish
novels in various shades of humor—sick, black, and blue—by
Philip Roth, Bruce Jay Friedman, Wallace Markfield, and Norman Mailer; plus collections of Jewish jokes, humorous Yiddish
expressions, absurd posters (a bearded Hasid wearing Super-
man's costume), and the collected works of such Jewish humorists as Jules Feiffer, David Levine, and the various comedians,
headed by Lenny Bruce, whose paperback collection of bits and

pieces was a best-seller in New York and on college campuses all over the country. What you couldn't find in the bookstore, the authentic oral intonations and accents and "timing" of Jewish humor, you could obtain in record stores, which displayed albums by Nichols and May, Shelley Berman, Mort Sahl, Mel Brooks, and Carl Reiner, to name just a few. Leaving the record store and descending into the subway, one stared at huge posters of a Chinese or a black proclaiming, "You don't have to be Jewish to love Levy's rye." Switching on the radio or TV, you were amused by the clever concoctions of the Jewish advertising writers eager to keep pace with their colleagues in show biz. Yiddish, once a dying language, received a shot of adrenalin as it was picked up and exploited by journalists. Even the kind of Jewish joke that was once confined to the garment district suddenly surfaced in the privileged purlieus of the Jet Set.

As the Jewish Mama and the Jewish Boy and the Jewish Princess and the Jewish Doctor became the familiar *dramatis personae* of American humor, lo and behold! a cultural miracle was wrought. For the first time in modern times the minute particulars of a little minority's life-style suddenly proved out as the "universals" of American culture. Far from regarding the jokes of the Jewish humorists as offensive or self-serving or unintelligibly parochial, Americans embraced Jewish humor and the Jewish *schlemiel* as a perfect rendering of themselves and their own problems. *Portnoy's Complaint,* the masterpiece of the genre, became one of the greatest best-sellers in the history of American publishing; and its author, after years of trying to write distinctly American fiction, was acclaimed as one of the greatest living American writers on the strength of his depiction of a hopelessly neurotic and hysterical Jewish boy.

Time has shown that this embrace of Jewishness was just the first in a series of minority-group identifications that has now expanded to include the Negro, the hillbilly, the American Indian, and other despised or proscribed groups. In making such identifications, Americans are motivated by a complex mixture of emotions ranging from profound feelings of guilt and penitence through their own sense of alienation, persecution, and self-hatred to the simple longing to belong to a group small enough and tight enough to provide its members with a true sense of personal identity. Being simply an American has not satisfied many souls; however, nobody is willing to be patronized as a member of a minority; hence the characteristic modern way of having your social-cultural cake and eating it too: the flight into ethnic masquerades via jokes, jargon, costume, and music.

Today the Jew is losing some of his prominence in American culture, his fad having worn itself out and his own identity showing signs of yet further transformations through the continuing process of assimilation. (Today's Portnoys typically marry their gentile sex goddesses instead of worshiping them from afar; the resulting offspring are not apt to suffer from having been reared by a Jewish mother.) Having scored heavily in all the cultural and social occupations to which they once aspired, American Jews are now eager to excel in pursuits that would have seemed startlingly alien to their ancestors. The most idealized Jewish hero of the early 1970s was neither a scientist, businessman, entertainer, or artist: he was Mark Spitz, a sensuously beautiful swimmer, the male equivalent of the traditional *shiksah* "cheese cake"—what is now called "beefcake."

The golden age of modern humor has also come to an end as American culture enters upon a new utopian phase in which the sense of impotence and the baffled anger that breed great satire are supplanted by the philosophy of activism and social amelioration preached by countless ecologists, conservationists, consumer protectionists, women libbers, etc., etc. The role of the comedian or humorist in this new social order is obviously far less important than it was in the days of Eisenhower stagnation and apathy. The once-familiar figure of the night-club comedian has virtually vanished along with the clubs in which he entertained. The cabaret theater has also disappeared. The big TV comedy shows have given way to situation comedies with their neatly formulated plots and trivializing attitudes. Only in an occasional film by Woody Allen does one still see anything of the genius of Jewish comedy. Philip Roth has continued to extend the resources of black humor in books like *Our Gang,* the mordant satire on Richard Nixon, and *The Great American Novel,* a burlesque of American baseball myths and stereotypes; but Roth's finely honed satire of Jewish society—perfected in a long sequence of brilliant tales and novels, from *Goodbye, Columbus* to *Portnoy's Complaint*—seems to have finally worn itself out for lack of fresh material.

How far, how wide, how deep, the impact of the latest outburst of Jewish humor has reached in terms of the enduring structure of American culture is a matter on which it is still too early to pronounce. Nothing ages more rapidly than jokes; nothing is more ephemeral than a cultural fad. Yet there is no denying the basic fact that the current crop of Jewish comic geniuses has attained through the obsessive assertion of their own Jewishness precisely the same breadth of appeal and universality of interest that was achieved in previous generations by comics who didn't dare even to hint that theirs was the perspective of a special and persecuted minority. Everything that was once strictly taboo in the comedy business is now routine, accustomed, and almost positively enjoined. The determination to smash through the remaining barriers to a total expression of the once shamefully repressed fantasies of the modern urban Jew remains strong largely because it has been so strongly endorsed by the society as a whole.

This may be a good thing for the Jewish comic or writer, if he has anything left to say. It certainly is not a good sign for Americans. The word "paranoid" is on everyone's lips today. Precisely! What greater evidence of the paranoia of the average American could be found than the fact that he identifies so glibly with the Jew?

LENNY BRUCE

Shpritzing the *Goyim*/Shocking the Jews

SANFORD PINSKER

> Now I neologize Jewish and *goyish*. Dig: I'm
> Jewish. Count Basie's Jewish. Ray Charles is
> Jewish. Eddie Cantor's *goyish*. B'nai Brith is
> *goyish;* Hadassah, Jewish. Marine corps—
> heavy *goyish*, dangerous. Koolaid is *goyish*.
> All Drake's Cakes are *goyish*. Pumpernickel
> is Jewish, and, as you know, white bread is
> very *goyish*. . . . Black cherry soda's very
> Jewish. Macaroons are *very* Jewish—very
> Jewish cake. Fruit salad is Jewish. Lime jello
> is *goyish*. Lime soda is *very goyish*.
>
> —from *The Essential Lenny Bruce*[1]

"The words of a dead man," W.H. Auden tells us, "are modified in the guts of the living." He had a fellow-poet, William Butler Yeats, in mind, but the sentiment holds true as well for Lenny Bruce. For some time now we have been modifying (or, to use a fancier term, "transmogrifying") Lenny Bruce, reimagining him—on stage, on screen, in biographies and critical articles—as prophet, as guru, as rabbi, as satirist, as stand-up comic, but, most of all, as martyr.

Let me begin by considering him as "neologist," a word he used shamelessly and without credentials, but which suggests something of the cultural landscape he both came from and forever changed. A neologist either invents new words or discovers new meanings for old ones. Lenny Bruce did neither. He did not invent the word *"shpriptz,"* although he was no doubt its most important popularizer; nor was he quite the innovator, the daring linguistic pioneer, that the term "neologist" implies. But *words* were what mattered to him, especially if they could take on the improvisational energy of a Charlie Parker or the go-for-broke abandon of the streetcorner wise-cracker. Words, showers of them, unleashed, sprayed, machine-gunned at the audience until they "cracked up," couldn't *stand* it anymore . . . that was Lenny Bruce's brand of neology whether he was "working a room" or talking on the telephone.

Here, for example, is Bruce *shpriptzing* the *goyim* in one of his most famous "bits"—Religions Incorporated. The scene is the headquarters where the movers-and-shakers (Oral Roberts, Billy Graham, Patamunzo Yogananda, Danny Thomas, Eddie Cantor, Pat O'Brien, General Sarnoff, and others) are conducting some heavy business. Bruce begins in parody—in this case, the syrupy southern voice of H. A. Allen—but he ends in pure *shpritz,* a torrent of images and off-the-wall associations:

> Now, gentlemen, we got mistuh Necktyuh, from our religious novelty house in Chicago, who's got a beautiful selluh—the gen-yew-ine Jewish-star-lucky-cross-cigarette-lighter combined; an we got the kiss-me-in-the-dahk *mezzuzah;* an the wawk-me-tawk-me camel; an these wunnerful lil cocktail napkins with some helluva saying theah—"Anuthuh mahtini faw Muthuh Cabrini"—an some pretty far out things. . . . (p. 62)

Bruce was hardly the first satirist to equate hucksterism with piety, to point out the dollar signs in officially God-fearing eyes, but he was probably the first comic to turn these observations into *shtick.* Of politics, there had been humor aplenty; about religion—especially the sort that named names and imagined Mother Cabrini cocktail napkins—there had been a conspicuous vacuum before Lenny Bruce. His *shpriptz* turned organized religion into a big, Spencer Gifts business.

If scat singers like Ella Fitzgerald or Mel Torme can turn the human voice into a wailing saxophone, or a screeching trumpet, Bruce's *shpritz* used words as if they were drumsticks: *bam—bam—bam.* The result was a rapid-fire rhythm that broke the rules of timing older comics like George Burns and Jack Benny had lived by, but Bruce's manic energy, his relentless pounding, also "broke up" the crowd.

To be sure, *shtetl* humorists were also "verbal," but with some important differences. They "unpacked their hearts" within the religious, cultural, and socio-political frameworks of the Jewish community, giving vent in *words* to frustrations that often arrived with the sanction of law or at the end of a gentile fist. Reviewing Sholom Aleichem's *Motl the Cantor's Son,* Saul Bellow put it this way:

> Powerlessness appears to force people to have recourse to words. Hamlet has to unpack his heart with words, he complains. The fact that the Jews of Eastern Europe lived among menacing and powerful neighbors no doubt contributed to the subtlety and richness of the words with which they unpacked.[2]

By contrast, subtlety was hardly Bruce's strong suit. His *shpritz* was designed to overwhelm, overpower, overkill. It thrived on confrontation, on making painfully "public" what *shtetl* humorists thought and said privately, with caution and, of course, in Yiddish.

That is why Bruce, for all the Yiddishisms he peppered through his monologues, bears but a slight resemblance to the traditions of Yiddish humor. He is too brassy, too cocksure of himself, finally too *American.* He learned the fine points of *shpritzing* not from Mendele Mocher Seforim or Sholom Aleichem (writers one has every reason to suspect he never read or, for that matter, knew about), but, rather, from a legendary character named Joe Ancis. As Albert Goldman's biography-as-*shpritz/shpritz*-as-biography would have it, Bruce met Ancis, the Ur-sick-comic, at Hanson's, a hang-out for comics that doubled as a drugstore/luncheonette. In 1947, a quarter would buy an egg cream and all the *shtick,* the patter and talk about the *business* that a down-on-his-heels comic could want. If New Orleans gave birth to the blues, Hanson's is where *shpritz* first went semiprofessional. Ancis eyeballed Bruce and decided to give him the Jewish version of what Blacks call "playing the dozens." He pinned a young woman against the counter and, in Goldman's reconstruction of those times, that place, neologized her as follows:

> "Oi, is this a fucking grape-jelly job! Varicosities on the legs. Sweat stains under the arms. Cotton panties from Kresge's with the days of the week. Always wears the wrong day. Schleps home to Carnarsie every night. Her old man beats her up while the mother listens to the

radio in a wheelchair. Supper is ham and eggs and grits and all that Southern-dummy-cheapo-drecky-dumbbell shit."[3]

Ancis cracked the joint up—with enough pure cataloging to make Walt Whitman envious, but, unlike the sonorous bard, delivered with a manic energy that always seemed on the edge of going completely out of control . . . and yet never quite did. In short, Ancis was the consummate *shpritzer,* an artist who had enough hidden verbal reserves to outlast even the toughest competition.

What Ancis lacked, however, was the raw courage or, if you will, the *chutzpah* necessary to work as a professional stand-up comic. *That,* as it turned out, Lenny Bruce had in abundance. He was a Brooklyn version of the frontier braggart who could reel off outrageous claims faster than his listeners could either digest them or register their dissent.

In a word, Bruce *overwhelmed* his audiences. But, unlike the ring-tailed roarers so dear to the heart of southwestern humorists, Bruce was more prone to direct his scathing commentary "outward." At the same time, ironically enough, he was perhaps the first Jewish stand-up comic to make regular raids on his autobiography. Instead of appropriating, and appealing to, the insular life of the Jewish community (as Yiddish humorists from Mendele Mocher Seforim to the Borsht Belt vaudevillians had, in effect, done), Bruce turned stage-center into a forum for free associating about them and us, the *goyim* and the Jews. The result coarsened Jewish material. At the same time he sharpened its public sting. When Bruce insists, for example, that "Pumpernickel is Jewish and, as you know, white bread is very *goyish,*" he both reduces "difference" to a matter of supermarket preference and makes it clear that the Jews were hipper, smarter, superior, *chosen*—because they saw their corned beef through a rye, darkly. At the same time, when Bruce explains that his irreverence results from having "no knowledge of the [Jewish] god . . . because to have a god you have to know something about him, and as a child I couldn't speak the same language as the Jewish god" (p. 44), the ignorance he glibly equates with alienation may well be the central truth of American-Jewish assimilation. If these quotations smack of contradiction, Bruce, like Whitman, did not especially worry: *"So I contradicted myself,"* I can hear his ghost *shreiing, "so what?"* He, too, contained multitudes—in this case, the popular culture he absorbed half by osmosis, half by catch-up reading; the American-Jewish "culture" he regarded as albatross and badge of honor; the hipster ethos he lived, and died, for.

Irving Howe, clearly as admiring as he is embarrassed by Bruce's mean-spirited, unrelentingly public attacks on *Yiddishkleit* describes the Bruce phenomenon this way:

> Humor of this kind bears a heavy weight of destruction; in Jewish hands, more likely self-destruction, for it proceeds from a brilliance that corrodes the world faster than, even in imagination, it can remake it. A corrupt ascetic is a man undone. Bruce remained a creature of show biz, addicted to values he despised, complicit at the "upper" levels of his life in the corruption of the big time and yielding at the "lower" levels to the lure of drugs and chaos.[4]

Mordecai Richler, the comic novelist, puts the matter more bluntly: "Lenny Bruce did not die for my sins."

To *shpritz* the *goyim*/to shock the Jews—that is to describe what Bruce did, rather than to turn his self-styled neology into a modern jeremiad, his neuroses into the stuff of martyrdom. If Mort Sahl used the evening newspaper as a source for "material," as a prop for his comic timing and as a way of juxtaposing liberal (Jewish?) values against American hypocrisy, Bruce often resorted to that last refuge of the freshman essay—"definition," according to Webster:

> Now, a Jew, in the dictionary, is one who is descended from the ancient tribes of Judea, or one who is regarded as descended from that tribe. (p. 40)

That, of course, is the definition, but the culture knows better and, moreover, it operates—just below the surface of polite, liberal pieties—on what it *knows*. As Bruce puts it, with a matter-of-factness that usually preceded his more trenchant observations: "but you and I know what a Jew is—*One Who Killed Our Lord.*" Long before blowing the whistle on this-or-that conspiracy, on this-or-that official cover-up, Bruce used the *emmis,* the truth, to pack them in at the hipper nitespots:

> Alright, I'll clear the air once and for all, and confess. Yes, I did it, my family. I found a note in my basement. It said: "We killed him. Signed, Morty." (pp. 40–41)

An older generation of Catskill comics—who did material of the Jews, for the Jews and, most important of all, *in* "Jewish"—knew instinctively that some things were tasteless, *schmutzike* ("dirty"), not funny—even at Grossinger's. But in front of "mixed" crowds like those at nightclubs like the "hungry i"? Unthinkable! There was simply too much history, too much felt pain, packed into their immigrant bones, much less into the more conventional bones of their audiences. Besides, if Bruce could shock such Jews by aping the affected talk of reform rabbis ("Today, on Chin-ukka, with Rose-o-shonah approaching . . .") and letting us in on the "truth" about God (rabbi: "What cheek! To ask [if God exists or not] in a temple! We're not here to talk of God—we're here to sell bonds for Israel!"), he could also misfire rather badly: "A *mezzuzah* is a Jewish chapstick. That's why they're always kissing it when they go out." The first examples are the stuff of satire and, of course, the occasion for predictable charges about self-hatred; on the other hand, the wisecrack about chapstick *mezzuzahs* falls flat, embarrassing in its ignorance and sheer pointlessness.

Bruce, of course, put as much distance as he could between himself and the conventional, the timid, the fainthearted. His appeal was a willingness—indeed, a compulsion—to tell the *emmis* (the truth) as it was, and still is. "Maybe it would shock some people," Bruce insisted, moving toward the sermon that often replaced the punch line of conventional comics, "to say that we killed him at his own request, because he knew that people would exploit him. . . . In Christ's name they would exploit the flag, the Bible, and—*whew!* Boy, the things they've done in his name" (p. 41).

His riff on Blacks that began "By the way, are there any niggers here tonight?" shows that Bruce understood that language is power, and also that the words that hurt can be words defused, exhausted by repetition (e.g., "That's two kikes, and three niggers," Bruce would begin, in the guise of a Southern tobacco auctioneer, "and one spic. One spic—two, three spics, One mick. One mick, one spic, one hick, thick, funky, spunky boogie. . . ." The point, of course, is that

if President Kennedy got on television and said, "Tonight I'd like to introduce the niggers in my cabinet," and he yelled "niggernigger-niggerniggernigger" at every nigger he saw and "boogeyboogeyboogey, niggerniggernigger" 'till nigger lost its meaning—you'd never make any four-year-old nigger cry when he came home from school. (p. 16)

Litany, then, became for Bruce a species of exorcism, a way to purify the language by purgation.

The rub, of course, is that there was more to Bruce's *modus operandi* than "shock" and certainly much, much more than labels like *sick comic* could cover. For the hipster, the world divided (a bit too neatly) into the "with-it's" and the squares, into those who dug *real* jazz (Charlie Parker) and those who bought Montavani records. Those "in-between," as it were, wore madras shirts and belt-in-the-back pants, owned *all* the Brubeck albums, thought of themselves both as liberal and as majoring in the liberal-arts. They swelled the crowd on weekends and, not surprisingly, a high percentage of these medium-rollers were Jewish.

For them, Bruce was a clean break from the tedious, predictable patter of the Borsht Belt comics their parents still found funny. This guy could really do a number on bigots, on religious hypocrites, on the smug complacencies of a smug, majority culture. To walk out complaining that Bruce was a "toilet mouth," that "enough-was-enough" was to put yourself on record as the enemy. To laugh, to clap approvingly or, better yet, to simply nod and let out a soulful "yeaaaa" was to be on the side of the left-thinking angels.

Shtick about Nazis became the acid test. Long before Mel Brooks gave us the outrageous production number from *The Producers* called "Springtime for Hitler," Bruce had thrown this bit of off-the-cuff analysis at his audiences:

Eichmann really figured, you know, "The Jews—the most liberal people in the world—they'll give me a fair shake." Fair? *Certainly.* "Rabbi" means lawyer. He'll get the best trial in the world. Eichmann. *Ha!* They were shaving his leg while he was giving his appeal! That's the last bit of insanity, man. (p. 35)

It was, of course, easy to sit through Bruce's put-downs of middle America, with its small towns ("You go to the park, see the cannon, and you've had it.") and small minds (working a Milwaukee club, Bruce figures "these are the *Grey Line tourers,* before they leave! This is where they *live*."), but send-ups about the Holocaust were more than the over-thirty Jewish crowd could

take. What he said about Eichmann was not only "tasteless," it
was forbidden, taboo, altogether unacceptable.

To be sure, Bruce, being Bruce, was never at a loss for words,
especially for those words which explained, which rationalized,
which put whatever he said under the large protective covering
called "satire":

> But here's the thing on comedy. If I were to do a satire on the
> assassination of John Foster Dulles, it would shock people. They'd
> say, "That is in heinous taste." Why? Because it's fresh. And that's
> why my contention is: that satire is tragedy plus time. You give it
> enough time, the public, the reviewers will allow you to satirize it.
> Which is rather ridiculous when you think about it. And I know,
> probably 500 years from today, someone will do a satire on Adolf
> Hitler, maybe even showing him as a hero, and everyone will
> laugh. . . . And yet if you did it today, it would be bad. (p. 116)

What Bruce didn't figure on, however, was the distinction
between a satirical sketch about John Foster Dulles's assassination—where terms like "tasteless" and "sick" were sure to follow—and *shtick* about Hitler that raised the issue of self-hatred.
Consider, for example, Bruce's "fantasy" about Hitler's "discovery" by a quasi-Jewish, fast-talking talent agent ("I like dot first
name—Adolf—it's sort ov off beat. I like that."). But
Shicklegruber? A last name like that will never do:

> Ve need something to, sort of, hit people. . . . Adolf Hit—No.
> Adolf Hit-ler—zat's a vild name, right? A-d-o-l-f H-i-t-l-e-r. Five and
> six for the marquee—nice and zmall. Dot's nice. Dot's right. Ve get a
> little rhythm section behind him, it'll sving dere. Jonah Jones,
> maybe. (p. 137)

Bruce, of course, knew about pseudonyms first-hand, having
come into the world as Leonard Alfred Schneider. Lenny
Bruce—with its back-to-back first names and requisite number
of spaces for the marquee—was a monicker with *snap* to it—
quick, no-nonsense and, best of all, not stuck in the immigrant
world of exhausted, defeated Schneiders. Like the Great
Gatsby—who metamorphosed himself from his unlikely, humble
origins as Jay Gatz—Bruce "sprang from his Platonic conception
of himself." The difference, of course, is that while Gatsby's
forward motion is fueled by a deep, unquestioning belief in the
American Dreams that ultimately destroyed him, it was the sub-
culture that kept Bruce hopping. He took corrosion, rather than

innocence, as his special province and, as such, his manic energy had a decidedly Manichean edge. The Princes of Good and Evil warred within his best material, as "definitions" of each—what Bruce liked to call the *emmis*—did acrobatic leaps across the conjunction.

In short, he was out to exorcize whatever impulses toward Jewishness, toward "restraint" still clung to his bones. If an immigrant generation believed that God gave us bodies so that our heads wouldn't fall off, if the observant wore *gartels* (sashes) to divide the higher portions (the holier) from the lower (the profane), Bruce was out to liberate—yea, to *celebrate*—the fleshly:

> Now, lemme hip you to something. Lemme tell you something. If you believe that there is a god, a god that made your body, and yet you think you can do anything with that body that's dirty, then the fault lies with the manufacturer. *Emmis.* (p. 287)

For Bruce, *Emmis* is akin to *"Selah,"* to *"Omayn."* In philosophical argument, it would be represented *Quod erat demonstrandum* ("which was to be demonstrated"). Either way, Bruce hath spoken and matters of the body need not detain us any longer.

Bruce's wide-openness encompassed more than the mouth and the genitals—what one said and, sexually speaking, whatever one chose to do. It also included, in increasing doses, whatever one could smoke or swallow or shoot-up. The body's excitement, rather than Jewish fearfulness, was alone worth exploring, worth the Faustian challenge. What Alexander Portnoy *kvetches* about in *Portnoy's Complaint,* Philip Roth's testament to American-Jewish emancipation ("The guilt, the fears—the terror bred into my bones! What in their world was not charged with danger, dripping with germs, fraught with peril?"), Bruce turned into shock, into *shpritz* and into what, in California, is called a "lifestyle":

> I think that a lot of marriages went West, you know, they split up, in my generation, because ladies didn't know that guys were different . . . to a lady [cheating] means kissing hugging and liking somebody. You have to at least *like* somebody. With guys that doesn't enter into it. . . . Like, a lady can't go through a plate glass window and go to bed with you five seconds later. But every guy in this audience is the same—you can *idolize* your wife, just be so

crazy about her, be on the way home from work, have a head-on
collision with a Greyhound bus, in a *disaster* area. Forty people
laying dead on the highway—not even in the hospital, in the *am-
bulance*—the guy makes a play for the nurse. (pp. 193–94)

It's very possible that—— ——is *very* sexual. He's just probably a
very horny cat—makes it with guys, chicks, mud, sheep, anything:
his fist. He's a real *haisser*—that could be, couldn't it?
Like all of us: me, you, you, you—put us on a desert island for five
years, no chicks, you'll ball mud. *Emmis.* You *have,* man. *Knotholes.*
(p. 217)

Moreover, his view from the sleazy underbelly of show biz
credentialled the *emmis* of what he said, in roughly the same way
that the "cult of experience" had authenticated people like Stephen Crane or John Steinbeck or Ernest Hemingway. "Bruce
was *there,* man. He had *seen* it."—which, for twenty-year-old
college students is, presumably, all that needs to be said.

The trouble with confusing so much patter with so much
"truth," of course, is that Bruce's monologues are to the hip
what Kahlil Gibran's *The Prophet* is to the square. Pearl K. Bell
once wrote a shrewd review with the intriguing title "Philip Roth:
Sonny Boy or Lenny Bruce" (*Commentary,* November 1977). In
it, she says this of the Roth who provided David Kepesh, *The
Professor of Desire,* with the temper tantrums we recognize as
vintage Roth:

> Roth seems to believe that the only two choices of being available
> to a grown Jewish man are Al Jolson's sonny boy or Lenny Bruce. In
> fact, the erudite professor sounds oddly like soap opera, where
> people fall in and out of love as though life were a swimming pool (so
> life is *not* like a swimming pool).

To be sure, Roth is a sit-down comedian, a *writer,* whose "influences," anxiety-producing or otherwise, are more likely to be
Kafka or Gogol or Chekov, rather than a Lenny Bruce. Besides,
Bruce shed early whatever *persona* might have separated him
from Leonard Alfred Schneider. His "act," as it were, was his
life. Roth has always insisted—usually without much success—
that he is *not* Neil Klugman, *not* Alexander Portnoy, *not* Nathan
Zuckerman.

What the two culture heroes have in common, however, is a
wide streak of the Puritanical, albeit turned upside-down. Roth,
apparently, would like nothing better than to add Jewish pro-

tagonists who do the unthinkable—that is, run wild, unbridled, restlessly unsatisfied—to the official canon of tame "Jewish books." But the enterprise has a desperate ring about it, as if Roth were trying too hard to be morally liberated. Bruce, on the other hand, insisted on having his self-righteous cake at the same time he *shtupped* it into his mouth. Guilt was, presumably, other people's hang-up, yet Bruce's flights into hedonism (usually by way of various "fantasies") had a way of being coupled with "instruction." His aphorisms, his epigrammatic wit, slipped easily—perhaps *too* easily—into large pronouncements:

> If I could just rob fifty words out of your head I could stop the war. . . . (p. 227)
>
> The reason I got busted—arrested—is I picked on the wrong god. (p. 266)
>
> My concept? You can't do *anything* with anybody's body to make it dirty to me. Six people, eight people, one person—you can do only one thing to make it dirty: kill it. Hiroshima was dirty. Chessman was dirty. (p. 288)

That *Playboy Magazine* found this "good copy" is hardly surprising. Everything conventionally thought and said about the 1950s suggests that repression was long overdue for the gospel according to Hefner. The Playboy "Bunny" was, in this sense, a stroke of (advertising) genius that, for far too many, became associated with genius *per se*. The magazine published long excerpts from Bruce's autobiographical romp, *How to Talk Dirty and Influence People,* and a seemingly endless mish-mash of the liberal and the hedonistic called "The Playboy Philosophy." Bruce, the entertainer, was in danger of being taken seriously as Bruce, the prophet, as Bruce, the discerning social commentator. Even more important, Bruce was in danger of taking *himself* seriously, of becoming that saddest of all tricksters—the con man conned. In this respect, Buddy Hackett—yet another pioneer in the popularization of "dirty words" and blunt, tasteless talk—has fared better. Partly because he is roly-poly, partly because his physical brand of clowning exudes little boyishness, Hackett stands outside the pale of censorship. He is, in a word, *funny*— rather than "one of us."

At the end, of course, Bruce found himself cast in the role of defendant, pleading his case to audiences that had come to see his old bits: "Religions, Inc.," "The Lone Ranger," "Father

Flotsky," "Tits-'N-Ass." Instead, their cover charge bought them readings from the transcripts of his trials and his anguished, Joseph K-ish responsa. Those with a fascination for the stuff of legend, who understood that, in America, nothing succeeds like failure, sat transfixed through Bruce's harrowing: others, expecting yuks, shot the ragged-out, black-suited *maggid* (preacher) a sour look and headed toward the exits. The Bruce who had *shpritzed* the *goyim,* who had shocked the Jews, ended by boring both.

Since Bruce ODed during the long, hot summer of 1966, other martyrs have followed in his footsteps, most notably Freddie Prinze of "Chico and the Man" fame and John Belushi, the resident wild-man of "Saturday Night Live." With these cases, videotape provides a performance record that can be judged dispassionately, when the "sympathy vote" is finally in. For better or worse, Bruce's best work was *live*. There are record albums, of course, and a few attempts to "catch" his act on film, but the overall effect is rather like trying to judge a legendary tenor like Caruso from a scratchy 78. Moreover, Bruce on the printed page is hardly Bruce at his finest. The material not dated by its references to that time, those places, has a stilted, sophomoric ring if read aloud today. What it lacks is Bruce's timing, his gestures, his pauses, even his nervous "you know's."

Nonetheless, Bruce continues to matter—not only to those true believers who would insist that Lenny Bruce was "murdered" because he told the truth or to those who would place his ideas ahead of William James's or Alfred North Whitehead's, but also to those more modest souls who see Bruce in the context of what he was, what he did and what he made possible. A stand-up comic like George Carlin, for example, continues Bruce's satiric investigations into our language—the words we "forbid" as well as those we use without thinking. Troupes like "Second City" (best known in their incarnations on SCTV) continue the parodic romps through our popular culture that Bruce pioneered without elaborate props or the aid-and-comfort of repertory players. In a word, Bruce made stand-up comedy as it is currently being practiced at clubs like "Catch a Rising Star" or the "Comedy Store" possible. Granted, he did not create our permissive, no-holds-barred environment single-handedly (the cunning of history, especially as the Vietnam War divided our country into culture versus counter-culture, can lay greater claim to these dubious benefits), but it is fair to say that he paid dues—heavy dues—early.

And yet, after we have laid our obligatory wreath on Bruce's tomb and pointed to those aspects of his career that were unique and important, there are continuities worth mentioning. If Bruce was a phenomenon that only the 1950s could have created and only the 1960s could have loved, he was also some very old Manischewitz wrapped inside a new brown paper bag. The urban vaudeville comic knew that "American humor" put its emphasis on the adjective, that ethnic stereotyping (e.g. the drunken Irishman, the shuffling "darky" and money-hungry Jew) was always good for a laugh.

For turn-of-the-century Jewish comics, it meant that charm gave way to meanness. Take, for example, two representative "fire stories," the first firmly within the Yiddish tradition:

> A Jew pays a call on the rabbi of a small community and tells him a heartbreaking story. He has been the victim of a terrible fire, one that destroyed his house and everything he owned. In short, he has been reduced to penury and now he travels from town to town collecting what charity he can. "Can you help me, rabbi?" the poor man asks.
>
> "And have you a document from the rabbi of your town testifying that you are, indeed, a fire victim?" the suspicious rabbi inquires.
>
> "Absolutely. Without question," the man replies, "but, unfortunately, it too was burnt."

Granted, the victim/beggar's "deception" is paper-thin, but the wit, the *fiction,* if you will, makes measures of dignity possible both for the giver and the receiver of "help." The question, in short, is not Who was hurt by the ruse? but rather, How can even a joke speak for man? The alternative, after all, is *charity*—that which often leads to self-righteousness in the do-gooder and a robbed humanity in the done-to.

By contrast, here is how East Broadway turned the typical "fire story" into its sleazy American cousin:

> One Jew meets another on the street and says: "So, Abe, I hear you had a fire in your store last week."
>
> "Quiet, quiet," Abe replies, "it's *next* week."[5]

Granted, vaudeville humor had a rough edge—evidently one with staying power, if the sales figures for *Truly Tasteless Jokes* are any indication—but the hidden agenda just behind the cheap laughs was clear: shed your ethnic differences, assimilate into mainstream America, in a word, *melt*. When an Abie meets an Ike, what they invariably talk about is how they cheated the *goyim*—by torching a store, by swapping the goods or by simply overcharging. These stage Jews were smart all right, but they were also unethical, unsavory, just plain greedy. Who did *they* hurt? This time the answer was clear: America, which is to say, the *goyim*.

Bruce knew the tradition, and he insisted that it was "cruel":

> The comedy they had *before,* I think, actually was cruel. . . . There was the Jew comic, they used to call them; the Wop comic, they used to say; they used to do the blackface, real stereotype Uncle Tom Jim Crow with the curls and fright wig. . . . I think the comedy of today has more of a liberal viewpoint. (p. 133)

Bruce, of course, *began* with stereotypes and then went on to give them the send-up, the *shpritz* they deserved. His Negroes insist, for example, that "the furst ting I gwine do when I gwine get to Hebbin is fine out what a 'gwine' is" (p. 33). But without Blacks, without Catholics, without homosexuals and, to be sure, without Jews, Bruce had no act.

To be sure, Bruce's comedy was light-years beyond the predictability of easy punch lines and socko finishes. In the lingo of exasperated agents, Bruce "played to the band"—meaning that he *shpritzed* a good many curve balls that conventional audiences simply didn't catch. But, at bottom, his were differences of degree rather than of kind. He went after those with identifiable religious affiliations not only because he found them hypocritical, but because, for him, liberalism was religion enough; he went after the middle-class not only because they were smug, but because they weren't hipsters; he went after southerners not only because they were racists, but because *any* regionalisms (outside New York City) were suspect. In short, Bruce imagined a tea-colored, compassionate America, one that would *swing* and that would not hassle people if they talked "dirty" or smoked a little dope. Best of all, Bruce imagined that this better America would be neither Jewish nor *goyish*. And like most people who dwell on the "big picture," Bruce preferred to think that God was made in *his* image, rather than the other way around:

> He's any kind of god you want him to be, god, that's what he is . . . he's a pumpkin god, he's a halloween god, he's a good sweet loving

> god who'll make me burn in hell for my sins and blaspheming, he's
> that kind of god, too. . . . And he's a god that you can exploit and
> make work for you, and get you respect in the community, and get
> St. Jude working for you, and all those other Catholic priests,
> Jewish—Eddie Cantor, putz-o exploiter, George E. Jessel and Kiss-
> it-off Santas. Yeah, he's a god that'll look at this culture and say,
> "*Whew!* What were they *doing,* man? They've got people in prison
> for thirty-five years!" (pp. 292–93)

Not surprisingly, this last "god"—the hip one, with a social
conscience—sounds like a dead ringer for Lenny Bruce.

What "shocked" in Bruce was his unrelenting attack on the
values Jews and non-Jews alike had melted into—the pieties of
organized religion, the conventions of heterosexual marriage, the
world according to *Time* magazine. His *shpritz* was the word-as-
weapon, the "free association" (often freer than it was asso-
ciative) that played over everything—the autobiographical, the
socio-cultural, the sacred and the profane—without compromis-
ing, or "believing" any of it.

Only Bruce could tell an audience that he was *"going to piss
on you"* ("You can't photograph it—it's like rain.") or ask a big
hand as he "introduced" Adolf Hitler. He may have squirmed
under the label of "vomic" or felt that a word like "sick" belonged to the culture at large rather than to him, but outrage
buttered his bread and bought his dope.

Among his more reflective moments, this one may be the most
permanently revealing:

> Today's comedian has a cross to bear that he built himself. A
> comedian of the older generation did an "act" and he told the
> audience, "This is my act." Today's comic is not doing an act. The
> audience assumes he's telling the truth. . . . [And] when I'm inter-
> ested in a truth, it's really a *truth* truth, one hundred per cent. And
> that's a terrible truth to be interested in. (p. 111)

For Bruce, the need to shock the Jews, to "go public" with their
secrets; the need to *shpritz* the *goyim,* to exorcize all their
"Southern-dummy—cheapo-drecky—dumbbell shit," all their
white bread Protestantism, raised comedy-as-hostility and com-
edy-as-tragic catharsis to new levels, and to new expectations.
Since Bruce's untimely exit, put-downs of mass culture have
hardened into formula (the rise-and-fall of "Saturday Night
Live," for example), and professional defenders of the Jewish
faith have had Philip Roth's continuing efforts to kick around.
But Bruce got to the sensitive nerves first, and in ways that can

still *shpritz* the *goyim* into helpless laughter and shock the Jews
into uncomfortable worry. As Bruce once put it: "All my humor
is based upon destruction and despair" (p. 112). A good deal of
the "destruction and despair" came from, and was restricted to,
Bruce's life; but sizable portions were, and continue to be, part of
ours as well.

NOTES

1.   John Cohen, ed., *The Essential Lenny Bruce* (New York: Ballantine
Books, 1967), pp. 41–42. Subsequent references to Bruce's monologues are
to this edition, and pagination is provided parenthetically.

2. Saul Bellow, "Laughter in the Ghetto," *Saturday Review of Literature*
36 (May 30, 1953): 15.

3. Albert Goldman, *Ladies and Gentlemen: Lenny Bruce* (New York:
Ballantine Books, 1971), p. 146.

4. Irving Howe, *World of Our Fathers* (New York: Harcourt Brace
Jovanovich, 1976), p. 573.

5. For a fuller discussion of "fire stories," traditional and American, see
Jacob Richman's *Laughs from Jewish Lore* (New York: Hebrew Publishing
Company, 1954), pp. xi–xxv.

THE UNKOSHER COMEDIENNES

From Sophie Tucker to Joan Rivers

SARAH BLACHER COHEN

Jewish women comedians are brazen offenders of the faith. Their behavior violates the Torah's conception of *tzniut* or feminine modesty. Rather than being shy and humble, they unashamedly bask in the public's eye, clamoring for all the attention they can get. They do not heed the Talmudic injunction: *"isha lo tikra batorah mipnei kavod ha'tsibur"* (*Megillah* 23a; "a woman should not read the Torah out of respect for the congregation"). From their self-erected pulpits, they shock the community with their risqué sermonettes, their unorthodox learning, their bastardization of scripture. By invading the holy sphere of the Jewish male comic, they usurp his audience and so diminish his self-esteem. Their humor of camouflaged aggression disturbs their female spectators as well, for it clashes with the code of *edelkeit* or gentility observed by respectable Jewish women. But worst of all, the comediennes disbar themselves from performing Judaism's central commandment for women: the enforcement of the ritual of *kashrut*—keeping kosher, keeping clean. As creatures of unclean lips, they make dirty, they sully, they corrupt.

Yet their foul mouths not only tarnish our life, but add zest to it. They infuse the bland with the spicy, the sterile with the racy, the staid with the forbidden. The dual aspects of their humor, its contaminating and liberating effects, can be seen in one of their jokes: "A woman tells of a man who goes to the village rabbi and says he wants to divorce his wife because she has filthy habits. 'Everytime I go to piss in the sink, it's always full of dirty dishes.'"[1] This joke is a disguised expression of the woman's anger. But it is also an explosive flaunting of the taboo of grossness which we secretly admire but which our internal censors prohibit. What is permitted, however, is uncomfortable laughter.

Of all the Jewish women comedians of this century, the pioneer flaunter of taboos, who made illicit laughter more comfortable, was Sophie Tucker. In her autobiography, *Some of These Days,* she informs us of her origins: "I was born on the road. Not on the Orpheum, the Pantages, Keith, or any of the other circuits I've traveled since . . . but on the long rutted track from Russia across Poland to the Baltic. . . . In one of the big, canvas-covered wagons carrying poor emigrants bound for America."[2] Though Sophie Abuza made her first American appearance when three months old in Boston, she grew up in a Yiddish-speaking home in Hartford, Connecticut, where from age eight to sixteen she helped her destitute parents run a kosher-style restaurant. Serving the traveling show people the "borscht to blintze five course meal for a quarter," she sang songs for them and vowed never to duplicate the life of her over-worked mother whose husband gambled away their hard-earned money. At thirteen Sophie already weighed 145 pounds, but this did not deter her from performing at amateur concerts to help support her family and gaining instant affection from the crowds. When people yelled for the "fat girl to do her stuff," she began to realize that in "show business size didn't matter if you could sing and make people laugh."[3] At sixteen, her fat self wanted romantic love as well as applause. Without parental consent, she married a young neighborhood boy, Louis Tuck, the first of many men in her life who would be a replica of her father, weak and irresponsible, expecting her to be both wage earner and domestic servant. The birth of a son made her feel more trapped, desperate to emancipate herself. Desecrating the role of Jewish mother and homemaker, denounced by the neighbors as a whore, she left the baby with her parents to break into New York show business.

In 1906 she began her career by singing in rathskellers, performing fifty to one hundred songs a night and catering to individual tastes. She graduated to burlesque and vaudeville where in black-face she was billed as "Sophie Tucker, Manipulator of Coon Melodies" because she was too big and ugly to sing as a white woman. But she made her distinctive contribution as a Jewish comedienne with her "red hot mamma" songs in the intimate quarters of cabarets and night clubs. There she incorporated the tastes of her burlesque hall audiences: "Folks weren't so high brow," she said. "They wanted to let down their hair and unbutton their vests and be natural. They wanted to laugh at sex. Sex was funny, not necessarily intense and tragic the way the playwrights such as Ibsen made it out to be. Why, weren't the best jokes in the world the ones that played on sex?"[4]

Sophie Tucker's sexual numbers were funny for a number of reasons. Weighing in at two hundred well-corseted pounds, swaying suggestively to the sensual music, she was a caricature of the torch singer. She capitalized on the Rabelaisian humor of her huge bulk and her correspondingly huge sexual appetite. Calling herself a "King-sized Lollabrigida," she sang, "I've put a little more meat on. So what, there's more schmaltz to sizzle when I turn the heat on."

Sophie was also a comic assaulter of the Gentiles' puritanical society. With her raucous, gravel-throated voice, she belted out those prurient desires suppressed by the strait-laced public. Parading her vulgarity, she over-turned WASP gentility with her plebeian ways and racy gutter idioms. As Eddie Cantor said of her, "Sophie's style and material are hardly what you'd want at a Holy Name Breakfast. . . . She has no inhibitions. . . . She sings the words we used to write on the sidewalks of New York."[5]

In particular, Sophie Tucker mirthfully shattered the idols cherished by her Jewish audiences. Because of her girth, she assumed the pose of the Jewish mother figure. Indeed her most winning number was her tearful rendition of "My Yiddishe Mamme." Though Jews viewed sex not as a sin but as a virtuous act to be enjoyed within the framework of marriage, they still did not expect their food-pushing mammas to be starved for sex, let alone publicly announce their craving for sex. "If the Jewish young woman is generally portrayed as sexy before marriage but frigid afterwards," Sophie Tucker "turned the maternal-frigid image on its head: the Jewish mother needed and wanted sexual attention just like the attractive, slim Jewish girl."[6] The incongruous spectacle of a large Jewish mother in heat initially

produced shame in the audience, but since she so wittingly
exaggerated her needs, their shame quickly dissolved into laughter.

When Sophie Tucker wasn't the red-hot mamma complaining
of her ice-cold papa, she performed a musical minidrama of a
forlorn woman seduced and abandoned by a faithless lover. Married and divorced three times, she had sad personal experience
to draw upon. But she transformed these romantic disasters into
drollery by employing her inimitable humor of verbal retrieval.
We can see this humor operative in excerpts from one of her
most popular routines:

> Mistah Siegel, you'd better make it legal, Mistah Siegel
> *Mazel Tov:*
>
> Something happened, accidently.
> Consequently, we should marry.
>
> No, no, it isn't a mistake.
> I'm swearing I should live so.
> It wasn't Sam or Jake.
>
> A *klug tzu Columbus,* what you made from me.
> My mamma told me yesterday that I'm gaining weight.
> It's not from something that I ate.
>
> You said, "Come'on make whoopy, come'on, just one little kiss."
>
> *Ich hob moira far da chupah*
> (I'll be afraid at the wedding canopy.)
>
> *Vet dos zein bei uns a bris.*
> (We'll have a circumcision ceremony instead.)
>
> Mistah Siegel, Mister Siegel, in my *boich is schoen a kiegel.*
> (In my belly is already a noodle pudding.)
>
> Mistah Siegel, make it legal for me.

Sophie Tucker comically reduces the wretched circumstances
of the fallen woman to a Jewish domestic scandal. The culprit is
not a dashing gigolo, but a Jewish paterfamilias out for a fling.
The pregnant woman is not a seasoned professional, but a com-
pliant ingénue out to catch a husband. Her immigrant-fractured
English parodies the complaints of other wronged women. Her
use of the Yiddish curse, *a klug tzu Columbus,* allies her with
other greenhorns foolishly duped by America the *gonif,* the thief.
Her equation of the growing fetus inside her to the Yiddish *kiegel*

or noodle pudding ludicrously converts the product of her sin into a gastronomic anomaly. The song's constant refrain, "Mistah Siegel, make it legal" is a mocking commentary on the need for women to barter sex for the respectability of marriage and man's reluctance to honor the terms of the agreement.

In another of Sophie Tucker's songs, "When Am I Getting the Mink, Mr. Fink?" the more emancipated secretary of the garment district wants material goods for her services, not marriage. Devoid of romantic illusions, sex for her is strictly a business transaction. Toughened by experience, she minces no words in demanding what's due her:

> You made a deal with me
> I kept it faithfully
> I gave you credit for what is always C.O.D.
> You promised to give me the mink in July.
> It's three months overdue and so am I
>
> A silver fox you're offering me.
> You're such a heel
> Look at all the room rent I saved you
> In the back seat of your automobile.
> No, I won't settle for a stole.
> Don't forget, you cheapskate lover,
> The whole of me you've got to cover.
> Now I want my mink, Mr. Fink, right now.

The humor in this number lies not in the mock pathos of Mistah Siegel's forlorn pregnant lover, but in the brassiness of an uncouth woman who performs the unmentionable and mentions the unmentionable. A feisty lady, she knows her own worth and will not be short-changed by men.

This same comic bravado of a spunky woman who does not depend on men, but fends for herself is prevalent in other Sophie Tucker songs such as "I'm Living Alone and I Like It," "I Ain't Takin' Orders From No One," "Never Let the Same Dog Bite You Twice" and "No One Man Is Ever Going To Worry Me." A woman's liberationist ahead of her times, she urges spurned females to leave faithless lovers, make a life for themselves, and triumph over adversity. Yet she does not underestimate the high cost women pay for independence. With rueful humor, she states: "Once you start carrying your own suitcases, paying your own bills, running your own show, you've done something to yourself that makes you one of those women men may like and call a pal and a good sport, the kind of woman they tell their troubles to. But you've cut yourself off from the orchids and the diamond bracelets, except those you buy yourself."[7]

Yet as a "pal" and "good sport" Sophie Tucker continued to amuse nightclub audiences all through her sixties and early seventies. Though she was still the fat and foul-mouthed chanteuse, the new addition to her humor dispelled the myth of the sexually non-active senior citizen. She shocked people with the improprieties of a randy old lady, but she also appealed to their "longing to make life over, to live it more fully and freely. To have more love and a lot more laughs."[8] Thus she raised their eyebrows and their spirits when she sang, "I'm having more fun since I'm sixty, than I had all the rest of my life," or "I'm starting all over again and I'm hotter than I've ever been," or "Plenty of boys want me, as my engagement book confirms, then I'm not going to save it for the worms." From Sophie Tucker's New York opening in 1906 to her finale in 1966 when she died at the age of seventy-nine, she was an irrepressible force, a Jewish female version of the comic buffoon, "the indomitable living creature . . . the personified *elan vital* . . . now triumphant, now worsted and rueful," but ultimately bouncing back.[9] Or as she says in one of her songs, "You can't deep-freeze a red-hot mamma, cause you can't get her temperature down."

Sophie Tucker's song-writer, Fred Fisher, convinced her that if she sang about sex she would not offend or titillate anyone since her size would make any smutty song she sang immediately funny. Moreover, singing her songs in the first person, she would make the audience laugh at her own distress. These "hot numbers" she regarded as "all moral. They have to do with sex, but not with vice."[10]

Belle Barth, the nightclub entertainer who followed in Sophie Tucker's footsteps was not moral, for her routines have to do with sex and vice. Called the "Hildegard of the Underworld," and the "doyenne of the dirty line," the former Belle Salzman was born in New York's East Harlem area in 1911, appeared in vaudeville during the 1920s and performed at the Catskills, Atlantic City, Las Vegas and her own Belle Barth Pub in Miami Beach until her death in 1971. Though she wanted to be remembered as a female Victor Borge, she created the greatest stir with recordings of her ribald comedy routines, "My Next Story is a Little Risqué" and

"If I Embarrass You, Tell Your Friends," which sold 400,000 copies, despite an unofficial ban on its display in record stores.

Before predominately Jewish audiences, Belle Barth put into practice the title of Lenny Bruce's autobiography, *How to Talk Dirty and Influence People*. Only she employed more Yiddish to talk dirty than he, especially in her scatological humor of bodily excretions. Since scatology represents a form of aggression against propriety, against society's insistence that certain human activities are not to be spoken of in public, she playfully masks her violation of cultural restrictions in two ways. Calling herself an MD, a *Maven* on *Dreck* (an expert on feces), she first bluntly describes the tasteless and then augments its filth quotient by providing the vulgar Yiddish equivalent of it. For example, she gleefully changes the lines of "Home on the Range" to "Show me a home where the buffalo roam and I'll show you a home full of *pishartz* (urine)." Or in mock anger she complains: "This drink tastes just like *pishartz*." Sometimes in more lengthy scatological routines she substitutes outrageously crude detail for obscene Yiddishisms to gain her broad comic effect as in the joke about the dying ninety-year-old Jewish man who has to be fed through a rectal tube. "He tells the nurse. Please bring two tubes. You've been so nice to me. I want you should have dinner with me before I die." This joke, however, is inoffensive compared to the gross one she tells about the man who claims to sing through his rectum. When his agent asks him to perform, "the guy drops his pants and messes the whole floor. The agent says, What, are you nuts or something? This is a $6,000 rug! The guy replies, I had to clear my throat, didn't I?" These scatological jokes subvert the iron-clad rules of toilet-training. They burst open the tightly locked doors of the bathroom and catapult the hidden, shameful activity of the private sphere into the social sphere: the anti-septic hospital room and the expensively decorated agent's apartment. And it is Belle Barth, the unkosher comedienne who originates these excremental jests. With them she defies anal taboos and loosens her audiences' choked respectability so they can laugh at these shattered prohibitions.

Belle Barth is the most graphic bedroom as well as bathroom iconoclast of all the Jewish comediennes. In her many embarrassing nightclub acts, she is a master of the smutty joke, a form of obscenity which Freud likened to "the denudation of a person of the opposite sex toward whom the joke is directed. Through the utterance of obscene words," Freud claims, "the person attacked is forced to picture the parts of the body in question, or the sexual act, and is shown that the aggressor himself pictures the same thing." For Freud, the joke-teller is usually a man and the person "attacked and denuded" is generally a woman, so "that the telling of jokes in this way is intended as a modified form of rape: verbal rape rather than physical—a sort of seduction or preparation of the woman for the man's actual physical approach."[11] However, Belle Barth, the pudgy Jewish woman who originates the smutty joke, reverses the process. She attacks and denudes the male, making public his privates. But she does not want to verbally rape her naked prey. She intends, rather, to make risqué comments about men's genitalia and amusingly shock the audience with what a naughty Jewish girl she is. She begins her bawdy penis jokes with two one-liners. The first one is: "Only two words you have to learn in the Yiddish language and that is *Gelt* (money) and *Schmuck* (penis). Because if a man has no, he is." The use of the Yiddish equivalent for penis in this context deflates the sexual component of it and transforms it into the playfully hostile personification of the male as a nonfunctioning organ, the male devoid of potency, i.e., money. Barth's other one-liner, "I heard a great group in Israel called the foreskins," does not have the negative connotation of the first joke, but covertly jests about the sexual inadequacy Jewish males feel because they have been circumcised.

In a more lengthy joke Belle Barth comically treats the middle-aged Jewish woman's confrontation with the male's free-floating penis. She tells of a devoted daughter who gives her visiting mother a roasted chicken in a zippered bag to take with her to Florida. When the mother gets on the train, she puts the chicken beside her. Dozing, she does not notice that a man sits down next to her and puts the chicken on the floor. Meanwhile, the mother unzips his pants and puts her hands on his penis. She quells: "What a daughter I have: The neck of the chicken is still warm."

The humor of the joke rests upon the incongruity of the stereotypical Jewish mother, whose nurturing instincts have totally replaced her libidinal instincts, caught in the act of fondling a strange man's penis. The situation is made even more funny by her tactile misperception, her mistaking a warm chicken neck for a male's aroused penis. Beneath the surface humor of the joke, however, there is also the underlying hostile element. Belle Barth, in the process of comically denuding the male, is also stripping away his power. She is saying that what we construe as the male's formidable penis, the instrument of his uncontestable virility, is in actuality as flaccid as a limp chicken neck.

Belle Barth not only pin-pricks our inflation of the prick, but she punctures our erotic illusions connected with the sexual act in general. For example, she states that "the most difficult thing for a woman to do on the first night of her second marriage is to holler it hurts" and for the new husband "to tie his feet to the bed so he doesn't fall in and drown." Or she invents a new slogan for the wife of the T.V. Western hero, Palladin: "Have crack, will shack, until the *schmuck* with the gun gets back." Thus she reduces voluptuous sexual experience to crude anatomical acts, the stuffing of organs into cracks. Humans for her are mechanical beings who frenetically screw and unscrew their parts. Subscribing to Bergson's definition of humor as the mechanical encrusted upon the living, Belle Barth makes us grin and grimace at our malfunctioning sex machine.

Not all audiences appreciated Belle Barth's tough vulgarian routines in which she was fouler than any male comedian. When she died of stomach cancer in 1971 at age fifty-nine, they preferred the self-deprecating humor of Totie Fields who made her fat body the butt of her jokes. Born Sophie Feldman, the 4'10", 190 pound comedienne began her career in 1944, touring the Borscht Belt at fourteen, and working as an all-purpose *tummler* in Boston strip joints before she was twenty. She soon realized she got the biggest laughs when she criticized her own anatomy. She would say, for example, "I look like a pregnant bouquet in this dress, don't I?" or "do you think it is easy pushing fat Jewish feet into thin Italian shoes?" Unlike Sophie Tucker who blamed men for being inept lovers, Totie Fields benignly mocked her own lack of sex appeal. She claimed that when a beauty expert told her "to stand naked in front of the mirror and list her assets and liabilities, she immediately went bankrupt." Presenting herself as the most undesired female, Totie Fields so craved male attention that the hilarious bids she made for sexual attention in the 1970s would infuriate today's feminists. "I'm so tired of being everybody's buddy," she said. "Just once to read in a newspaper, Totie Fields raped in an alley," or "I had to smack six Italian men. Not one of them would pinch me, so I pinched them."

Totie Fields also assumed the pose of the inept bargain-hunter who ends up with shlock merchandise, yet deludes herself into thinking it is still worthwhile. For example, she is proud of the fact that she bought fifty pairs of stockings at twelve cents a pair only to discover that the seams go up the front. "But for twelve cents a pair," she consoles herself, "I can learn to walk backward." As for the bra she bought for eighty-nine cents, it has three cups, but then she tells herself, "maybe someday my cup will runneth over." Rather than strive to correct her errors of judgment and fallible ways, in her routines she accepts her imperfect, bungling self. For, as she says, "happiness is finding a library book that's three weeks overdue and that you're not," or "happiness is going out to dinner with friends and getting a brown gravy stain on a brown dress."

Since comedy makes us feel superior to those more wretched than ourselves, Totie Fields, whose spills never miss "because the target is so big," made her audiences feel positively lofty. But when a protracted bout with phlebitis forced doctors to amputate her left leg above the knee and she made her come-back on an artificial limb as a stand-up comic once again, audiences looked up to her as a valiant woman who had the courage to surmount adversity. She continued to jest about her maladroit body, only the body, through lengthy hospital stays, had now slimmed down to 120 pounds. So in place of fat jokes, she substituted her own brand of prosthetic humor, transforming her recent misfortune into mirth. "I never had good legs anyway," she cracks. "You never heard people say, Geez, what a pair of gams that Totie Fields has." Because Totie Fields was so brave, yet so vulnerable, her audiences during the last year of her career could not respond with that total "anesthesia of the heart" which Bergson says comedy requires. They felt her pain, though she tried to convince them in her famous foghorn voice that she just lost a leg, not her sense of humor.

Though it was difficult not to have a wooden response to Totie Field's wooden leg, audiences still laughed at the ugly persona she created. Like Sophie Tucker and Belle Barth, she relied on her former girth for her mirth. She emphasized the ravages of age on a body yearning to be young. She repeatedly acknowledged her romantic defeats, her sexual fiascoes. It's as if for her and other comediennes that age and ugliness were the credentials required to permit them to be funny, "to show audiences that they have lived long enough to suffer the circumstances they were joking about."[12] They also had to camouflage their good looks, or, in a sense, neuter themselves so they could mock the sexual and not destroy the comic effect by being too seductive themselves.

Joan Rivers, as Jewish comedienne, defies the somatype and appearance of Sophie Tucker, Belle Barth, and Totie Fields. She is not fat, but a svelte 110 pounds. Not a caricature of a femme fatale, but a femme fatale herself, she appears stylishly coiffed, elegantly outfitted in designer gowns and radiantly beautiful, profiting from every nip and tuck of the latest cosmetic surgery. But to hear her tell it, she still sees herself as the ugly duckling of the past. Born Joan Molinsky in 1933 and raised on Brooklyn's Eastern Parkway, she was eleven when her physician father and extravagant Russian emigré mother moved the family to Larchmont, New York. There she claimed to be "overshadowed by her beautiful older sister with great legs" who was a straight A student, while she, with an occasional A-minus, was designated "The Dumb One." Then being "the token Jew in all Christian schools," she developed complexes and "swelled to 130 pounds on her five-foot two-inch frame."[13] Or as she says in one of her routines, I was "so fat I was my own buddy at camp." Similarly, Joan Rivers has difficulty seeing herself as the reigning queen of American comedy who has been the most successful guest host of Johnny Carson's "Tonight Show," a Las Vegas headliner, a Carnegie Hall sell-out hit, and, most recently, the luminary of her own program, "The Late Show Starring Joan Rivers," on the new Fox Broadcasting network. She still considers herself the prodigal daughter who rebelled against the wishes of her conservative, affluent parents to become a starving comedienne. She still fixates on the first seven lean years of her career, when she began doing "stand-up comedy for $6 a night in Mafia strip joints so tough she was afraid to say, 'Stop me if you've heard this one.'" Or "if a trash can had a bulb in it,"[14] she appeared there. Fired from every job she had the first year, she still persisted in her calling and after seven rejections succeeded in getting on the Johnny Carson show in 1965. Yet she cannot forget the cruel words of the agent who tried to discourage her: "You're too old, too many people have seen you. If you were going to make it, you'd have made it by now."[15] Thus, despite twenty years of steadily escalating success, the Joan Rivers we see on stage today is not the self-possessed comedienne confident of her finely honed sense of humor, the deft igniter of explosive laughter. Rather, she is a mass of insecurities who has been described as hurling "herself into each monologue with the energy of a cheerleader tempered by the desperation that comes from a life spent leading cheers for herself. In a gown that weighs nearly a fifth of what she does (110 pounds, she says, slightly less than she weighed at birth), she hurtles across the stage as if fleeing the Cossacks. . . ."[16] This conception of self as the insulted and the injured, which internalizes and magnifies the world's rejection, which frenetically tries to advertise personal flaws before they are jeered at by others, is at the core of Joan Rivers's identity as a Jewish comedienne. As she told one reviewer, "The loneliness of being left out, being thrown out, which I always fear and dread— is a great deal of my humor. I'm upset and angry and sensitive about everything. The last angry woman. When you've had a lot of unkindnesses done to you, you become a walking wound."[17]

Joan Rivers artfully camouflages this wound and transforms her powerless self begging for pity into a powerful *schlemiel* figure earning sympathetic laughter by cleverly exposing her weaknesses and exaggerating her vulnerabilities. By controlling the reenactment of her inadequacies, she determines the kind of response she receives from her audience. Her fallible being is not at the mercy of their unexpected raillery, but through her shrewd sense of self-preservation, she is psychically prepared for the ridicule she solicits. "As Freud has shown, people side with us when they laugh at something with us, and this solidarity exists even when we encourage them to laugh with us at us."[18] Thus Joan Rivers regales us with lines and lines of self-deprecating humor whose principal target is what she conceives of as her damaged body:

> On our wedding night, my husband said: "Can I help with the buttons?" I was naked at the time.
>
> You've heard of A Cup, B Cup, and C Cup. Well, you're looking at demitasse.
>
> My boobies have dropped so far, I now use the left one as a stopper in the tub.
>
> They show my picture to men on death row to get their minds off women.

> Three stagehands saw me naked. One threw up and the others turned gay.

> My body is so bad, a Peeping Tom looked in my window and pulled down the shade.

> Dress by Oscar de la Renta, body by Oscar Meyer.

Obviously, Joan Rivers exaggerates the defectiveness of her body for the purposes of comedy. Eager to prevent herself from suffering cruel rejection, she manufactures far-fetched censure which cannot be taken seriously. The body images she projects may be pathetic or absurd, but she transcends the weakness she depicts. For her verbal ingenuity, a sign of her hidden strength, allows her to fashion a humorously defective self she can accept and even covertly admire.

Joan Rivers's humorous somatic invention not only wards off her own anxiety about aging, but it also helps her audience laughingly tolerate the imperfections of their own deteriorating bodies. "I'm a common denominator," Joan Rivers claims, "for a lot of people, especially women. Isn't it nice that some little lady somewhere can hear another lady on television say, 'Hey, it's okay to get a little older; it's okay if your body's not perfect! it's okay to say you're not happy sexually.' We're all in the same boat and I want to shake people up a little. Maybe then a woman can laugh about her problems."[19]

Just as Joan Rivers aims her playful barbs at her own body to ward off the onslaught of more painful ones, so she takes harmless potshots at her own people, the Jews, to forestall the more lethal blows of anti-Semitism. As a replacement host for the "Tonight Show," she was very much aware of the contrast between her Jewish acerbic self and the genial Gentile, Johnny Carson. The Jewish humor she employs is an expression of her uneasiness at usurping the WASP's domain, and she uses this humor as a self-protective device to prevent her from being stung. It is also an assurance to the non-Jew that she knows her place and does not presume to permanently invade the premises. Thus, as ethnic jester for the night, she felt free to utter such disparaging Jewish wisecracks as: "I want a Jewish delivery—to be knocked out in the delivery room and wake up at the hairdresser." "A Jewish porno film is made up of one minute of sex and six minutes of guilt." "A flying saucer has never landed on a

Jewish lawn cause we would turn it over to see who made it."
"Jews get orgasms in department stores." "It's a Jewish com-
puter. You punch in three times five and it says three times five
equals fifteen, but for you twelve dollars and ninety-five cents."
These remarks are mildly self-hating, but their levity provides
comic relief from the anxiety Joan Rivers feels as the interloper
Jew. This levity also temporarily numbs the severity of anti-
Jewish hostility.

When it comes to attacking other people, however, Joan
Rivers's hostility is not particularly numbed. In addition to her
self-mockery, she is able to turn her aggression outward and jest
about the real and imaginary flaws of others. In this respect, she
shows a great affinity to the Yiddish *yente,* "a woman of low
origins or vulgar manners . . . a shallow, coarse termagant" who
is an inveterate "scandal-spreader and rumormonger."[20] But,
unlike the *yente,* Joan Rivers does not indiscriminately tongue-
lash everyone. She directs her caustic wit, what Aristotle called
"educated insolence," at celebrities, people of high degree, who
would not be diminished by her clever belittling. For example,
she declares that Liberace is gay, information the public already
has, but then she amusingly invents the outrageous consequences that "Liberace is carrying Truman Capote's baby and
couldn't come tonight because of a yeast infection." Or she
comically exploits the stereotype of the beautiful but dumb
blonde and claims that "Bo Derek studies for the Pap Test and
turned down the role of Helen Keller because she couldn't remember the lines." Or she lampoons such an august figure as the
Queen of England and reduces her to an unkempt loose woman
who doesn't shave between her legs and leaves her tiara marks
on her date's stomach. But Joan Rivers's most scathing character
assassinations rely on her hyperbolic criticisms of anatomy. Here
she most resembles the *shtetl yente* who often called humorous
attention to people's bodily deformities and sardonically named
them according to their principal defects. In the same way that
the *yente* spoke of Berl the Hunchback, and Itke with the big
behind, Joan Rivers referred to Walter Mondale and Geraldine
Ferraro as "Fritz and Tits," who if elected would make "three
boobs in the White House." And just as the *yente* never intended
to shame the individual by underscoring his deformity, Joan
Rivers does not intend to heap scorn on, for example, Elizabeth
Taylor in her fat period, but fabricates the many ludicrous reper-

cussions from her being fat. Thus, she claims that Elizabeth Taylor's "thighs are going condo," that "she wears stretch caftans," that she has "more chins than a Chinese phone book," that she "blew up like a major balloon whom you could put Goodyear on and use at the Rose Bowl," that "mosquitoes see her and scream, 'buffet'" and that "she put on a yellow dress and thirty kids tried to board her." Or Joan Rivers focuses on the potentially unattractive features of prominent figures and magnifies them to their most ridiculous extreme. "Isn't Nancy Kissinger a horse?" she asks. "When I met her, she was wearing a saddle from Gucci." Of Christine Onassis, she observes, "People thought she had a fur coat on, but she was wearing a strapless gown. When she raised her arm, they saw the Greek National Forest."

For many, Joan Rivers's *ad hominem* insults are so ingenious and divorced from probability that they are benignly satirical. As with comic curses, the more extravagant they are, the less venom people assume they contain. Yet for others Joan Rivers is the "meanest bitch in America,"[21] the tough, brassy lady more brutally cutting than inoffensively cute. She, however, defends her big-mouthed "Harriet Hostile" persona. Answering the charge that her humor is "abrasive, tasteless, profane," she explains: "You have to be abrasive to be a current comic. If you don't offend somebody, you become pap. . . . Humor is tasteless. These are tasteless times. Everybody is frightened, grabbing out, values gone, losing all restraint. And I've ridden right on that crest."[22] In a way Joan Rivers's not-so-camouflaged anger has given voice to the public's deeply ingrained anger, its envy and contempt for the media-endowed attributes of the celebrities. Aware that her audience bitterly contrasts their ugly lives with those of the beautiful people, she uses large doses of unsparing satire to vicariously express their feelings of vengeance against the privileged. The more savage, grotesque and crude she is in her character vilifications, the more uproarious is the audience's response. It is not so much that they are shocked by what is said, as that they are shocked that Joan Rivers, regaled in all her feminine finery, has the impudence not only to swear in public, but to crassly utter the vicious things about dignitaries that need saying. In her role as comic reprimander, she functions as a cosmetic and cosmic moralist, prescribing the ideal way high and mighty people should look and act in this world. She feels entitled to ridicule the famous if they do not measure up to the lofty standards they have led the public to expect of them. "If you're going to accept the accolades and payoffs for being a celebrated beauty," she argues, "you should *be* beautiful. If you're going to let yourself be treated as a national institution, then you should behave that way."[23]

For ordinary people Joan Rivers also applies the *yente's* moral standards. She has a nose for dirt, frenetically sniffing out all particles of scandal besmudging past and present reputations. Establishing instant intimacy with her "can we talk," she pries into people's private affairs, getting them to answer the most embarrassing questions. She is especially meddlesome when proffering advice to women. She cautions the bright ones to be wary of men who seem overly infatuated with their brains for she says, "No guy put his hand down a girl's chest to look for a library card." She warns all women not to sell themselves cheaply, but to barter their sex for the most lucrative material possessions and the respectability of marriage. To a young new-lywed, she shrieks, "You're a Jew and you took that shitty ring. It's a piece of shit on four prongs." To the older woman, she admonishes: "Marry rich. Buy him a pacemaker, then stand behind him and say boo!"

In these jokes reflecting Joan Rivers's *yente* morality, women are shrewd business operators, always calculating what is to their best interests, exacting the most favorable price for their favors, never giving anything away free. Because Joan Rivers exaggerates the attributes of this morality—its hard-nosed prag-matics, its stifling of sexuality, its curtailment of spontaneity, she arouses laughter in her increasingly uptight audiences who are all too familiar with the restrictive aspects of this morality in their own lives.

To prevent the *yente* from dominating her routines, Joan Rivers creates an opposing character, Heidi Abromowitz, the *kurveh,* the Yiddish tramp. The term, *kurveh,* taken from the Hebrew word, *karove,* means a "strange woman who comes very close."[24] And indeed Heidi Abromowitz, a scandal raiser, comes very close to, is, in fact, the obverse side of the *yente,* the scandal monger. Inspired out of the envy Joan Rivers had for Marilyn Abrams, the prettiest and most popular girl in her high school class, Heidi Abromowitz is Rivers's comically spiteful portrayal of the nice Jewish girl's direct opposite whose motto is "Never put off for tomorrow who you can put out for tonight."[25] In her best-selling book, *The Life and Times of Heidi Abromowitz,* a Jewish low comedy version of another prostitute's saga, Defoe's *Moll Flanders,* Rivers chronicles the stages of Abromowitz's development as "Baby Bimbo," "Toddler Tramp," "the Elementary Piece," "The Tramp at Camp," "Teen Tart," "the Sophomore Slut," "Senior Strumpet," "The Broad Abroad," "Career Chippy" and "Hooker Housewife."[26] As *yente,* Rivers gleefully discloses the lascivious conduct of Heidi Abromowitz from her earlier years, when "she did things with her pacifier that most women haven't done with their husbands,"[27] to her adulthood, when she listed herself in the Yellow Pages under "Public Utility."[28] Rivers delights in spreading the most malicious gossip about Heidi Abromowitz to titillate both herself and her audiences. For Heidi, who never lets herself "get tied down to housework," if she "can get tied down to a bed instead"[29] is the sexual transgressor whom we outwardly condemn but covertly like to emulate. Her actions are comically incongruous with her Jewish-sounding name, for instead of striving to be the biblical *eyshes chayil* (the dutiful women of valor), she is the liberated whore with the heart of gold. Devoid of moral constraints, she can take the lid off her id and fly away on the wings of an ego. And we, who are grounded by our multiple repressions, are temporarily seduced into flying away with her.

Joan Rivers's graphic caricatures of the sharp-tongued *yente* and the loose-tongued *kurveh* have offended some feminists who find them very unflattering depictions of women. To placate these critics she has added a new persona in her routines: an abrasively funny Gloria Steinem type who mocks patriarchal society for putting down women. The chief offender in her eyes is the gynecologist. Operating under the assumption that for women "bravery is to make a gynecologist's appointment and to show up," she hyperbolically recounts her own experience: "I wonder why I'm not relaxed. My feet are in the stirrups, my knees are in my face and the door is open facing me. And there's always a guy in the waiting room you went to high school with. . . . My doctor always tells jokes. Dr. Schwartz, at your cervix. You know what it's like to be in the stirrups and your doctor walks in wearing a snorkle. I'm dilated to meet you, says he. . . . Nurse Kelley, come here. Want to see some cob webs. Bring that Endust. . . . We have spent the whole morning taking a bath, showering, powdering, perfuming, shaving and douching and that son of a bitch has the nerve to wear a rubber glove. Who is he?" (From Joan Rivers's recording, *What Becomes a Semi-Legend Most?*)

The hostile humor of this routine is not directed inward at the supposed defects of Joan's body, like her self-deprecating *schlemiel* humor. Rather it is retaliatory humor, angrily striking back at the male power structure for subordinating and demeaning women. It is especially aimed at the hubris of the gynecologist, the doctor as superior being who makes women assume the most debasing positions, who sees them not as respectworthy persons but unsanitary sexual organs. Part of this humor is also directed at the women themselves for internalizing the low esteem men have of them, for resorting to desperate measures to gain male approval and for being willing accomplices in their own humiliation.

Joan Rivers, however, refuses to confine herself to any one kind of humor, be it the feminist, *schlemiel, yente,* or *kurveh* variety. An effervescent mocking bird, she flits from one kind of raillery to the next and often goes out on a limb to take new risks. For she believes that is the only way she can grow as a comedienne: "I think you have to go too far to know where you're going. I listened to what I talked about ten years ago and what I talk about now. Totally different. I hope in five years it will again be totally different. You've got to go too far and you don't know until they tell you."[30] And we, her audience, are eager to hear what this unpredictable mockingbird will squawk or *kvetch* about next.

When asked why female comics are in such short supply, Carol Burnett replied: "It's because you have to be kooky to be funny. You have to roll your eyes and throw yourself around and generally be aggressive."[31] There is another reason for the shortage of Jewish comediennes. Not only do they have to be "kooky" and "aggressive," they have to be unkosher, violating the most sanctioned ritual performed by the Jewish woman. Sophie Tucker, Belle Barth, Totie Fields and Joan Rivers have had the *chutzpah,* the nerve, to be unkosher comediennes. Rather than being tamed domestics who are properly clean, they have transformed themselves into unkosher *vilde chayes* (wild beasts) leaping over the boundaries of Jewish respectability. Yet they have not alienated audiences with their breaches of decency. Rather than offend sensibilities, their big mouths have created a memorable tumult and their innovative *schmutz* (filth) has left an indelible mark.

NOTES

1. G. Legman, *Rationale of the Dirty Joke,* First Series (New York: Grove Press, Inc., 1968), p. 17.

2. Sophie Tucker, *Some of These Days* (New York: Doubleday & Co., 1945), p. 1.

3. Ibid., p. 11.

4. Ibid., p. 54.

5. Eddie Cantor, *Take My Life,* p. 34, quoted in Lewis A. Erenberg, *Steppin' Out* (Westport, CT: Greenwood Press, 1981), p. 196.

6. June Sochen, "Fanny Brice and Sophie Tucker: Blending the Particular with the Universal," in *From Hester Street to Hollywood: The Jewish-American Stage and Screen,* ed. Sarah Blacher Cohen (Bloomington: Indiana University Press, 1983), p. 48.

7. Tucker, *Some of These Days,* pp. 126–27.

8. Ibid., pp. 95–96.

9. This description of the comic buffoon was formulated by Susanne K. Langer, *Feeling and Form* (New York: Charles Scribner's Sons, 1953), p. 342.

10. Tucker, *Some of These Days,* p. 96.

11. Legman, *Rationale of the Dirty Joke,* p. 12.

12. In conversation with psychologist Sam Janus, "who spent ten years and $20,000 of his own money traveling around the country to interview top comedians and give them psychological tests." Some of his findings appeared in "Analyzing Jewish Comics," *Time* (October 2, 1978), p. 76.

13. Cliff Jahr, "No Kidding, Joan Rivers is the Queen of Comedy," *Ladies Home Journal* (November 1983), p. 89.

14. Jerry Adler with Pamela Abramson and Susan Agrest, "Joan Rivers Gets Even With Laughs," *Newsweek* (October 10, 1983), p. 59.

15. Lee Israel, "Joan Rivers and How She Got That Way," *MS Magazine* (October 1984), p. 112.

16. Adler, *Newsweek,* p. 58.

17. Richard Meryman, "Can We Talk? Why Joan Rivers Can't Stop" *McCalls* (September 1983) p. 64.

18. Albert Goldman, "Boy-man, *Schlemiel:* the Jewish Element in American Humour," in *Explorations,* ed. Murray Mindlin and Chaim Bermant (London: Barrie and Rockliff, 1967), p. 13.

19. Jahr, *Ladies Home Journal,* p. 89.

20. Leo Rosten, *The Joys of Yiddish* (New York: McGraw-Hill, 1968), p. 426.

21. Gerald Clarke, "Barbs for the Queen (and Others)" *Time* (April 11, 1983), p. 85.

22. Meryman, *McCalls*, p. 64.

23. Ibid.

24. Rosten, *The Joys of Yiddish,* p. 198.

25. Joan Rivers, *The Life and Times of Heidi Abromowitz* (New York: Delacorte Press, 1984), p. 10.

26. Ibid. Titles from Table of Contents.

27. Ibid., p. 10.

28. Ibid., p. 60.

29. Ibid., p. 74.

30. Joan Rivers, quoted in *MS* (October 1984), p. 110.

31. Sarel Eimerl, "Can Women Be Funny?" *Mademoiselle* (November 1962), p. 151.

WOODY ALLEN

The Neurotic Jew as American Clown

GERALD MAST

> "Doc. My brother's crazy. He thinks he's a chicken."
> "Why don't you turn him in?"
> "I would. But I need the eggs."
>
> *Annie Hall*

The American clown-star of movie comedies has always been a separate breed of being, different from everyone else around him—similar to others in his aspirations, perhaps, but wildly different in his looks, dress, and demeanor. The clown announced his distance from the culture that contained him with his clothing, which mirrored his odd habits of mind, and with his thinking, reflected by his bizarre external appearance and gestures. Chaplin's Tramp costume declared his spiritual independence from bourgeois materialism while Keaton's dead-pan face and pork-pie hat hid a furiously inventive imagination beneath the dour WASP surface of some archetypal Grant Wood midwesterner. Harold Lloyd's round glasses, insistent smiles, and aggressive schemes; Harry Langdon's floppy round hat, puffy face, and baby hands; Groucho's bouncing eyebrows, bristling moustache, and battling cigar; W.C. Field's fancy clothes and swollen nose; Jerry Lewis's nebbish glasses, knobby knees, and nasal twang—all were trademarks that not only defined their

bearers as funny, but funny in a particular way about particular
kinds of things.

To be a star American film-clown meant to look different from
everyone else (the way that the star clown always looked different in the music-hall, circus, vaudeville, and burlesque—the
"universities" that produced the early generations of film-
clowns). But the funny look was not merely a gag and a getup; it
was a comic way of viewing everybody else, who looked (and,
consequently, acted) normal—whatever that meant—and which
the clown's very being undermined. The great film-clowns were
always some deviation from an Aristotelian "Golden Mean" of
contemporary comportment—suggesting either too much (like
Keaton, Lloyd, and Groucho) or too little (like Chaplin, Langdon, Fields, and Lewis), an excess or a deficiency, of what
everyone else believed necessary for a meaningful life.

That Woody Allen descends from this tradition is obvious
from his eyeglasses alone, which link him with Harold Lloyd,
Groucho Marx, and Jerry Lewis. Glasses suggest three male
stereotypes in movies and in our culture: the blindness of childhood naiveté (Lloyd, or Cary Grant's glasses in *Bringing Up
Baby*), the sophistry of intellectual dexterity (Groucho), or the
clumsiness of physical weakness (Lewis). (For women in movies,
glasses suggest a single stereotype that parallels Jerry Lewis—
the ugly duckling becomes a swan when the glasses come off—
except in Alfred Hitchcock movies.) Having made the movie
house his "university," Woody Allen learned enough about
"glass characters" (as Lloyd called them) to use all three implications: the Allen "glass character" is a childish weakling intellectual.

But it isn't simply that Allen looks odd or funny in comparison
to everyone else—although he is physically smaller, like Chaplin,
Langdon, and Keaton, than most others around him and, like
them, looks powerless to defend himself against anyone or anything. Like his predecessors, Allen's clownship is more depen-
dent on what he is rather than how he looks, how he thinks
rather than how he appears. And what Allen is, is Jewish. Allen,
unJewish, is as unthinkable as Chaplin without his cane,
Groucho without his cigar, or Fields without his nose.

Woody Allen is the first great American film-clown for whom
being Jewish was not simply a hereditary accident but a way of
life. The Marx Brothers were Jewish, and the anarchic irra-

tionality of their film plots (such as they were) and personae grew directly from Jewish roots in burlesque—in the turn-of-the-century "Dutch" acts of Joe Weber and Lew Fields or the Howard Brothers, when "Dutch" was a euphemism for *Deutsch,* and *Deutsch* was a euphemism for Yiddish. It was during this Weber/ Fields period that Mama Minnie Marx first put together an act for her boys. But Harpo's angelic silence and Chico's Italianate malaprop puns balanced Groucho's sophistic weeds that sprang from "Dutch" soil. The Marxes' fast and crazy parodies grew, however well disguised, from crazy comedy's Jewish roots in Weber/Fields burlesque, and Mel Brooks's film parodies of the 1970s represent a second-generation disguise that sprang from the same roots. Jerry Lewis was also Jewish, but as Lewis rose from Borscht Belt nightclubs to the duo with Dean Martin to his own solo comedies, he also increasingly disguised his Jewish roots (those characters in television sketches named Melvin, in contrast to Dino, the smooth *goy*) as he came more and more to embody the unspecified genus *shleppus Americanus.*

Before Woody Allen it was box-office poison for a film comedian to seem "too Jewish" (which is to say, at all Jewish). In the earliest, primitive era of film comedy, the improvisational 1910s of Mack Sennett's Keystone Comedies, there were plenty of broad Jewish types in comic films. There were also plenty of other ethnic comic types—Irishmen named Riley, Germans named Fritz and Schultz, Blacks named Rastus—and Jews named Cohen. This ethnic humor was always based on the most stereotypic traits—the Irish were always ready for a brawl, the Germans drank beer and ate Limberger cheese, the Blacks fainted every time a white sheet moved, and the Jews counted their shekels. This crude humor (by today's sensitive standards) obviously appealed to a largely immigrant, working-class audience in the early days of film comedy—who could laugh at themselves and at other immigrant groups at the same time. The humor went quickly out of fashion when the movies became a more genteel, middle-class entertainment after World War I, and when unassimilated immigrants became suspicious as "foreign"—in fact or in spirit—to American middle-class values.

The film career of Ernst Lubitsch provides an instructive example. Lubitsch was the son of a tailor, born in the Jewish ghetto of Berlin. After training with the great Max Reinhardt, Lubitsch began a series of short comic films in 1913 as "Meyer," a roly-

poly comic Jew, whom Lubitsch—at five-feet-four with high
forehead and large nose to match—stereotypically resembled.
After five years of success as both star and director of this low-
comic series, Lubitsch moved up to the stylish historical epics,
starring his discoveries, Emil Jannings and Pola Negri, which
made him famous worldwide as the "humanizer" (i.e., sex-
ualizer) of history. He came to Hollywood in 1923 and, until the
Second World War, served as America's most stylish chronicler
of the lives, loves, and mores of European high society—the
hedonistic highlife of earls, counts, barons, princesses, lords,
and ladies, from which he himself, the Jewish son of a tailor, had
always been excluded. Lubitsch's satirical deflation of the shal-
lowness and emptiness of this upper crust may well be an oblique
reflection of his earthy Jewish distance from it, but the literal
Jewishness of this director, one of the most successful in Hollywood history at combining stylistic integrity and commercial
popularity, is invisible. Only with the war in Europe could
Lubitsch move to the more familiar and familial mercantile world
(The Shop Around the Corner) and an overt attack on the anti-
Semitism of the Nazis *(To Be or Not To Be)*.

The Hollywood moguls of the 1920s and 1930s, either Jewish
immigrants or the sons of immigrants themselves, became understandably nervous if their movies seemed "too Jewish." The
concerted campaign for federal censorship of motion picture
content, fueled by the first wave of Hollywood sex and drug
scandals in the early 1920s, was a thinly veiled (and sometimes
not so veiled) anti-Semitic attack against the Jews who ran the
movie business. Many of the organizations which agitated noisily
against "the freedom of the screen," like the Women's Christian
Temperance Union, also suggested that the Jewish infidels were
about their usual business of poisoning the wells (this time moral
and spiritual wells) of a Christian nation. It was no accident that
in 1922, when the Jewish moguls banded together to combat this
attack (and eventually to write the famed Hollywood Code which
successfully protected the movies from federal censorship), they
appointed a Presbyterian elder, Will H. Hays, to run the organization, two Catholics, Martin Quigley and Daniel Lord (a Jesuit
priest), to write the Code, and another Catholic, Joseph Breen, to
administer it.

Although Jewish characters were appropriate for "serious"
film stories like *The Jazz Singer* (written by Samson Raphaelson,

who became Lubitsch's witty scriptwriter), Jews seemed inappropriate—too vulgar or too touchy a subject—for comedies. The one exception in the early years of synchronized sound was Eddie Cantor, the Jewish star of musical comedy imported from Broadway to Hollywood by Samuel Goldwyn. Jewish humor had always been a part of Cantor's stage act, accompanying him up the show-business ladder from burlesque to vaudeville to Broadway. Fanny Brice, who climbed the same ladder with the same Jewish comedy, never succeeded in movies, and when she became a star of radio and television it was not as a Jewish adult but as a "Baby Snooks." The anti-heroic, anti-romantic Cantor, whose tiny body made him the perfect comic foil for all the physical menaces of life, depended heavily on his trademark—his bulging "banjo" eyes, which bulged as much as they did because they sat between his high "Jewish" forehead and large "Jewish" nose. If Cantor was scant of body (like Chaplin, Keaton, and Allen) he was also (exactly like them) quick of wit. For Cantor, that wit was frequently Jewish.

In his first film, *Whoopee!* (1930), Cantor plays a weakling in the wild West, the friend of a half-breed Indian banished from the sight of his white lady love. When the Indian insists to Cantor that he has been raised as a white—"I've gone to your schools"—Eddie replies incredulously, "An Indian in a Hebrew school?" Later in the film, Eddie masquerades as Big Chief Indie Horovitz on the reservation, haggling with tourists over the price of Indian blankets. In *Roman Scandals* (1933), Cantor dreams himself into the society of ancient Rome as a slave named Eddiepuss. On the block at the slave auction, Eddie tries to interest prospective buyers in his virtues, despite his tiny size: "Look at these skins," he remarks, patting his arms and legs, "imported from Russia." But as Cantor films progressed through the thirties, Goldwyn steadily invested less in their budgets and made even less at the box office. Not coincidentally, Cantor's explicit Jewishness declined with his films' grosses (the cause or the effect of the decline?), until, by his last film of the Goldwyn cycle, *Strike Me Pink* (1936), Eddie is still small, weak, cowardly, and clumsy, but not at all Jewish. In the 1940s, when Goldwyn recycled Cantor into Danny Kaye, another Jewish musical-comedy star from Broadway, he rewrote the same plots (comic klutz embroiled in dangerous, deadly intrigue) without any suggestion that the klutz might be Jewish. Kaye would leave both Goldwyn and the Goldwyn formula to make his offbeat, highly personal attack on anti-Semitism, *Me and the Colonel,* in 1958. But by this point in his career, Kaye was not only through with Goldwyn but, like Cantor, through with movies and ready to be recycled for television.

Woody Allen's films, unlike Cantor's, increasingly define his persona as Jewish. In *Take the Money and Run* (1968), the first "true" Woody Allen film ("true" because he wrote it, directed it, and starred in it), Allen plays Vergil Starkwell, the caricature of some *goyish* criminal (like a Richard Speck or the Truman Capote subjects of *In Cold Blood*) in a parody of a crime film. Like all his early films, *Take the Money* parodied some other kind of film: *Bananas* (1971), the Banana-Republic Revolution film; *Sleeper* (1973), science fiction; *Love and Death* (1975), *War and Peace*. Allen played characters (Fielding Melish and Miles Monroe, for example) whose traits and names were clearly parodic but not particularly Jewish. The first extended comic sequence based on Allen's Jewishness is in *Sleeper,* and it would point the way toward the goal of Allen's mature comedies: the creation of psychocomedy, translating personal painful experiences into comic fictions, by exploring the differences between the Jewish Allen and the *goyim* who become his lovers and friends.

While Allen (as Miles Monroe) and two sidekicks (Allen's quintessential *shiksa,* Diane Keaton, and the blond Teuton, John Beck) flee their Brave New World pursuers, the three pause to perform a playlet in the woods. Miles passes out the scripts, and the three sit down to reenact the scene of that fateful Passover *seder* when Monroe (i.e., Allen) informed his parents that he and his wife were separating. The whining rage, the pushy insistence, the domineering pressure of the parental responses in Allen's dialogue play in counterpoint with the young, smooth gentile faces and the flat American accents of the actors, who parody the Yiddish-immigrant English of the parents. The ludicrousness of their pronunciations and the inappropriateness of the setting—outdoors in bright sunlight rather than indoors in the parental dining room—distance the painful and personal scene into the detachment of Shavian or Brechtian comedy. In this odd combination of "Dutch" comedy (performed by amateurs) and his own psychoanalytic traumas, Allen had discovered the angle of his comic perspective.

Allen's collaboration with scriptwriter Marshall Brickman and cinematographer Gordon Willis on *Annie Hall* (1977) created the team that consistently allowed him to balance the whiningly personal psychoanalytic confession with the objective detachment of comedy. Built around the differing conversations of Jews and Gentiles at dinner and contrasting cramped urban interiors with brightly open rural exteriors, *Annie Hall* became Allen's most sincere, most personal, and most richly comic statement about both his life and his art. For the first time, the character Allen plays in the film, Alvy Singer, is as close to him as any fictional character could be. Like Allen, Alvy began as a gag writer for others, then performed his own material as a stand-up comic, then created complete comic fictional works like movies and plays. Like Allen, Alvy is forty and twice divorced. Like Allen, Alvy has left Jewish women for *shiksas*: Alvy's first wife was a Jewish American Princess with literary aspirations; his second, a "New York Jewish liberal intellectual—Central Park West, Socialist summer camps, father with Ben Shahn drawings." Annie Hall, Alvy's third serious romance, is played by Diane Keaton, who became Allen's third wife. Even the names of Woody Allen and Alvy Singer are congruent—a two-syllable first name ending in the diminutive y and a two-syllable surname. (However, Alvy Singer never changed his name, as Woody Allen—born Allen Konigsberg—did.)

The *seder* of *Sleeper* leads directly to the split-screen dinner scene of *Annie Hall,* which compares and contrasts the different habits at table (and, by implication, the different approaches to life) of the gentile Hall family and the Jewish Singer family. The Halls take their meal at midday, bathed in the bright light that pours in through the windows, a reminder of the outdoors and nature which surround the Hall farm. The Singers take their meal at an unspecified evening hour, enclosed in a cavelike interior tinted by the amber glow of electric light bulbs. Nature is nowhere to be seen—except perhaps on the flower-print dresses of the women. The Halls, however, wear and live within patternless, colorless neutrals—whites, off-whites, beiges, grays—the tasteful "earthtones" that Allen always associates with *goyim* (and which become an important leitmotif of *Interiors,* 1978). The stark, clean lines of the Hall dining room—echoed by the rectangular photographs of Annie's apartment—make a sharp visual contrast with the messy clutter of the Singer's dining room, beyond whose tacky yellow walls lie not the fields and trees of nature but the rollercoaster of Coney Island. The Halls speak, if they speak at all, quietly and politely, one conversation at a time, about such earth-shaking topics as the weather; the Singers all chatter at once, a noisy, semi-articulate babble, concerning such pleasant subjects as hospital visits and terminal diseases.

No wonder Alvy feels a freak at the Halls' table (they are, after all, eating ham). In one of the film's most memorable subjective images, Allen depicts Alvy in the guise of an *Hasidic* Jew, complete with black hat and coat, red beard and *payos*—a vision of the most extreme form of unassimilated American Jewry, often embarrassing to Jews themselves. On its surface, the vision of *Hasidic* Alvy has a clear meaning—the freaky, tacky foreignness of Jews, strangers in the strange American heartland of the clean, bright, open, tasteful, stylish, normal Halls.

But Allen gives this clear contrast several twists below its simple surface. The shot of *Hasidic* Alvy does not really convey the Halls' view of him; instead, it mirrors the way Alvy feels the Halls feel about his presence at their table. It is an image of Alvy's own self-consciousness in their gentile midst, not an image of the Halls' gentile consciousness. Indeed, the Halls probably lack the actual experience with Jewish looks and types to fashion any clear image of Jewish or *Hasidic* appearance. (Friends of mine from Hall-type backgrounds—American farms and small towns—tell me that, although they often heard sneering references to "Jew York City," they had no precise image of what a Jew looked like.) Only an American Jew could imagine himself as a freak in the guise of the *Hasidim*. Alvy's vision relates less to the clear contrast of Gentiles and Jews than to his (and Allen's?) paranoia and persecution complex, his own insecurities and discomfort (totally self-induced or accurately inferred from the "vibes" at the dinner table?). The parenthetic question marks in that sentence, which may or may not have clear answers, contribute to the richness of that striking image.

Although Allen associates any number of pleasing visual images with *goyim* —sunlight; nature; tasteful shades, shapes, furniture, *objets d'art,* and clothing—he also implies spiritual deficiencies to accompany the tasteful imagery. The Gentiles are cold, unpredictable, frivolous, and suicidal. The quiet at the Halls' table is gracious but deadly; the noise of the Singer table is tacky but vital. While life with the Halls is both lovely and lifeless, the life of the Singers has all the noise and the bounce of a rollercoaster—loud and bumpy but it moves, up as well as down as well as up. The Halls remain static within frames whose lines are evenly horizontal. A frequent reaction to the character Pearl (Maureen Stapleton), in *Interiors,* is that she represents a Jewish reaction to the gentile family of the film's focus (Allen's shifting his concern in his next film to the mystical gentile world of the Halls could only be accomplished by eliminating himself from the film.) There is, however, no evidence that Pearl is Jewish; she only seems so because her warmth, vitality, vulgarity, and clothing (a red dress in contrast to the others' earthtones) are consistent with the terms Allen had defined in *Annie Hall* for Jews in contrast to Gentiles.

Allen also draws a complex distinction between the view of Jews and Gentiles toward death. Alvy (like Allen) is obsessed with death. On their first date, Alvy buys Annie two books: *The Denial of Death* and *Death and Western Thought.* When the pair splits up and divides their belongings, Annie tosses "all the books on death and dying" into Alvy's pile. Alvy's favorite movie is *The Sorrow and the Pity,* and one of Allen's favorite film sequences is the opening deathdream of Ingmar Bergman's *Wild Strawberries* (which he parodies in *Bananas*). While Jews think and talk a lot about death, the Gentiles in Allen's films more actively pursue it. Only Gentiles commit suicide in Allen films *(Interiors),* while Annie Hall's demented brother, Dwayne (Christopher Walken), is a suicidal maniac with a yen to swerve his automobile into oncoming highway traffic. As Alvy informs Dwayne after his bedroom confession, "I have to go now, Dwayne, 'cause I'm due back on the planet earth." If Jews whine about death, Gentiles seem to hold life more cheaply. Jews are fatalists, not fatalities.

For Allen, Gentiles are also more faddish, flippant, and unpredictable. They go for faddish religions like Rosicrucianism, while Alvy "can't get with any religion that advertises in *Popular Mechanics.*" Both Annie and Rob (Tony Roberts) can change their clothing as easily as their lifestyles when they move from coast to coast. Annie can switch from indoor New York delis (even if she does eat her pastrami sandwiches on white bread with mayo) to outdoor health food restaurants where they serve alfalfa sprouts and natural yogurt. But the bright sunshine, open spaces, and white outfits of Los Angeles—those styles and

shades always associated with nonJews—make Alvy physically
ill. No matter when or where, Alvy always dresses the same (in
wrinkled tweed jackets), and looks the same (as if no ray of
sunlight ever brushed a freckle of his perpetual pallor). The
Hollywood party at the home of Tony Lacey (the record pro-
ducer played by Paul Simon), who may represent Allen's vision of
a Jew transported and converted to Hollywood, is flooded with
sunshine (like the Halls' dining room) and white-clad guests in
loose, oddly shaped garments. Even Lacey's Los Angeles Christmas tree is white, while Alvy's and Annie's Christmas tree in
New York is a traditional green. (And why does Alvy have a
Christmas tree? Well, if he's going to have one, it will be old-
fashioned—Alvy's style—and natural—Annie's style.)

Somewhere beneath these clear contrasts of Jews and Gentiles, indoors and outdoors, East Coast and West Coast, life and
death, Allen also invokes Alvy's (and his own) persecution ma-
nias. Allen is not only a self-conscious creator and performer; he
is self-conscious of his self-consciousness. Alvy sniffs anti-Semitism everywhere—in the looks of the Halls, the mutterings under
strangers' breaths, even in the simple question, "Did you?"
elided in the vernacular American pronunciation as "Djew?" In
this paranoia, Allen both recognizes and criticizes the knee-jerk
Jewish tendency to overreact to even comical anti-Semitic
slights. As Rob informs Alvy, "Every time some group disagrees
with you, it's because of anti-Semitism."

Alvy is eaten by self-doubt: he has been in analysis, "just for
fifteen years." He can't abide drugs or alcohol as sexual season-
ings because they make him feel "unbearably wonderful"—so
wonderful that the sex must be dirty and will make him feel
guilty. Alvy's sexual fantasies are visual—black-lace underwear
and a red lightbulb—not sensual; they are ideas (and pretty
unoriginal ones), not sensations. Allen, like Alvy, seems frozen
by his doubts, contradictions, and irresolution: he can't make up
his mind about which woman he wants in *Manhattan (1979),* nor
whether he can remain faithful to any one woman; he can't make
up his mind about his fans, his critics, his art, and his dreams in
Stardust Memories (1980); he wonders if he, like *Zelig* (1982), is
merely a chameleon man, a figure of multiple guises and poses
who stands for nothing at all.

Unlike the silent clowns before him—Chaplin, Keaton,
Lloyd—Allen is incapable of action, of *doing* anything. All he

performs is his performance and all he has are his inner thoughts
and his external comments (like Groucho and W.C. Fields). His
only action is acting out his cultural commentary. His life, like his
comic art, turns inward; the two are indistinguishable. He rewrites the final scene of parting between Alvy and Annie as the
climactic scene of his new play and casts it with two types who
resemble them as theater "types" resemble actual people (the
boy a more conventionally young and handsome "Jewish type"
than Alvy, and the young woman an actressly glamorized Annie).
After listening to the "Alvy-type's" marriage proposal, the "An-
nie-type" accepts it. Alvy then turns directly to the camera and
apologizes for his own sentimental emendation: "What do you
want? It was my first play." But *Annie Hall* is not Allen's first
movie, and its interweaving of performer and persona, actual
experience and fictional episode, personal pain and comic detachment, self-consciousness and self-expression is as complex a
depiction of neurotic but cathartic Jewish inwardness as has ever
been seen on a movie screen.

In the films that follow the pivotal *Annie Hall*, Woody Allen
wavers between his neurotic doubts and his cathartic affections.
Although *Broadway Danny Rose* (1984) and *The Purple Rose of
Cairo* (1985) may not be Allen's two best films after *Annie Hall,*
they are certainly his most affectionate. Both return to Allen's
second most important personal commitment (after being Jewish): being an entertainer. And both imply a nostalgic affection
for oldtime entertainments that have passed from the earth: the
oddball variety acts that once found a home on the Borscht Belt
circuit, and the escapist movie romances that once found a home
in Depression America. Danny Rose, a theatrical agent who
handles very odd specialty acts, provides the transportation for a
sentimental journey into Allen's own Borscht Belt past—to the
Catskill resorts where young Allen Konigsberg caught his first
glimpse of show-biz glitter watching such acts, and where Woody
Allen's own career as a comedian began. The film collects a
gaggle of oldtimer yocksmiths to reminisce at Broadway's Stage
Deli—Corbett Monica, Morty Gunty, Jackie Mason, Henny
Youngman—all veterans of the Catskills. And the film collects a
troupe of oldtime performance oddities—a stuttering ventriloquist, balloon sculpturists, a water-glass instrumentalist, a so-
prano parrot, and the booze-bloated, womanizing Italian singer
with incomprehensible appeal for middle-aged Jewish ladies—

who spring from Allen's memory and dreams and who have otherwise vanished from the earth. (Occasionally these odd specialty acts turn up on cruise ships, which have become the floating Borscht Belt.)

Broadway Danny Rose is conscious of itself as an homage to a vanishing breed of entertainment and entertainer. Set in the early 1960s and filmed in black-and-white (a stylistic kin and contemporary of Martin Scorsese's *Raging Bull*), *Danny Rose* is the story of an anachronism who finds himself caught between the Borscht Belt and *The Godfather*—a kind-hearted Jewish loser entangled in a Sicilian battle for honor and revenge. How else can you get a Jewish *shlepp* into an Italian gangster movie? *Broadway Danny Rose* also seems conscious that the personalized little entertainments represented by those Borscht Belt specialty acts have been replaced by big blockbuster movies with superstars from Hollywood like *The Godfather*. Danny Rose's battle with the Mafia clans is not unlike Woody Allen's own New York battle with the Hollywood Goliaths like Francis Coppola, George Lucas, and Steven Spielberg. For whatever reason, mixing Jews and gangsters has become the newest variant of the genre, not only in *Broadway Danny Rose* but in *Once Upon a Time in America* and *The Cotton Club*. Perhaps the Italians (like Sergio Leone and Coppola) have grown weary of the Italian gangster myth, particularly since that myth sprang primarily from the four Jewish Warner brothers and their Jewish stars, Paul Muni and Edward G. Robinson. *Broadway Danny Rose* is less interested in attacking the genre myth than in manipulating it as an affectionate means to bid farewell to an odd corner of the show-business world.

The Purple Rose of Cairo also accepts a myth and explores it affectionately—two myths actually (and both of them very much gentile myths). One is the film's off-screen technicolor world of social "reality"—working-class America during the Depression, where the wife supports her husband as a waitress in a diner because the plant where her husband worked has been closed by hard times. The Jewel, the town's movie house, provides her one glittering escape from such a world, and no matter how grim her life at home, the movie replaces the tears in her eyes with a twinkle. The other myth is the on-screen black-and-white world of movie romance, "The Purple Rose of Cairo," where characters have no jobs or worries except to gather their mythical rosebuds, dividing their lives between pyramids along the Nile and nights at the Copacabana. That these two worlds are equally mythical in the film becomes clear when one asks exactly *where* in New Jersey is this "real" town supposed to be? How close is it to New York? Why must these characters work in a plant or a diner? Why don't they own a struggling Mom and Pop store (which was the reality for many Jews during the Depression)? The "reality" of *The Purple Rose of Cairo* very much represents a Jewish vision of a *goyish* Depression myth.

The reason Woody Allen cannot appear in this film becomes clear. *The Purple Rose of Cairo*—no less than *Interiors*—deliberately confines itself to a gentile world. It is also, like *Interiors,* a woman-centered film (another consequence of removing Woody Allen from a film is to shift its gender focus). Its male embodiment of mythic *goy*dom is Tom Baxter (Jeff Daniels), the African explorer (like Groucho Marx's Captain Spalding in *Animal Crackers*), who steps off the black-and-white screen and into the technicolor "real" life of the superfan, Cecilia (Mia Farrow). Baxter combines the logical perfection of a Pirandello character, the naiveté of Carroll's Alice on the unfamiliar side of the looking glass, and the amazement of Keaton's Sherlock Jr., who gets similarly confused between on- and off-screen worlds. Whatever Tom Baxter is, it is obvious what he is not: he is the very opposite of Woody Allen. He has no sexual desire (passion obligatorily ends for Tom at the fade-out); he has never even heard of God (the concept of whom reminds him of his script writers, Irving Sax and R.H. Levine); he has never thought about unemployment, poverty, prostitution, disease, or death. He exists by logic—deducing his conduct from traits written into his character and locations where he has been filmed (somewhat limited to an Egyptian tomb, a New York penthouse, and the Copacabana nightclub). He is completely clear about the ultimate goal of existence—true love crowned by eternal marriage— and nothing else. In his perfectly handsome, *goyish*ly beautiful face and perfectly placid moral convictions, he is a 1985 Jewish mythic vision of a 1935 American Dream. Without any neuroses, doubts, insecurities, ambivalences, morbidities, or cynicism, Tom Baxter is Woody Allen in negative.

Why or how can the opposite neurotic inwardness of Woody Allen seem cathartic? And why or how can it appeal to American audiences who are not primarily Jewish? These questions have both historical and cultural answers. For one thing, the neurotic insecurity of Woody Allen seems much more perceptive, honest, and human than the bland optimism of Tom Baxter. After five decades of Hollywood films that implied the Tom Baxterish homogeneity of American life—the oneness of American experience despite our differing ethnic roots—American films and television in the 1970s suggested an alternative view: an America not merely flavored, but energized by ethnic difference and variety. The growing middle-class and the suspicion of foreigners in the 1920s, the need to stick together in response to the Depression in the 1930s and the War in the 1940s (those platoons of mythic American soldiers: different ethnic types who become a single fighting unit), the conservative retreat accompanying the move to the suburbs of the 1950s—all contributed to Hollywood's homogenization of American life in its films. But 1970s television (from "Archie Bunker" to "The Jeffersons" to "Hill Street Blues") and comedy (from Richard Pryor to the late Freddie Prinze) recognized the ethnic differences (in effect, class differences) that needed to be faced honestly if social prejudices and their consequent injustices were to be eradicated. The classic American metaphor of the "melting pot," in which assorted ethnic ingredients boil down together into a consistent cultural stew, was replaced by an open recognition of the different ethnic meats in the kettle. Woody Allen came to embody the quintessential Jewish chunk.

The Dickensian stereotype of the money-counting Jew came to be replaced by a healthier, if no less stereotypic, image—of Jewish intellectuality. So many of the ways we have come to think about modern life have come from the thoughts of Jews: from Marx's analysis of economics and history, to Freud's psychoanalysis, to Einstein's physics, to Kafka's paranoid surrealistic fantasies of absurdity. So many of these forces can be seen in Woody Allen's films (from his dependence on his analyst, to the relationship of his art and his dreams, to his concrete references to Jewish intellectual superstars like Susan Sontag, Irving Howe, and Saul Bellow in *Zelig*). Woody Allen is the clown who *thinks* about the ways we think. If there is Freud in Allen's psychocomedy and Kafka in his films' imaginative spatiotemporal leaps, the Marx in Woody Allen comes less from Karl than from Groucho—the smart-ass, big-mouth commentator on social inanities. In a world in which we have all become self-conscious of our value systems and their limitations, the Jew-ishness of Woody Allen seems an appropriate general emblem of self-consciousness, which all moderns—Jews and Gentiles—share.

The self-conscious inwardness of Woody Allen becomes especially striking in comparison to the alternative comedy of Eddie Murphy, the most interesting and arresting Black comedian ever to appear in American films. Murphy, who heads his own production company, is very much the primary creator of the world of his films, just as Allen is. While Allen is an essentially passive figure, responding to and commenting upon the culture surrounding him, and his films contain no action other than their self-conscious meditation upon themselves as films and artworks, Murphy plays active, goal-oriented roles in action-packed genre films (the type which critics fondly call movie movies). While Allen's gags and comic routines are modernist reflections (on Allen himself, or his relationships, or his art, or movies, or cultural beliefs), Murphy's gags and comic routines all play functional roles in advancing the plot and the character toward their goals. For example, when Murphy, in *Beverly Hills Cop,* impersonates "Ramon," the swish who claims to be the lover of the film's villain, he is using the comic routine to get past an obstacle and more toward the goal of capturing that villain. Murphy uses cultural presumptions about Blacks—that they are crooked, or stupid, or guileless, or dangerous—in comic sketches to defeat those who make the presumptions. It is as powerful an image of Black power—of active Blacks and their social strategies—as Allen is as an image of passive Jewish reflection. (Even in *Broadway Danny Rose,* Allen's gangster movie, the only thing Danny *does* is run away from trouble.) While Allen is a character of pure mind who is tortured by self-conscious doubts about his body, Eddie Murphy takes his body for granted with such casual grace that he scarcely knows there is a difference between mind and body.

Of course these current stereotypes of black resourcefulness and Jewish reflectiveness are, like all cultural images, hyperbolic myths. But more interesting than the questionable accuracy or validity of these myths is the cultural power of these two comic personae as emblems of opposite cultural necessities—the need to think about the culture and the need to do something about it. In this paradigm, it is no accident that the embodiment of passive reflection is the self-conscious clown who is as obviously Jewish as Murphy is Black and is clever in the way that Jews are believed to be clever. If so many of us respond to that cleverness, it is probably because, whether Jew or Gentile, we can recognize the insanities of life and love but cannot renounce the struggle with them. Like Allen, we still "need the eggs."

DEAR MR. EINSTEIN

Jewish Comedy and the Contradictions of Culture

MARK SHECHNER

> The oldest form of social study is
> comedy. . . . Comic irony sets whole
> cultures side by side in a multiple exposure
> (e.g. *Don Quixote, Ulysses*), causing
> valuation to spring out of the recital of facts
> alone, in contrast to the hidden editorializing
> of tongue-in-cheek ideologists.
>
> HAROLD ROSENBERG[1]

In a fantastical and funny story by Philip Roth entitled "On the Air," Milton Lippman, a talent scout, writes to Albert Einstein to ask if Einstein would agree to star on "The Jewish Answer Man," a radio program that Lippman hopes to negotiate with the networks. It will demonstrate to the world that "the Greatest Genius of all Time is a Jew." When his first approach to Einstein goes unanswered, Lippman bravely writes again:

Dear Mr. Einstein:

I can understand how busy you must be thinking, and appreciate that you did not answer my letter suggesting that I try to get you on a radio program that would make "The Answer Man" look like the joke it is. Will you reconsider, if the silence means no? I realize that one of the reasons you don't wear a tie or even bother to comb your hair is because you are as busy as you are, thinking new things. Well, don't think that you would have to change your ways once you

become a radio personality. Your hair is a great gimmick, and I
wouldn't change it for a second. It's a great trademark. Without
disrespect, it sticks in your mind the way Harpo Marx's does. Which
is excellent. (Now I wonder if you even have the time to know who
The Marx Brothers are? They are four zany Jewish brothers, and
you happen to look a little like one of them. You might get a kick out
of catching one of their movies. Probably they don't even show
movies in Princeton, but maybe you could get somebody to drive
you out of town. You can get the entire plot in about a minute, but
the resemblance between you and Harpo and his hair and yours,
might reassure you that you are a fine personality in terms of show
business just as you are.)[2]

This is a splendid routine, taking Albert Einstein for a quiz
show star and his Harpo-esque coiffure for a commercial logo.
So fantastic are its premises that this comedy borders on the
absurd, and indeed, as the story of Lippman's pilgrimage to
Princeton unfolds, it takes on increasingly surreal dimensions.
Consider the very incongruity of the proposition! Milton Lippman to join forces with Albert Einstein: the man who revolutionized our understanding of space and time to be managed and
marketed by this *landsman,* this marginal hustler and jobber
whose voice keens with the desperate wisdom that comes of
2,000 years working bum territories: Egypt, Spain, the Pale of
Settlement, New Jersey.

But why is this funny, and what, if anything, can we say is
"Jewish" about it, besides the fact that Einstein and Lippman
are both Jews and that a Jew, Philip Roth, has conjured up the
entire phantasmagoria? For years now I have been gathering
notes on "the Jewish imagination," prompted by a curiosity
about Jewish culture and an appreciation of the role of humor
and comedy in it, both as a typical product and as an expression
of its deeper patternings. Indeed, I'm inclined to regard comedy
as an index to culture, a *via regia* into the collective unconscious
of a group no less revealing than dreams are of the individual
unconscious; for in the comic, where all is essentialized and
drawn in bold strokes, the basic terms of a culture are most
available for inspection. Comedy discloses culture the way x-rays
disclose bones or iron filings trace the force fields of a magnet,
mapping its auras and trajectories, its nodes of energy and its
fingers of attraction. A culture's manners, values, fears, taboos,
tempos, climates, and radiations constitute the very medium of
comedy, and the comedian immerses himself in this medium in

the spirit of an anthropologist immersing himself in an alien culture. The comedian's golden rule is, *the more familiar, the more strange*.

Some time ago I set out to write an essay on contemporary Jewish writers in America in an effort to determine whether there was anything decisively Jewish about the writers I was dealing with apart from their lineage and the cultural reference points in their books, and whether, in our current state of cultural homogenization, we could even distinguish between the fiction of Jewish writers or, speaking more cautiously, writers of Jewish descent and that written by other Americans.[3] Is it possible, I wondered, to speak of a Jewish imagination without invoking universals, properties common to all people that just happened to be embedded in Jewish circumstances, or without citing the authority of the merely circumstantial—*shtetls,* rabbis, *dybbuks,* tailors, *gonifs,* cutting rooms, egg creams, chicken soup, or chicken fat—details that dissolve every generation or two as the circumstances and locales of Jewish life alter.

If geographical sign posts and social manners do not of themselves define a "Jewish" imagination, what about themes: the ethical imagination, the Bible, the exile, the wrath of Jehovah, the covenant, pogrom, the Holocaust? What of moods or tonalities, like lamentation? Here we would seem to be on firmer footing, since there is scarcely an expression of the Jewish imagination for the last 2,000 years that was not drenched in the basic premises of Jewish life. And yet even here we're bound to note that these premises, persistent though they be, are also perishable. The exile, for the time being, is over; the covenant has lost its authority for most modern Jews; and though pogrom has given way to jihad, a seemingly indifferent exchange of assaults, Jews now have tanks and aircraft. As for the Holocaust, it is already appropriated by others who see in it the potential for major statement. We have *Sophie's Choice*. The Bible? The God of Israel? To see these as uniquely Jewish themes is to make Jews out of those American Protestants for whom the Old Testament and the exactions of the Almighty have long been the mainstay of their Christian faith. And as for suffering and martyrdom, they don't distinguish Jews in America from others who've known hard times. The Psalms may have given us lamentation, but it was Black America, steeped in biblical tonalities, that gave us the blues. (Israel may have crossed the Jordan, but it is the Baptists who sing about it.) Nor does sorrow as a distinctively "Jewish" note tell us much about Jewish resilience, ingenuity, and resourcefulness, which are at least as historically evident as Jewish martyrdom. It doesn't help us understand Israel.

If details or themes do not alone define a cultural imagination, what might suffice? Or are we destined to shuttle back and forth between the universals of the human imagination (archetypes, deep structures, universal biological or developmental determinants) and the specifics of the individual—the sediments of personal experience and personal history? I want to propose, if only as a stopgap, that an alternative approach to the cultural dimensions of the imagination might be through its characteristic structures, the *forms* taken by experience, for it is by the mediation of cultural forms that universals are filtered into the workaday and the particulars of experience charged with the generic. Culture packs the mind with rules of meaning, and it is through those rules that the raw data of life become our experiences of it. I do not claim that these configurations of imagination are timeless, for they too are products of history, and as history changes so do they. But because they are embedded in lore and ritual, and because family and culture pass them down, they are tenacious; they resist easy uprooting, and one may find in them anachronistic remnants of past times and conditions. The structures of imagination lag behind the times, sometimes by generations, and continue to order the priorities of mind long after the conditions of life that had formed them have passed into oblivion.

I have written elsewhere about a structure of perception that seems to me to sustain a particular sort of Jewish imagining, and I stress *particular sort,* since it should be evident that the Jewish mind is not and has never been a simple entity. I call that structure "ghetto cosmopolitanism"[4] and think of it as a conjunction of identities within the same individual: contrasting internal frames of reference whose abutment and interplay give form and inspiration to Jewish imagining. Ghetto cosmopolitanism arose out of the striking conjunctions of oppression and spirituality in the ghettos and *shtetls* of Ashkenazic Jewry in Eastern Europe and Russia, and it persists among contemporary American Jews whose lives are no longer in thrall to Old World conditions. The ghetto cosmopolitan is at once an insular and a worldly individual. He combines a parochialism bred of poverty and confinement with a universal consciousness bred of study and intellectual ambition. In him, vulgarity and sensibility go hand in hand; his coarseness of manner is not inconsistent with high orders of intellectual and aesthetic discrimination. Socially rude, even coarse in his demeanor, he is attuned to world events and is at home discussing Hegel or Henry James.[5] His character is a puzzle to non-Jews, for whom education implies refinement, decorum, *breeding,* but among Jews he is accepted as a standard intellectual type.

Other cultures may have analogous forms; Lévi-Strauss has taught us that such dualisms in myth, in value, in character, are universal properties of culture, and it stands to reason that a form akin to ghetto-cosmopolitanism may prevail elsewhere, though the special conjunction of learning, spirituality, and material deprivation that formed the Ashkenazi character was not common to Europe. It was more oriental. "The ancient Semite," C.M. Doughty, the British Arabist once remarked, "sits in a cloaca up to his neck, but his brow touches the stars." Backward, poor, living amid the most wretched circumstances, these pariahs were a God-intoxicated and studious people, the most literate of all Europe's peoples through the close of the nineteenth century, however unworldly their learning may have been.

The Ashkenazim of Eastern Europe dwelled in two worlds simultaneously. One was the world of labor and trade, money, politics, love, marriage, family, trouble, death. Its domain were the six days from Saturday night through Friday, and its language was commonly Yiddish, though the Jews also spoke Polish, Russian, Czech, Magyar, German, Ukrainian, and to some degree had their imaginations shaped by those languages as well. The other was the world of the Sabbath, the world of prayer and study, Torah and Talmud, faith and prophecy. It was exalted and transcendent, and it had its own language, Hebrew.

The Yiddish scholar Max Weinreich spoke, in a famous formulation, of the "internal bilingualism" of the Ashkenazi Jews,[6] which placed them, imaginatively, in sharply opposed worlds, the one reverential, austere, bound by duty, ritual, and awe, the other ironic, playful, mischievous. In practice, the languages tended to fuse, as Yiddish penetrated the language of prayer and Hebrew formed a sacred canopy over common speech, so that each language was flavored by the other. The literature of the Yiddish renaissance reflects vividly this contrast at the heart of Jewish life. Its typical figures were the *shlemiel* who was also a saint, the victim of misfortune who was a hero of endurance; the impecunious scholar or rabbi who was the exalted moral arbiter of his people; the peddler, the shopkeeper, or *luftmensch* down on his luck who was also a visionary. I. L. Peretz's Bontsche the Silent, Sholom Aleichem's Tevye the Milkman, Isaac Bashevis Singer's Gimpel the Fool are all expressions of this same doubleness. The macaronic language of that literature also reflected the interpenetration of realms. It was a literature in which, as Maurice Samuel once observed, "Well-worn quotations from sacred texts mingle easily with colloquialisms, and dignified passages jostle popular interjections without taking or giving offense."[7] What one finds in a mind nurtured upon a higher and a lower language is one that is rather accustomed to shuttling between the transcendent and the worldly and defining its relationship to reality in terms of the ironies generated by such travel.

Although American Jews are no longer bilingual and the startling contradictions of ghetto life have melted into the suburban continuities of the American middle-class, habits of mind that were fostered in the old country stubbornly remain as structures of consciousness. Just as certain primal hungers persist long after every Jew has filled his stomach and has even joined weight-watchers in order to be hungry again, so too the habit of self-irony remains long after the disparities of the ghetto have either faded or been transformed. The contradictions of Doughty's ancient Semite no longer apply, though the ironies of cultural change and generational succession have partially replaced them. There was scarcely a Jew born of immigrant parents in America who did not in his or her lifetime experience a change of station so drastic as to feel like a rise from the cloaca to the stars. Thus the prose of American Jewish writers is marked by the same signatures of timbre, register, and tempo that marked the Yiddish. Irving Howe has described its elements as:

> Yoking of opposites, gutter vividness with university refinement, street energy with high-culture rhetoric . . . a deliberate play with the phrasings of plebian speech, but often, also, the kind that vibrates with cultural ambition, seeking to zoom into regions of higher thought.[8]

This "demotic upsurge," as Howe calls it, into high culture, might best be illustrated by a remark I once heard made by an art collector, an elderly Jewish lady who, when informed of an opportunity to purchase another Picasso, answered, "No thank you, dear. I'm up to my ass in Picassos already." Here it isn't the brow that touches the stars but the ass that touches the Picassos, and where else but in America would you ever hear such a thing? For it is a by-product of American upward mobility: the language of Delancey Street brought up into the drawing rooms of Sutton Place where it sounds as if it had always been there. Whether it be the result of a border crossing or a sudden leap in social station, the Jew in modern times has had his consciousness formed by more than one set of rules and conditions. Where the circumstances are not absolutely tragic, the attendant discrepancies become ironies, sources of the comic doubletake. We need only turn to the Jewish comics or the novelists who have taken lessons from them for vivid examples of the comic doubletake in operation. Thus, Lippman to Einstein:

> Perhaps I should have told you that my fee is ten percent. But truly and honestly I am not in this business for money. I want to help people. I have taken colored off the streets, shoeshine kit and all, and turned them into headline tap dancers at roadhouses and night-clubs overnight. And my satisfaction comes not from the money, which in all honesty is not so much, but in seeing those boys getting dressed up in dinner jackets and learning to face an audience of people out for a nice time. Dignity far more than money is my business.[9]

Such comedy is hooked right into Jewish history: the people of the book were also the people of the deal. What Roth has done here is to draw out the comic ramifications of this encounter of learning and business in the same culture.

The comic doubletake is a standard technique of Jewish humor. Here are some routines by one Jules Farber, the comedian hero of Wallace Markfield's novel, *You Could Live If They'd Let You,*[10] a book in praise of stand-up comedy and the desperation for which it stands:

> And they shall beat their swords into plowshares—and then, then first they'll give it to you with those plowshares.
>
> By the waters of Babylon I sat down and I wept that I have not bought a little property.
>
> If your brother should weaken and fall, don't move him until you first have at least two witnesses.

Then spake Rabbi Israel: And the sages do say that we shall weaken their vitals, yea, with fish sticks and red hots shall we pierce their bowels. For hath he not promised us, blessed be His Name of Names, that He will send us an angel, and the angel will put them in confusion and alarm, for He shall cause their shelves to be empty of Campbell's Soups, and we shall fall upon them, yea, we shall smite them with the slats from our venetian blinds.

Or this, which strikes me as one of the cleverest of Woody Allen's short routines:

And it came to pass that a man who sold shirts was smitten by hard times. Neither did any of his merchandise move nor did he prosper. And he prayed and said, "Lord, why hast thou left me to suffer thus? All mine enemies sell their goods except I. And it's the height of the season. My shirts are good shirts. Take a look at this rayon. I got button-downs, flare collars, nothing sells. Yet I have kept thy commandments. Why can I not earn a living when mine younger brother cleans up in children's ready-to-wear?"
And the Lord heard the man and said, "About thy shirts. . . ."
"Yes, Lord," the man said, falling to his knees.
"Put an alligator over the pocket."
"Pardon me, Lord?"
"Just do what I'm telling you. You won't be sorry."
And the man sewed to all his shirts a small alligator symbol and lo and behold, suddenly his merchandise moved like gangbusters, and there was much rejoicing while amongst his enemies there was wailing and gnashing of teeth.[11]

The fun here is of just the sort I have been talking about: a sudden thrusting downward from the exalted to the workaday, from the tragic to the trivial, from the Hebrew to the Yiddish, from the biblical cadence to the commercial slogan. It is the Lord who comes up with the alligator. But the indispensable element in each, without which these jokes would be scarcely more than routine exercises in ironic juxtaposition, is the cultural flavoring. Something of the humiliations and fears of Jewish life itself has been captured in these juxtapositions: the Jewish fear of violence, the sense of shame that underlies the show of pride, the fetish of insurance for a people who were vulnerable for 2000 years, the failing line of goods, the fear of a lawsuit in a world of shysters, the skepticism of a people who know from experience that anything, even a plowshare, can become a sword.

This acidic power of Yiddish makes it a powerful corrosive to the pieties of more genteel cultures. Its homely punch lines pack a potent wallop. Our comedian, Jules Farber, recalls once going with his Uncle Shermie to the movies to see a Western:

> I went one time to the movies with him—a western. With a scene—you know the scene? Morning, first thing in the morning. The gunslinger gets up. The gunslinger rubs his beard. The gunslinger takes out his razor. And he strops his razor, he gives himself a lovely shave and again he rubs his beard. He rubs his beard and he wipes his face and he wipes his razor. He finishes wiping the razor, he takes his coffee pot, he goes to the stream, he fills the coffee pot with water from the stream, he collects twigs, with the twigs he makes a fire, on the fire he makes coffee, he drinks a cup of coffee, he sloshes out the grinds, he finished sloshing out the grinds and he pours himself a second cup, he drinks the second cup—
>
> And my Uncle Shermie yells out, *"Nu, und pishn darft m'nisht?'* (Nu? And he doesn't have to piss?)[12]

That the cowboy in an American Western doesn't need to piss upon getting up is too much for this old-time Jew, for whom the willing suspension of disbelief, not to mention the willing suspension of water, is unheard of. Farber's conclusion is that Uncle Shermie's outburst is a victory for reality, and so it is.

Sometimes an entire story or poem may be the punch line to an absent text. Take this parody of T.S. Eliot's "The Love Song of J. Alfred Prufrock," composed as a lark some time in the 1940s by Saul Bellow and Isaac Rosenfeld. It was a party gag, and one recollection of its goes like this:

> *Nu-zhe, kum-zhe, ikh un du*
> *Ven der ovnt shteyt unter dem himl*
> *Vi a leymener goylem af tishebov.*
> *Lomir geyn gikh, durkh geselekh vos dreyen zikh*
> *Vi di bord bay dem rov.*
>
>   *Oyf der vant*
> *fun dem kosheren restorant*
> *Hengt a shmutsiker betgevant*
> *Un vantsn tantsn karahod. Es geht a geroykh*
> *fun gefilte fish un nase zokn.*
> *Oy, Bashe, freg nit keyn kashe, a dayge dir!*
> *Lomir oyfefnen di tir.*
> *In tsimer vu di vayber zenen*
> *Redt men fun Karl Marx un Lenin.*
>
> *Ikh ver alt, ikh ver alt*
> *Un der pupik vert mir kalt.*
> *Zol ikh oyskemen di hor,*

Meg ikh oyfesen a flom?
Ikh vel onton vayse hoysn
Un shpatsirn by dem yom.
Ikh vel hern di yom-moyden zingen khad gadyo.
Ikh vel zey entfern, Borekh-abo.[13]

Roughly translated, the parody sounds something like this:

Nu, let us go, you and I,
When the evening stands beneath the sky
Like a clay golem on Tisha B'av.
Let us go, through streets that twist themselves
Like the rabbi's beard.

On the wall
Of the kosher restaurant,
Hangs dirty bedding
And bedbugs dance in circles. There is a stink
Of gefilte fish and wet socks.
Oy, Bashe, don't ask questions, why bother?
Let me open the door.
In the room where the women are
They speak of Karl Marx and Lenin.

I grow old, I grow old,
And my navel grows cold.
Shall I comb out my hair,
May I eat a prune?
I shall put on white pants
And walk by the sea.
I shall hear the sea-maidens sing Chad Gadya.
I shall answer them: "Baruch Abba."

I can't imagine a transliteration of Eliot in French or German capable of this kind of comic domestication. A bedbug hanging in the boulangerie? The rathskeller? French and German are elevating languages and are just not geared for the crisp deflation of *"Ikh ver alt, ikh ver alt, un der pupik vert mir kalt."* Yiddish evolved in the old country without a pressing need for a vocabulary of idealization. Hebrew fairly monopolized the task of providing the Jews with idealizing and spiritualizing concepts and thereby of satisfying the portions of Jewish culture that traded in ennoblement—in *edelkeit*. The Yiddish Jew is the historical Jew; the Hebrew Jew the transhistorical, the transcendent Jew. Or, to borrow terms from the writer and historian Arthur Cohen, the one was the natural Jew, the other the supernatural Jew.[14] With the Hebrew hegemony over higher worlds established, Yiddish was free to evolve as a worldly and domestic language, remarkably free from high purpose and its attendant distortion, cant.

At his best, in his earlier films and routines, but especially in *Bananas, Play It Again Sam,* and *Love and Death,* Woody Allen was the master of comic techniques based upon these sudden collisions of perspective: the serious side of himself suddenly brought crashing to earth by the madman in him. The basic Allen joke is the lofty perspective laid low by the common desire. "My parents were very old world people. Their values were God and carpeting." "I have an intense desire to return to the womb. Anybody's." In *Play It Again Sam,* Allen (as Allen Felix) attempts to pick up a young woman in the Museum of Modern Art as both stand before a Jackson Pollack.

> Allen: What does it say to you?
> Woman: It restates the negativeness of the universe. The hideous lonely emptiness of existence. Nothingness. The predicament of Man forced to live in a barren, Godless eternity like a tiny flame flickering in an immense void with nothing but waste, horror and degradation, forming a useless bleak straightjacket in a bleak absurd cosmos.
> Allen: What're you doing Saturday night?
> Woman: Committing suicide.
> Allen: What about Friday night?[15]

This is American comedy of a sort that Groucho Marx or S. J. Perelman did between bites of a bagel: the mayhem of madcap juxtapositions, one frame of reference (popular, modern, awestruck) bombarding the other (classical, philosophical, reverent) with matzoballs. She's suffering an existential crisis; he just wants a date. The Yiddish theatre abounded in humor of this kind, because the Yiddish language was tuned for ironic deflation and was a perfect medium for the homely punch-line, even if God himself should be the butt of the joke. The lowly Yid who gets in the last word with God or death is a familiar figure in Jewish humor, as in an Allen routine, "Death Knocks,"[16] in which Nat Ackerman, visited by the Angel of Death, challenges him to a game of gin rummy in the hope of gaining an extra day of life, *and wins.* This Angel of Death is no big shot; he is a klutz who trips headlong over the windowsill upon entering Ackerman's house and cries out, "Jesus Christ. I nearly broke my neck." And he is a dreadful gin player. Ackerman not only beats him for a day of life but takes Death for twenty-eight dollars. Death has to leave empty-handed, but not before warning: "Look—I'll be back tomorrow, and you'll give me a chance to win the money back. Otherwise I'm in definite trouble." Nat: "Anything you want. Double or nothing we'll play. I'm liable to win an extra week or a month. The way you play, maybe years." The *Moloch ha-Movitz* takes a beating here along with Ingmar Bergman's *The Seventh Seal*.

Allen gives us some of the most baldly diagrammatic examples of this formula for comedy in his "Hasidic Tales"[17] in which Rabbi Baumel of Vitebsk embarks on a fast "to protest the unfair law prohibiting Russian Jews from wearing loafers outside the ghetto" or Rabbi Yitzchok Ben Levi, the great Jewish mystic, applies cabbalistic numerology to horse racing and hits the daily double at Aqueduct fifty-two days running. These inventions are naked formula: submit the exalted to the rule of the common and you've got a joke. But it is precisely in such cases where the humor is nothing more than the routine application of method that its machinery is most clearly exposed.

This dialectic at the heart of Jewish comedy recalls Van Wyck Brooks's conception of American culture as a divided realm: spiritual and practical, incorporeal and commercial, highbrow and lowbrow.[18] But where Brooks, in "America's Coming of Age," was describing a collision of values in American social life, the Jewish version of it exists *within the individual Jew,* who is highbrow and lowbrow unto himself. Maybe a more serviceable pair of metaphors for this cultural dualism is Philip Rahv's "redskin" and "paleface,"[19] in part because they suggest forms of reconciliation that are unavailable in Brooks's terms. Like Brooks's highbrow, the paleface in American culture is a product of "the thin, solemn, semi-clerical culture of Boston and Concord," and Henry James and T. S. Eliot its apostles in American literature. The redskin, on the other hand, is a product of "the lowlife world of the frontier and the big cities," for which Whitman and Twain were the classic spokesmen. However, though Brooks's and Rahv's terms describe the same cultural terrain, they suggest different forms of mediation, for if the synthesis of high and lowbrow is middlebrow, a term fixed for us by common usage, that of redskin and paleface is "redface," a term defined for us by Philip Roth.[20] The middlebrow, by common definition, is the commercial sublime, in which the trappings of high culture are thrown over the vacuities of popular taste like a Persian carpet over a trap door. A parody of high culture, the middlebrow novel or film takes world historical themes and straps them onto a romantic grid. The historical epic, or, nowadays, the space epic, are classic middle brow productions: martial music, pseudo-elevated speech, the grandeur of history or outer space serving as props for adolescent fantasies. Middlebrow art is a commodity; the middlebrow individual is its purveyor and consumer.[21]

The redface, however, as Philip Roth has defined him in an essay on himself, is the character in whom high and low are locked in powerful debate and who must define his own values by negotiating an uneasy detente between the two. He is a product of both cultures, and yet *"fundamentally ill-at-ease in, and at odds with, both worlds* although . . . alert to the inexhaustible number of intriguing postures that the awkward may assume in public, and the strange means that the uneasy come upon to express themselves."[22] Unlike the middlebrow, the redface never confuses high and popular. He has no interest in ennobling the ordinary or making tragic claims for the merely heartrending. He never uses words like "profound." He savors, rather, his own absurdity and relishes the idea of himself as a creature of unstable habits and volatile tastes. Middlebrowism strikes me as a uniquely American and commercial phenomenon, redface-ism a Jewish-American and psychological one.

A line of humor that runs through comedians as diverse as Jack Benny, Henny Youngman, Morey Amsterdam, Harpo Marx, Victor Borge, and Allen himself is built upon the premise of redface-ism, the self-conscious byplay of *Kunst* and candy store. Each of these comedians carries or carried a musical instrument as a prop, though Allen's clarinet is a hidden prop that has never been introduced into his comedy, and Harpo didn't always drag out the harp. But we know about them in any case; the instruments are their credentials as serious artists, the signs of their higher faculties. In all cases, the musical props are indications of a prior and abandoned vocation that bears specific cultural weight. These violins, cellos, and clarinets are the remnants of the European high culture that Jews sought to adopt as an avenue of escape from the ghetto. Such aspiration produced in our own day the great Jewish virtuosi of German and Russian music: David

Oistrakh, Yasha Heifetz, Yehudi Menuhin, Isaac Stern, Itzhak
Perlman, Vladimir Horowitz, Pinchas Zuckerman, Vladimir
Ashkenazi, et al., and the comedy that alludes to them is the
token of how successfully, and with how much guilt, their example has been evaded. In carrying his instrument on stage with
him, the comedian carries his past as a sight-gag, a mechanical
straight man that testifies to the stringencies of the ghetto and the
dreams of Jewish parents. The Jewish comedian and his violin
are not unlike the ventriloquist and his dummy, though roles are
reversed. Whereas the ventriloquist plays straight man to his
dummy, it is the comic who plays dummy to his violin, which is
also his muse, his past, his superego, his parent, his better half.
He brings it on stage in order to defy its sole command: *play me*.

Obviously, this strategy of splitting oneself up for comic purposes, when dressed in the colors of a particular history and
tradition in which such inner divisions are validated by a cultural
duality, can give rise to a humor in which the tradition itself is
interrogated and its own tensions brought into clearer focus. The
Jewish comedian is himself a one-man comedy team, an Abbott
and Costello, Smith and Dale, Burns and Allen, Bergen and
McCarthy, Caesar and Coca, Cheech and Chong all in one. That
is because at heart, and by historical design, he really is two men,
equally alive to God or the claims of high culture (our secular
substitute for God), and to carpeting or baseball or sex. The
comedian is one who is learning to negotiate the disparity between facets of himself and of the traditions in which he is
immersed for the purposes of amusement. From conflicts that
produce symptoms in others, he produces laughter. What others
suffer from, he exploits, which is not to say that he too doesn't
suffer from his material or isn't longing to be cured of it, but only
that by his routines he holds his afflictions at bay. Failing to
relieve himself by laughter, he may turn to psychoanalysis, and
may even, turning the screw another notch, treat psychoanalysis
to a dose of comic salts, as Roth did in *Portnoy's Complaint* and
Allen did in *Zelig*.

The larger point to be drawn from all this is that *culture is
comedy,* a perception shared by every man on the margin and
every shrewd comedian. It is the experience of the modern Jew,
an experience greatly attenuated of late, to be neither wholly or

comfortably Jewish nor cozily American, a predicament that renders the hyphen in his identity the cutting edge of his wit. Everything is alien to him; even the commonplace is incongruous, and he tends to approach the world with a tourist's sense of wonderment. *The more familiar, the more strange.* If he is an intellectual he may turn that wonderment into a formal treatise or some other form of high-level scowling (an intellectual should always be alienated); he may become a walker in the city like Alfred Kazin or a sociologist of the ordinary, like Bellow, or the Margaret Mead of his own life, like Roth, for whom coming of age in Newark bears comparison to coming of age in Samoa or the Fiji Islands. It is not for nothing that Saul Bellow, our most acclaimed chronicler of middle-class social rites, has a master's degree in anthropology to lend formal credentials, as if they were needed, to his native instinct for seeing the common in the light of the strange. For what the great novelist tells us, like the great comedian, is that the familiar really *is* strange, and if only for an instant the scales would fall from our eyes, we would see with the clarity of naked vision how outrageous is the world around us.

In a comedy of culture, then, the joke does not create the humor; it formulates a humor that is already there, defamiliarizing the familiar to make it seem suddenly alien. Cultural comedy is the disclosure of ironic conjunctions, not their invention. Where such a comedy is at its richest, the technique is the content; a heightening and distillation of common anomalies. Technique, to reapply an old formula for fiction, is discovery.

The relation of Jewish comedy to the Jewish religion, then, is apparent. It is its inversion, its negative, its shadow. The reversal of figure and ground. Where both comedy and religion acknowledge the interdependence of two worlds, a higher and a lower, each gives primacy to a different world. Religion subordinates this world to another; it translates upwards, while comedy undercuts the transcendent, criticizes it, subordinates it to the common. The one, in effect, Hebraizes, the other Yiddishizes. Which may tell us something about why that other great European comic tradition, the Irish, also arose in a culture in which religious authority has been central to cultural formation, and why in both cases the comedy should be so aggressive and so rude and should strike with such antinomian force at the heart of the exalted. Here again is Milton Lippman to Albert Einstein:

I think sometimes that the Bible stories of God talking from above
to the people down below is just what they had in those days instead
of radio. People, whether then or now, like to hear "the real thing."
Hearing is believing! . . . Today we don't *hear* God as they did in the
Bible—and what is the result? It is impossible for some people to
believe He is there. The same holds true with you, Doctor Einstein.
I'm sorry to say. To the general public, who is Einstein? A name
who doesn't comb his hair (not that I have any objection) and is
supposed to be the smartest person alive. A lot of good that does the
Jews, if you understand what I'm saying. At this stage of the game,
I'm afraid that if an election were held tonight between you and The
Answer Man, more people would vote for him than for you. I have to
be honest with you.[23]

There it is in a nutshell: God and Albert Einstein brought low
by radio and "The Answer Man." And we recognize right away
that the world is full of Milton Lippmans, who would put the
Lord himself on a quiz show if they could find sponsors to put up
the money. (And who would sponsor God? Who wouldn't?) Lippman speaks with a distinctly human and familiar voice. There
are people who talk this way—they are our parents; they are
embedded within ourselves—and though Lippman's entreaties
are fantastic, Roth need not have invented a word of them. This is
stone-cold realism and a program brought to you not by Philip
Roth or Procter and Gamble or Goodyear Tires but by the Jewish
people.

NOTES

1. Harold Rosenberg, "Community, Values, Comedy," in *Discovering
the Present: Three Decades in Art, Culture, and Politics* (Chicago: University of Chicago Press, 1973), p. 151.
2. Philip Roth, "On the Air," *New American Review* 10 (August 1970):
10.
3. Mark Shechner, "Jewish Writers," in *Harvard Guide to Contemporary American Writing*, ed. Daniel Hoffman (Cambridge: The Belknap
Press, 1979), pp. 191–239.
4. Mark Shechner, "Saul Bellow and Ghetto Cosmopolitanism," in
Modern Jewish Studies Annual II (1978): 33–44.
5. Portraits of the ghetto cosmopolitan as a social type abound in fiction,
but I might suggest a reading of Norman Podhoretz's autobiography, *Making It*, for a particularly rich distillation of the type.
6. Max Weinreich, "Internal Bilingualism in Ashkenaz," in Irving Howe

and Eliezer Greenberg, eds., *Voices from the Yiddish: Essays, Memoirs, Diaries* (Ann Arbor: University of Michigan Press, 1972), pp. 279–88.

7. Quoted in Irving Howe and Eliezer Greenberg, eds., *A Treasury of Yiddish Stories* (New York: Schocken, 1973), p. 47.

8. Irving Howe, "Introduction," in *Jewish-American Stories* (New York: New American Library, 1977), p. 15.

9. Roth, "On the Air," p. 11.

10. Wallace Markfield, *You Could Live If They'd Let You* (New York: Alfred A. Knopf, 1974). The novel is a compendium of borscht belt routines and repartee, and though not a particularly good novel, it faithfully reproduces the flavor and vibration, the timbre and pace, of Catskill comedy.

11. Woody Allen, "The Scrolls," in *Without Feathers* (New York: Warner Books, 1976), p. 27.

12. Markfield, *You Could Live,* p. 128.

13. Rosenfeld and Bellow's parody of "Prufrock" appeared anonymously in *Yiddish Studies and MJS Newsletter,* ed. David Neal Miller (Winter 1978): 1. It has been cited as an example of the warmth and effervescence of the Yiddish language by Chaim Raphael, in *Jewish Chronicle Literary Supplement* (London), June 6, 1980.

14. Arthur A. Cohen, *The Natural and the Supernatural Jew* (New York: Behrman House, 1962).

15. See *Woody Allen's 'Play It Again Sam,'* ed. Richard J. Anobile (New York: Grosset & Dunlap, 1977). pp. 88–89.

16. Woody Allen, "Death Knocks," in *Getting Even* (New York: Warner Books, 1972), pp. 37–46.

17. The "Hasidic Tales" are in *Getting Even* (New York: Warner Books, 1972), pp. 52–56.

18. Van Wyck Brooks, "America's Coming of Age: (1915)," in *Van Wyck Brooks: The Early Years. A Selection from His Works, 1908–1921,* ed. Claire Sprague (New York: Harper Torchbooks, 1968), pp. 79–158.

19. Philip Rahv, "Paleface and Redskin" (1939), in *Literature and the Sixth Sense* (New York: Houghton Mifflin, 1969), pp. 1–6.

20. Philip Roth, "On *The Great American Novel,*" in *Reading Myself and Others* (New York: Farrar, Straus & Giroux, 1975), pp. 82–84. This self-conception of being a cultural hybrid, half raw, half cooked, runs through the interviews with Roth in this book, and one can find there many formulations of the same idea.

21. It would take us far afield to discuss middlebrow taste at length here, but the reader might want to consult two of the classic formulations of it: "Dwight Macdonald's definition of midcult in "Masscult and Midcult," in *Against the American Grain* (New York: Random House, 1965), pp. 3–78, and Clement Greenberg's "Avant-Garde and Kitsch," in *Art and Culture* (Boston: Beacon Press, 1961), pp. 3–21.

22. Philip Roth, "On *The Great American Novel,*" in *Reading Myself and Others,* p. 83.

23. Roth, "On the Air," pp. 12–13.

THE JEWISH SIT-DOWN
COMEDY OF PHILIP ROTH

ALAN COOPER

Philip Roth owes a well-known debt to stand-up comedy. Critics have noted similarity between the "deliveries" of Alex Portnoy and comics like Lenny Bruce[1] and the great Yiddishizers of American humor: Sam Levenson, Myron Cohen, Milton Berle, Sid Ceasar, Mort Sahl, Buddy Hackett, Alan King, Woody Allen, and Jackie Mason.[2] Roth has said that what enabled him to write *Portnoy's Complaint* was coming to accept his long-suppressed affinity to Henny Youngman and to a local candy store owner of his youth, "Jake the Snake H., a middle-aged master of invective and insult, and a repository of lascivious neighborhood gossip."[3] But in addition to these stand-up comics, Roth credits another influence on the writing of *Portnoy,* "a sit-down comic named Franz Kafka."[4]

Since *Portnoy's Complaint* (1969) most of Roth's fiction has shown a mutual accommodation of stand-up and sit-down comedy: on the one hand, comic *shtick,* set pieces, one liners, *shpritz*es,[5] rapid changes and juxtapositions of subject matter; on the other, the extended monologue, "guilt as a comic idea,"[6] the hero as butt of some great cosmic joke, contention against some absurd authority, deft ironic reversal, and a sustained narrative that absorbs and gives shape to the stand-up material. It would be misleading to push the Kafka analogy too far, especially as it applies to *Portnoy's Complaint,*[7] for Roth assimilated Kafka to his own purposes during the late sixties and the

158

seventies, just as he had earlier assimilated Henry James, Theodore Dreiser, and a host of other writers. Yet, something of that demonic giggle, which, according to Max Brod, attended the composing of some of Kafka's grimmest stories, seems to echo through *Portnoy, The Breast, My Life as a Man, The Professor of Desire,* and the Zuckerman trilogy; and specific references to Kafka recur in these works and in his fantasy story, " 'I Always Wanted You to Admire My Fasting': or, Looking at Kafka."

Not that the public knows this entire body of work. Sales history suggests that *Portnoy's Complaint* and *Goodbye, Columbus* have been far more widely read that Roth's other twelve books and numerous magazine pieces combined. Still, readers take strong positions about Roth; either they find in his sit-down comedy a genuine criticism of life, or they regard his stand-up material as neurotic or thin, unchastened to the serious purposes of important fiction. Such purposes, say Roth's detractors, can be served only when the laughter moves one to a larger sympathy for mankind than Roth provides. They find his range narrow, his attacks personal, his comedy insufficient to achieve that sympathy. Moreover, the Jewish establishment has made him an offender of the faith; feminists, a misogynist; and certain reviewers, a case of arrested development. And to many, Roth convicts himself of these charges in his fiction by ranting of his innocence.

That the creator of Alex Portnoy, Word Smith, Nathan Zuckerman, David Kepesh, and Peter Tarnapol—plaintiffs all—should be the eternal defendant is fitting irony for Roth's comic muse. Roth's comedy is not romance; it reaches no happy endings, only surcease of pain. And part of the pain is the comedy itself: the reader laughs until it hurts, not innocently, but at other people's expense. Called ungenerous, immoral, Roth invites the raised eyebrow and then makes the raised eyebrow his target.

Indeed the plaintive voices of Roth's narrators have a nasty edge. It has always been there, from the jibes of Neil Klugman about Brenda's nose job, to the selfishness of Gabe Wallach, to what E. I. Lonoff recognizes in young Nathan Zuckerman— "You're not so nice and polite in your fiction. You're a different person." "Am I?" "I should hope so." Roth tempers that edge according to the requirements of his story: toward brash irony in "Goodbye, Columbus," toward wistful despair in *The Professor of Desire,* toward hysteria in *The Breast* and *The Anatomy Lesson.* But whether this nastiness is a fictive device or the real "Roth" coming through is part of the question of Philip Roth.

Another question is whether comedy itself doesn't unfit Roth to be taken seriously. Some readers regard *Portnoy,* and everything since, as part of a wrong turn, a wandering onto a false path from which Roth must return if he is ever to fulfill his real potentiality—at this point, in their view, a great unlikelihood. But everything since *Portnoy* has been overtly comedic, as everything before *Portnoy* seemed more or less "serious." So part of the reaction, especially the Jewish reaction, may be against Roth's very emphasis on the comic mode, acceptable as ironic counterpoint in Malamud and Bellow, but seen as reducing art to entertainment in Roth.

Of course, all good comedy is serious. And with the single exception of *The Great American Novel,* whose lampooning tone and parodic manner place it in the tradition of folk humor, all of Roth's fiction addresses real issues, the sit-down comic effects sparked by the relentless absurdity of life itself. (I exclude *Our Gang,* which is either a venting of spleen or an adolescent sketch, not a piece of fiction.) But if Roth's mordant serio-comic mixture has led to the charge of insensitivity, so has his inclusion in that mixture of subjects considered too delicate for comic treatment. Anne Frank, Jewish superiority as an element of chosenness, the fallibility of the rabbinate, the sanctity of Jewish motherhood, the exclusivity and permanence of the institution of marriage itself—these are hot potatoes for a writer whose characters proclaim themselves to be misunderstood innocents. Hot potatoes, Roth knows, are best juggled, not held. He juggles them by making them the stand-up *shtick* of his sit-down narratives. And for that reason, too, he faces the charge of superficiality: to work Anne Frank into young Nate's fantasy is not to confront the problem of the Holocaust, to have Alex wrestled into self-confrontation by an Israeli woman is not to grapple with Jewish national destiny, to have Zuckerman occupy several Manhattan studio apartments in childless liaisons is not to explore urban Jewish problems, and to scorn a secular leftist critic for writing a commercial Jewish history is not to declare one's own commitment to Jewish life. Roth's severest critics enjoy his humor, acknowledge his narrative "talent" (a word to chill the marrow of any artist), but see him mining a narrow range of personal concerns uninstructive for the great world. Roth's answer, if any, must be sought between the lines of his sit-down comedy.

> If ever there was a time to forget about propriety, decorum, and personal pride, this is it. But as these are matters intimately connected to my idea of sanity and to my self-esteem, I am, in fact, troubled now as I wasn't at all in my former life, where the style of social constraint practiced by the educated classes came quite easily to me, and provided real satisfaction.

Here is an attitude not uncommon to a narrator in Roth. There is some danger, perhaps the danger of too much liberty: Alex being offered his long-dreamt-of orgy, Tarnapol seeing a chance to flee from Maureen, Zuckerman, his back in spasm, trying to accept the sexual ministrations of one of his four Florence Nightingales. The narrator's straight-laced past is reaching through to spoil his libertine present. Culture resisting anarchy. A "former life" is being compared to a present life. The passage is from *The Breast*,[8] that Kafka-inspired fantasy panned by most critics. The metamorphosed David Kepesh, buried in a mass of adipose tissue, insists that though he is blind, motionless, and unrecognizable as a human being, he has no license for hysteria: he is bound by culture and judgment.

The issue in *The Breast* is not whether the metamorphosis is believable—Gregor Samsa's is not—but whether it is meaningful. Samsa as bug insists on nothing. He is a silent, externally scrutinized creation of a third-person narrator. Readers and critics are free to find meaning in him without hearing *his* two-cents' worth. And so he becomes one or another creeping family problem. But what Kepesh's transformation means (and he is the first to say it) is absurdity: Kepesh is mentally and emotionally sound; he has just reached that state after years of psychotherapy; he is not easily deluded, not even self-deluded, though now he can use some delusion, some non-self-acceptance. And the world would now excuse his being indulgently neurotic. He could undo that therapy and get away with some terrific wallowing. Still, his argument with himself is on moral grounds, as he sees both the tyranny and the salvation of culture. Who needs the restraints of rationalism and good behavior when you're a six-foot mammary gland slung in a hammock? Kepesh does. More than ever.

Kepesh cannot reason out, or out of, his predicament, although
the narrative is mostly his attempts to do so. As Job-like, he
rehearses the possibilities—physiology his Eliphaz, psychology
his Bildad, and moral philosophy his Zophar—he comes to appreciate the horrible joke that he is undeceivable. As in science
fiction or in Kafka, everything except the one impossibility is
utterly faithful to reality. Kepesh's reasoning and attempt at
denial; the responses of his father, his lover, his doctor, his nurse;
his slow relinquishings of the possibilities for productive life as a
paper grader or as a freak-show attraction—all these are utterly
believable and utterly absurd. At the same time they provide
opportunities for poignant stand-up humor, as in his rationale for
continuing to live:

> No, it is simply that having been terrified of death since the age of
> two, I have become entrenched in my hatred of it, have taken a
> personal stand *against* death from which I seem unable to retreat
> because of this. Horrible indeed This is; but on the other hand, I
> have been wanting not to die for so long now, I just can't stop doing it
> overnight. I need time. (p. 455)

The capitalized "This" is also parody, recalling Ivan Ilych's "It."
Kepesh makes no legal plea for the right to die, as in "Whose Life
Is It Anyway?" or for the ready pity owed an elephant man. He
may be blind, mouthless, and limbless, but he is not ugly. Ironically, he has assumed the shape of one of the most adored
objects in the life of a Jewish male, and he is regularly sucked by
a devoted lover and massaged to sexual climax, passively as in
pornographic fantasy.

Kepesh is closer to Job or Ivan Ilych than to Gregor Samsa
because he asserts rights. A post-World War II (or post-Israeli-
independence) Jew, he can complain and demand reasons. His
main difference from these three victims is in verisimilitude: Job
and Ilych have recognizable afflictions, and Samsa as bug has a
bug's limitations; but pubic rashes do not become aureolas, and
breasts cannot live independently of a body, or communicate
directly with a reader. However, Kepesh does not, as Joseph
Epstein suggests, "lack the requisite weight to compete with
Kafka's or Gogol's clown heroes."[9] Roth chose to turn Kepesh
into a breast for a no less "weighty" reason: the sheer absurdity
of it. Cancer might have been a better vehicle for questioning
God's justice, but it is too threatening for the comic treatment

Roth undertakes. Absurdity is everyone acting normally when normalcy will not help, when nothing will help, and culture reaching for deportment to keep itself intact. And the ultimate absurdity is the victim's seeing the joke and being forced, in spite of his pain, to laugh at himself. That is not what "Job" or "The Death of Ivan Ilych" is about, for these are orthodox evocations of God's justice. Roth's is the pain of a man released from God, and forced by the absence of answers to consider himself—now the most significant being there is—utterly insignificant.

The Breast is an extreme example of physical entrapment, a theme Roth also treats in "Novotny's Pain" and *The Anatomy Lesson*. But there is also other entrapment: Portnoy's in impotence (his complaint); Tarnapol's in a grotesque marriage; Word Smith's in a conspiracy to rewrite baseball history (or the delusion thereof); the young David Kepesh's (of *The Professor of Desire*) in waning sexual appetite; young Zuckerman's (of *The Ghost Writer*) in family expectation; middle-aged Zuckerman's in *Carnovsky* success. In all these stories, free will is stymied by custom, values by interests. An agreeable world inveigles the naive into its house of horrors. One accepts absurdity or writhes in opposition. Roth is the chronicler of writhing, his characters groaning in pain yet musing in paralyzed detachment.

Roth's comedy hurts because emptiness within reflects emptiness without; the authorities in his secular world deceive as badly as God. His characters sally forth into a world of quiz-show scandals, McCarthyism, wartime and cold-war profiteering, the false promises of the sexual revolution. The weapons offered them to slay these dragons are bigotry, Literature 101, and a shallow Jewish culture cut off from its rich European past,[10] noodles for swords. But though Roth uses, he did not invent, this empty world. The general absence of traditional values that strands his characters and leaves them writhing is as much a given of their condition as Kepesh's transformation is of his. In giving Kepesh his unwilled, inexplicable problem, Roth parallels his situation to socially determined entrapments but heightens the recognition of absurdity. Equally absurd, but blunted by custom, are more common situations such as those of Alvin Peppler in *Zuckerman Unbound* or the Czech Professor Soska in *The Professor of Desire*. Peppler, the Jewish, Newark-born ex-marine and memory expert who had been bumped from the nation's most popular quiz show in favor of a quintessential gentile aristocrat, is a victim of social power beyond his control. Professor Soska, politically blacklisted and retired to a subsistence pension at age thirty-nine, is also trapped in Kafkaesque absurdity. Indeed, here the absurd and the Jewish element in Roth share a common response: the flinch that follows defiance. Jewish literature, like Jewish history, chronicles danger along the edges of fallenness,[11] deviations from or conflicts with received Jewish tradition. And it is an unshakable or unreasonable received condition that creates absurdity. Soska, who dared to challenge the authority of the Czech government, is doomed to spend his time translating *Moby Dick* into Czech, though there is no hope of publishing his work and though a superior translation already exists; and Peppler, who defied the quiz show establishment, recounts his story like the Ancient Mariner to an indifferent world and is ready even to package it as a musical comedy. These are minor characters. The absurdity that Roth's main characters face is intensified by their being Jewish. They have that sense of fallenness that arises from every unkosher contact. (Any real difference between "Jewish-American" writers and "American writers who happen to be Jewish" is but the extent of the fallenness and the sensed extent of the danger.) Roth's characters, failing to see the hand of God in this absurdity, nevertheless wince at the awesome power of his self-appointed spokesmen—including, by anticipation, the reader—to wield his sword.

At the end of *The Breast*, Kepesh, undeceived, has only his wits, a vague sense that the worst is yet to come, and his insistence on his being human. It is wrong to read the work as an excuse for Roth to make some "adolescent proclamations" about unfairness "pass[ed] . . . off as a liberating act,"[12] just as it is wrong to read *Portnoy* without Dr. Spielvogel's final "punchline." *The Breast* represents the extreme of absurdity in Roth, an extreme that most reviewers rejected as exhausting itself in its very premise; nevertheless, it may illuminate stranger-than-fiction absurdities in his more "realistic" fiction.

In like manner Roth's other fictional fantasy, *The Great American Novel* (1973),[13] presents *in extremis* the high-spirited parody and aching bellylaugh that intertwine with more realistic subject matter throughout his fiction. Built out of the stuff of myth, this misalliance of baseball and literary lore limits its own audience to those who can "get" the allusions, a presumably small number.

But these twin lenses allow Roth a binocular look at the madness of American culture from a sufficient distance to make it un-threatening. Narrated by an eighty-seven-year-old, forcibly re-tired sports writer whose sanity is everywhere questioned, the story has a fictive premise with enough antic disposition to accommodate the wildest flights. Word Smith pleads for recogni-tion of the defunct Patriot League, a third major league whose glorious existence has been obliterated from history by a greedy plot, masked as anti-communist patriotism. The main tradition here is broad American humor of the redneck variety. Smith, an internal narrator, is writing his "Great American Novel," an exposé of the fate of the Patriot League's most defamed team, the Ruppert Mundys. Smith gushes together puns, exaggerations, and dialect stories from his opening line—"Call me Smitty"—to his closing letter to Mao Tse-tung. (He wants the Chairman to publish his blacklisted novel in China, just as the West has published Solzhenitsyn, blacklisted in Russia.) Baseball-adapted parodies of Melville, Hawthorne, Twain, Hemingway, and Poe launch the reader into a zany belles-lettrist world, where at any time he may meet literary allusion cleverly employed. For exam-ple, this about a disgraced former star who has been drifting incognito from town to town playing sandlot ball or coaching kids:

> He went around after Pearl Harbor trying to enlist, but always they would ask to see his birth certificate and always he would refuse to show it. . . . Then one day down in Winesberg, Ohio, unable to bear any longer his life as a lonely grotesque, he turned that self-in-criminating document over to the recruiting sergeant. (p. 340)

That quick conversion to a Sherwood Anderson grotesque is made by one Gil Gamesh, ancient mythic wanderer turned world's greatest pitcher, who disappears like Malamud's natural, and reemerges as manager of the Mundys to lead a Patton-like campaign of winning hatred and ruined lives. Roth's use of "the" for that recruiting sergeant, rather than "a," makes even a single-mentioned character sound like an agent of fate, reinforcing the mock mythic tone that works so well in this book. Other mythic names in the lineup include Astarte, Baal, Rama, Heket, De-meter, Pollux, and Kronos.

In *The Great American Novel* Roth makes tasteless but hi-larious use of physical handicaps, the kind that heighten tall tales

for fans and bench jockeys. By drawing upon baseball lore, and
setting most of the action during the wartime years of reduced
physical talent, Roth approaches the plausible, such as plau-
sibility is in this cock-eyed scenario. Along with the midgets and
the one-legged player, there is a one-armed outfielder, Bud Parusha, just one absurd step beyond the real-life Pete Gray.

> Unlike Gray of the Brownies, who had a stump of a left arm under
> which he could tuck his glove while he extracted the ball from the
> pocket, Bud (with no left arm at all) had to use his mouth. He was
> lucky to have a large one—"that old law of compensation," said the
> sports announcers—and a strong bite which he had further de-
> veloped over the years by five minutes of chewing on a tennis ball
> before going to sleep each night. After fielding a ball, he was able
> instantly to remove it from his glove with his teeth, and hold it
> clamped between them while he shook the glove from his hand; then
> he extracted the ball from his mouth with his bare right hand, and
> hurled it with Parusha-like speed and accuracy to the infield. (p. 119)

Roth's narrative imagination goes howlingly wild: fans, not quite
knowing what to make of Parusha's technique—looking as it did
"from a distance" like the act of a man "giving birth to something through the orifice in his head"—sometimes try to scare
him into swallowing the ball; and sometimes Parusha would get it
stuck in his teeth so that teammates would have to extract it,
always too late to make the big play at the plate. Roth makes
Parusha the darling of the handicapped—investing him with
Ruthian legends of visits to hospitals and plays dedicated to
specific unfortunates. The crippled faithful that come "banging
on the railings with their canes and crutches" literally fall out of
the stands trying to touch him. The fusion of pathos and wild
romp builds until

> in Kakoola, in fact, one fan was so inspired by Bud's example that
> after ten years in a wheelchair, he found himself up on his feet
> cheering wildly as Buddy made a shoestring catch in the bottom of
> the ninth. . . . "I'm walking!" the man suddenly cried out, even as
> Bud was extracting the ball from his mouth to fire it to first to double
> off the Reaper runner and end the game.
>
> CRIPPLE CURED AS RUPPERTS ROMP
>
> the Kakoola evening paper reported to its readers that night (p. 121)

What rescues this passage, and a whole book-full like it, from
bad taste is Roth's delving below the water line of public piety to

sink pretension. At the same time, the sheer invention, from recognizable materials, beguiles with a mirthful cleverness, and love of the game keeps Roth's perspective from becoming completely jaundiced. America—viewed from the depths of honky-tonk towns, freakish crowds, bedroom communities turned whorehouses, board rooms turned dens of conspiracy—becomes a whirling Bartholomew Fair; yet Word Smith, obsessed plaintiff, is such an endearing stand-up comic that he keeps the reader too entertained for bitterness. Alliterative excesses, which give Spiro Agnew a strident overkill in *Our Gang,* constitute merely a benign neurotic habit in Smitty, and are very funny. Moreover, the perspective, perhaps Roth's chief borrowing from Kafka (or maybe just a shared Jewish heritage), is always that of the outsider. Smitty has been excluded from the baseball writers. Gamesh is banished from the game. Port Ruppert, New Jersey (no doubt suggested by Ruppert field in Roth's boyhood Newark) is pulled out of the Patriot League, and the Mundys become a team without a home, the wandering Jews of baseball, doomed to play always as the visiting team, never to bat last or enjoy the cheers of the faithful. The opportunities for one liners, for headlines, for the gripping and fantastic imaginings that constitute stand-up comedy are legion. No one is spared. A Jewish baseball strategist is named Isaac Ellis, and the Black owner of the parallel Negro Patriot League is Aunt Jemima, complete with checkered babushka. Despite, or perhaps because of, all this hilarity, *The Great American Novel* topples of its own weight: it is too densely packed with laughs and too episodic for sustained reading. But it concentrates modes and techniques that leaven the later, leaner novels, and it gives a view of America that, though critical, is not unloving. No reader of *The Great American Novel* can come to Norman Podhoretz's conclusion that Philip Roth hates Americans or that Roth's appeal to his readers lies in an invitation that they join him in some "new class" of hypersophisticates scornful of the masses.[14]

Yet, it is not hard to see why Roth gets painted with that brush. From Jack E. Leonard to Don Rickles to Joan Rivers, a host of stand-up put-down artists have conspired with their audiences to disparage everyone else. And Roth is also fast-mouthed. Still, there is an element in sit-down comedy that saves his characters from being merely egoistic and acquits him of Podhoretz's charge. That element is embarrassment, what Roth has called the "red-face." It is a stance nervous with personal insecurity, and always eyeing itself critically through an external-internal double vision.

Young Nathan Zuckerman, of *The Ghost Writer* (1979),[15] is such a red-face. He badly needs an answer to his parents' charges of insensitivity to Jews, but it must be an answer acceptable to his own integrity as well. As he begins to salve his troubled soul with the fantasy that Amy Bellette is really Anne Frank, alive and available to him, his author places him squirming in the dark of Lonoff's study, directly beneath Amy's room. In his hand is a volume of Henry James.

> Within moments of hearing muffled voices coming from above my head, I stood up on the daybed—my finger still holding my place in the book—and, stretching to my full height, tried to make out what was being said up there and by whom. When that didn't help, I thought of climbing onto Lonoff's desk; it was easily a foot or so higher than the daybed and would put my ear only inches from the room's low ceiling. But if I should fall, if I should alter by a milimeter the placement of his typing paper, if somehow I should leave footprints—no, I couldn't risk it. I had gone far enough already by expropriating the corner of the desk to compose my half dozen unfinished letters home. My sense of propriety, not to mention the author's gracious hospitality, required me to restrain myself from committing such a sordid, callow little indecency.
>
> But in the meantime I had done it. (pp. 116–17)

Sit-down comedy is rationalism being explored minutely while being ignored grossly. It invites the reader into the character's head and at the same time holds him at bay to scoff at the character's awkwardness. Nathan's awkwardness has many inter-related dimensions. He has come on a literary pilgrimage, and he's acting like an adolescent voyeur. He wants to be a great writer, but he doubts the power of his own imagination. Of course he can fantasize and get a cheap, undisciplined release.

> That is easier by far than making things up at the typewriter. For that kind of imagining you don't have to have your picture in the *Saturday Review*. You don't even have to be young. You don't have to be anything.
>
> Virtuous reader, if you think that after intercourse all animals are sad, try masturbating on the daybed in E. I. Lonoff's study and see how you feel when it's over. (p. 112)

No, Nathan wants to clear himself with the Jews; he wants to be a disciple of high art, not a miserable onanist. Waiting for events to proceed above in Amy's room, he had unwittingly succumbed; and he had reached for the volume of Henry James as an act of atonement. As the scene continues, Nathan's embarrassment builds through a multiplicity of awarenesses. He sees himself as a miserable spy, prying into the privacy above; he senses Lonoff's stern authorial discipline here in this meticulous study; he is aware of the parallel to his own plight in James's "The Middle Years," which he has just been reading, the dying Dencombe's ironically double-edged words insinuating themselves into Nathan's literal situation:

> "We work in the dark—we do what we can—we give what we have. Our doubt is our passion and our passion is our task. The rest is the madness of art." (p. 116)

He feels all their judgments—his parents', Lonoff's, James's, Amy's, his own—and that of the reader standing nearby as treacherous accomplice and judge. Nathan is teetering on the desk.

> A woman was crying. Which one, over what, who was there comforting her—or causing the tears? Just a little higher and maybe I could find out. A thick dictionary would have been perfect, but Lonoff's Webster's was down on a shelf of fat reference books level with the typing chair, and the best I could manage under pressure was to gain another couple of inches by kneeling to insert between the desk and my feet the volume of stories by Henry James.
>
> Ah, the unreckoned consequences, the unaccountable uses of art! Dencombe would understand. But would Lonoff? *Don't fall.* (p. 117)

Roth keeps Nathan off balance and preserves his unheroic integrity by sit-down comic effects. They are devices of written fiction, a multiplicity of simultaneous perceptions unattainable in theater or movies, now that the aside and the soliloquy have been lost to realistic dramatization. They undercut high seriousness with comic absurdity. Without them or any other device for supplying the second perspective, even Roth's own television script of *The Ghost Writer,* was almost devoid of comedy.[16]

Roth's sit-down comedy differs from simple *schlemiel* stories. *Schlemiels* are lovable losers; the reader's response to them is a rueful shrug. They bungle along in a benign or indifferent world because they have never quite understood the rules. But Roth's comic protagonists have been taught the rules, or have consciously abandoned old rules for newly perceived principles, which should be applauded. Only no one is applauding, and the disillusionment is all the more bitter because they have marched forth firm in the conviction that a good (usually Jewish) upbringing has left them emotionally secure, armed against any buffetings that might come from a world not perceived as irrational. Now they find, at first to their irritation and then to their horror, that foreskinned is not forearmed. Worse yet, somewhere in their armor is a chink, perhaps a tribal defect, and under it is a rash. Very funny! Jewish sit-down humor necessarily plays off of, and seems to challenge, Jewish values. But that's because Roth's characters won't quit. "All right already" is not all right. *Schlemiels* would retire from the fray and settle for a hot roll and butter on Sunday norming, but Alex Portnoy must shed his impotence, which somehow comes from being the prisoner in some horrible Jewish joke; and Peter Tarnapol must regain his ability to write, which somehow he lost by fronting goyish cruelty with Jewish responsibility; and David Kepesh (in *The Professor of Desire*) who destroyed one paramour just by asserting the libertarian promises of the new society, cannot find contentment in unalloyed goodness and must suffer the inevitable loss of every newly-won desire. The humor, grim and abrasive, comes at the expense of a character so initially secure in his culture that he can rail at it for having betrayed him. But the railing, like the onanism, is Roth's contrivance for impotence, however much the character may use it for personal release.

Not all of Roth's characters' indictments are of society, though all become aware of its awesome competition. Some are indictments of self. Young Zuckerman ends his spying episode by combining the two in his contemplations.

> Oh, if only I could have imagined the scene I'd just overheard! If only I could invent as presumptuously as real life! If one day I could just *approach* the originality and excitement of what really goes on! But if I ever did, what then would they think of me, my father and his judge? How would my elders hold up against that? And if they couldn't, if the blow to their sentiments was finally too wounding, just how well would I hold up against being hated and reviled and disowned? (p. 121)

The answer to that question, provided in the rest of the Zuckerman trilogy, is *not very well.*

"If only I could have imagined the scene." That is not a
problem for Roth. Roth suffers from no paucity of imagination, as
Joseph Epstein has charged.[17] That "originality and excitement
of what really goes on," those very goings on in *The Ghost Writer*
are Roth's creations, however beyond the reach of Zuckerman
they may seem to be. What is awesome to Roth and beyond the
absurdities of literature are the absurdities of life. Would the
imaginary publisher of *Lickety Split* have concocted anything as
rich in pious hypocrisy as the forfeiture of the Miss America
crown or the million dollar escrow earnings of our purest ama-
ture olympic champions? Would Roth ever have given that strong
swimmer, Brenda Patimkin, with all her princessliness, a name
like Tiffany Cohen? Readers may be moved to read Roth's autobiography into Zuckerman's—and Kepesh's and Tarnapol's—life,
but it is Roth's imagined world, comparatively mild, that they
see.

Philip Roth's sit-down comedy is a response to an unfathoma-
ble world. It is a limited response, a refusal to will himself into
unwarranted optimism or to revile trends or social attitudes as if
they were people. He does not solve problems or resolve plots
because he does not think that the real world does either. He has
said of popular writers who do that, that while

> they are generally full of concern for the world about them . . . they
> just don't imagine the corruption and vulgarity and treachery of
> American public life any more profoundly than they imagine human
> character—that is, the country's private life. All issues are generally
> solvable, suggesting that [such authors] are not so much awe-struck
> or horror-struck as they are provoked by some topical controversy.[18]

Richly imagined character—the country's private life—is Roth's
indicator of the complexity of public life. And because most
people, most of the time, go on with their lives rather than
tragically end them, the duality of a comic vision, sustained by
the sureness of Roth's ear, best serves to present that awe-struck
or horror-struck response to life's absurdities. Roth's increasing
conviction that issues are not generally solvable may account for
his having omitted from his 1980 *Philip Roth Reader* any material

from the *Goodbye, Columbus* volume, where the short stories—
those "teachable gems" that have sustained college bookstore
sales—may tend to resolve themselves too easily. It may also
explain why Roth's comic works are generally short compared to
his highly resolved tomes of the mid-sixties.

Deftness, then, rather than fullness, has served Roth's latter-
day purposes. Short ironic jabs, parody, the single-line *stim-
mungsbrechung*, or the phrase that turns and shows the other
side of the coin are sit-down devices, not hilarious like the comic
one-liners or *kvetches*. Sometimes they complement the material
by being drawn from another world than the one immediately in
consciousness. Professor Kepesh, rising to leave a Prague café—
where late at night he has been composing his lecture on desire
for Literature 341—is addressed by one of two pretty young
prostitutes who have been observing him.

> "A letter to your wife?" says the one who strokes the dog and
> speaks some English.
> I cannot resist the slow curve she has thrown me. "To the chil-
> dren," I say.[19]

The baseball metaphor is apt. They are playing a game; she is
making a pitch. And Kepesh with his lie thinks that he has
escaped unknown. But Roth's slow curve is still breaking on the
reader: Kepesh, childless, disturbed by his attraction to what the
prostitutes represent (though he is not attracted sexually to
them), and fearful of marrying the wholesome Claire, who is
asleep in their hotel room, has scored only in a mental game.

In a brief sketch Roth presents the plight of the Jewish housewife a generation after Sophie Portnoy. Gloria, wife of Marvin, is
one of the ailing Zuckerman's comforters in *The Anatomy
Lesson*. A mother, and motherly, she also has sexual needs,
which, in post-sexual-revolution America deserve to be satisfied.
She ministers to Zuckerman naked, in heels, equipped from the
sex shop.

> "Times have changed," said Zuckerman, "since all you needed was
> a condom." "A child is sick," she said, "you bring toys." True, and
> Dionysian rites were once believed to have a therapeutic effect on
> the physically afflicted. There was also the ancient treatment known
> as the imposition of hands. Gloria had classical history on her side.
> His own mother's means for effecting a cure were to play casino on
> the edge of the bed with him when he was home with a fever. So as

not to fall behind in her housework, she'd set her ironing board up in his bedroom while they gossiped about school and his friends. He loved the smell of ironing still. Gloria, lubricating a finger and slipping it in his anus, talked about her marriage to Marvin.

Zuckerman said to her, "Gloria, you're the dirtiest woman I've ever met."

"If I'm the dirtiest woman you've ever met, you're in trouble. I fuck Marvin twice a week. I put down my book, put out my cigarette, turn out the light, and roll over."

"On your back?"

"What else? And then he puts it in and I know just what to do to make him come. And then he mumbles something about tits and love and he comes. Then I put on the light and roll on my side and light up a cigarette and get on with my book. . . .

". . . But it's hard fucking him, Nathan. And getting harder. You always think in a marriage, 'This is as bad as it can be'—and next year it's worse. It's the most odious duty I've ever had to perform. He says to me sometimes when he's straining to come, 'Gloria, Gloria, say something dirty.' I have to think hard, but I do it. He's a wonderful father and a wonderful husband, and he deserves all the help he can get. But still, one night I really thought I couldn't take it anymore. I put down my book and I put out the light and finally I said to him. I said, 'Marv, something's gone out of our marriage.' But he was almost snoring by then. 'Quiet,' he mumbles. 'Shhhhh, go to sleep.' I don't know what to do. There's nothing I *can* do. The odd thing and the terrible thing and the thing that's most confusing is that without a doubt Marvin was the real love of my life and beyond a doubt I was the love of Marvin's life and although we were never very happy, for about ten years we had a passionate marriage with all the trimmings, health, money, kids, Mercedes, a double sink and summer houses and everything. And so miserable and so attached. It makes no sense. And now I have these night monsters: no money, death, and getting old. I can't leave him. I'd fall apart. He'd fall apart. The kids would go nuts and they're screwy as it is. But I need excitement. I'm thirty-eight. I need extra attention."[20]

Roth does not attempt to solve Gloria's problem—she is but a sketch in the longer non-solving of Zuckerman's problem. But what a sketch! All those Jewish males who had been liberated into impotence, waning sexual desire, or writer's block by the right to say "I want! I want!" are now joined by Jewish females conflicted between traditional low expectations—summed up in "and although we were never very happy"—and the new bill of orgasmic rights. But the new high expectations are deceiving; they do not last. A decade of passion and the "trimmings" and then a nexus of materialism and not even the smell of ironing to bind the generations. Roth has caught the note of many a modern marriage. Gloria is not a cliché; she is a truism, one of several deftly sketched into *The Anatomy Lesson*.

That novel is another collection of traps—a writhing comic exploration of the unquiet desperation in which the great mass of modern men live out their lives. Roth returns to physical entrapment in a mysterious ailment to unify its themes. Like most of Roth's novels since *Portnoy*, it is about a man rooted in the middle class and economically able to make choices, who is considering his life as a man. Like the others it is about that absurdity of post-industrial life—perhaps the ultimate gift of Napoleon to the Jews in their release from the ghetto—the illusion of freedom. Professor Kepesh had thought (what does a Kepesh do but think?) that he could have both family (the fruit of the womb, out of Claire Ovington, whose very smell, look, taste is of apples) *and* desire. He finds he cannot have both. Young Zuckerman had thought that he could write about real, flawed Jews and have the respect of the Jewish community. He finds that they want "topical controversy" and him always on the "right" side. Middle-aged Zuckerman, flush with *Carnovsky* success, finds that his novel has been taken for an autobiography and that the world has become his devil—in a brilliant parody of Blatty's *Exorcist* he gets a note containing the very curse hurled at the young priest in that novel who feels responsible for his mother's death. Similar guilts are now hounding Zuckerman into surrender: he will give over the sin of literature and become a good Jewish boy, a doctor.

Zuckerman, of course, is defeated in trying to act out his fantasy. One does not get a chance to replay one's life differently, or even to explain it. The only doom is to live it. But frustrated and imaginative young men may fantasize, as Kepesh does of Kafka's whore and young Zuckerman does of Anne Frank. And Roth uses these fantasies to draw together many threads of the conflict in his novels without raising false expectations of resolution. In *The Professor of Desire* Kafka is a central awareness and the ultimate mystery. Kepesh, as a professor of literature concerned about desire, may plan to use Tolstoy, Flaubert, and Mann as the central authors of his proposed course, but he is also K., with problems, like K.'s, involving sex and marriage. In Prague, where past meets present and East meets West, he compares his supposed freedom with Professor Soska's constraint. He sees the prostitutes. He is writing a lecture employing the tone of Kafka's "A Report to an Academy," "an account of the life I formerly led as an ape," the very tone that Kepesh is using in this whole first-person-narrated novel. He would get to the heart of everything by getting to Kafka, but Kafka is dead and his mystery with him. In Kepesh's fantasy, Kafka's whore, now in her eighties, will reveal all. Before he is finished, he brings together all the libidinous crew of his early life, the three B.'s—Bratasky, Birgitta, and Baumgarten—and rests the survival of free enterprise before the onslaught of communism on the issue of whether or not to touch her genitalia. But, of course, he gets no answer to his question. It is a brilliant device.

And young Zuckerman's fantasy of Amy Bellette as Anne Frank? Its very outrageousness is clearly part of Roth's intent in *The Ghost Writer*. The independent life of Anne's diary underscores the book's thesis of "the madness of art"; a live Anne as his bride is Zuckerman's fantasized defense against charges of anti-Semitism: the perfect bride to please Jewish parents—and the perfect challenge to hurl at critics. Roth's having the older Zuckerman go beyond imagining, to acting out his fantasies, is a way of imagining one further step. What if the critics had defeated the comic writer? What if they had driven him into "topical controversy" and easy resolutions? What if they had gotten him to deny the absurdity of the absurd? In inviting the raised eyebrow and making that his target, Roth keeps alive the integrity of sit-down comedy.

Roth's comic muse is not likely to retire before the demands of serious fiction. It is much more likely to continue to serve those demands with its stereoscopic view of absurdity. There are no sterner moralists in his readership than the moralizing side of his own characters. Readers who, like the moralizers in his novels, think the fit aspect for a serious writer is a frown, are likely to continue being disappointed by Roth; and those who respond only to the stand-up comedy may see him as a lightweight. Sit-down comedy carries a burden of misunderstanding. Roth might have to say of his readership, especially of his Jewish readership, what Job says of God:

> Though [they] slay me, yet will I trust in [them], but I will maintain mine own ways before [them.]

but "they slay me" would have a crisp vaudevillian edge.

NOTES

1. Howard Junker, "Will This Finally Be Philip Roth's Year?" *New York Magazine* (January 13, 1969): 46.

2. Irving Howe, "Philip Roth Reconsidered," *Commentary* 54 (December 1972): 69–77; and Sanford Pinsker, *The Comedy That "Hoits"* (Columbia: University of Missouri Press, 1975), pp. 55–71.

3. Philip Roth, *Reading Myself and Others* (New York: Farrar, Straus and Giroux, 1975), pp. 30–31.

4. Roth, *Reading Myself and Others,* p. 22.

5. "The spontaneous satire that gathers momentum and energy as it goes along, spiraling finally into the exhilarating anarchy of total freedom from inhibition." Albert Goldman, quoted in Irving Howe, *World of Our Fathers* (New York: Harcourt Brace Jovanovich, 1976), p. 571.

6. Roth, *Reading Myself and Others,* p. 94.

7. See Sheldon Grebstein's excellent "The Comic Anatomy of *Portnoy's Complaint*" in *Comic Relief: Humor in Contemporary American Literature,* ed. Sarah Blacher Cohen (Urbana: University of Illinois Press, 1978), pp. 155–56.

8. In this and all other references to *The Breast,* I cite the revised version contained in *The Philip Roth Reader* (New York: Farrar, Straus and Giroux, 1983), reduced by one-third from the 1973 edition and infinitely superior; p. 454.

9. Joseph Epstein, "What Does Philip Roth Want?" *Commentary* 77 (January 1984): 67.

10. "Hardly any Jew today is without some Jewish past. Total amnesia is still relatively rare. The choice for Jews as for non-Jews is not whether or not to have a past, but rather—what kind of past shall one have.

". . . The suburban Jewish past of the characters in the fiction of Philip Roth is also a Jewish part, only as meager as the span of a generation or two and infinitely more distasteful, because so much more trivial." Joseph Hayim Yerushalmi, *Zakhor: Jewish History and Jewish Memory* (Seattle: University of Washington Press, 1982), p. 99. Yerushalmi's use of "suburban" suggests that, like most readers, his exposure to Roth is limited, perhaps to *Goodbye, Columbus.*

11. "Modern Jewish historiography cannot address itself to those Jews who have not 'fallen.' The potential dialogue of the historian is with those who, consciously or unwittingly, have tasted of forbidden fruit and have never been the same. I think these are the majority. . . . Franz Kafka, fallen modern Jew that he was, 'with a fierce longing for forebears' that neither his own father nor the synogogue could assuage, read Graetz 'eagerly and happily,' yet another search that, like so much else in his life, never attained its goal." Ibid., p. 98.

12. Pinsker, *The Comedy That "Hoits,"* p. 84.

13. Philip Roth, *The Great American Novel* (New York: Holt, Rinehart and Winston, 1973). All citations in the text are from this edition.

14. Norman Podhoretz, "Laureate of the New Class," *Commentary* LIV:6 (December 1972): 4–6.

15. Philip Roth, *The Ghost Writer* (New York: Farrar, Straus and Giroux, 1979). All citations in the text are from this edition.

16. I personally interviewed some dozen viewers within a day or two of the airing on PBS. Those who had not read the novel were universally surprised to hear that there are comic dimensions to the book.

17. Epstein, "What Does Philip Roth Want?" p. 67.

18. Philip Roth, "Writing American Fiction," in *Reading Myself and Others,* p. 122.

19. Philip Roth, *The Professor of Desire* (New York: Farrar, Straus and Giroux, 1977), pp. 185–86.

20. Philip Roth, *The Anatomy Lesson* (New York: Farrar, Straus and Giroux, 1983), pp. 120–22.

STANLEY ELKIN AND
JEWISH BLACK HUMOR

MAURICE CHARNEY

Stanley Elkin defines himself "as a writer who happens to be Jewish, happens to be American, and happens to be a writer."[1] This is charmingly disingenuous, if not actually a way of thumbing one's nose at all critical affiliations. Elkin has emphatically separated himself from the ghetto of Jewish-American (and Jewish-Canadian) writers, all comic and all black humorists: Roth, Richler, Heller, Bruce Jay Friedman, and others. Yet there is a catch to his separation: "I don't identify myself with Jewish writers. However, you know, I resent it if I see an anthology with Jewish writers, and I'm not included."[2] Similarly, he is repelled by the term "black humor," which he claims was invented by *Time* magazine,[3] but his resistance has definite limits: "I resent the term 'Black Humor' tremendously. I hate that term. I don't know what it means. Yet if there is an anthology of Black Humorists I resent it if I'm not included in the anthology."[4] It is obvious that Elkin is cultivating paradox. The two issues, Elkin's Jewishness and Elkin's black humor, are intertwined, because to be a Jewish writer almost necessarily implies that you will work by means of an ironic self-consciousness that is essentially comic. Insofar as the Jewish writer makes claims upon us for his Jewishness, he also casts himself in the role of the alienated observer of a scene to which he only partly belongs. He looks at American or Canadian life from the outside, with comic detachment and ironic indulgence. From this perspective everything is absurd and grotesque almost by definition.

In *Bright Book of Life,* Alfred Kazin shows contemporary

Jewish writers one way to resolve the dilemma of their relation to their own Jewish background. The concept of "constructed folklore" applies with special force to Elkin's Jewish black humor:

> Jewishness as the novelist's material (which can be quite different from the individual material of Jews writing fiction) is constructed folklore. It is usually comic, or at least humorous; the characters are always ready to tell a joke on themselves. With their bizarre names, their accents, *their* language, they are jokes on themselves. And so they become "Jewish" material, which expresses not the predicament of the individual who knows himself to be an exception, but a piece of the folk, of "Jewishness" as a style of life and a point of view.[5]

If Jewishness is a style of life and a point of view, we don't need to insist on historical, liturgical, or ritualistic detail, or authenticate the materials the writer of fiction is drawing from his own "Jewish" experience. In Kazin's telling phrase, the folklore is not natural and spontaneous but artful and constructed. It is a fiction of Jewishness—the quality of being Jewish in America, the sense of a Jewish character with a gamut of defined traits, a special language and syntax that is neither Yiddish nor Standard English—rather than an accurate report on Jewish life. And the charm of "constructed folklore" is that the characters don't have to have Jewish names or be specifically identified as Jews.[6]

In *After the Tradition: Essays on Modern Jewish Writing,* Robert Alter is much too ready to get rid of myth and to refer Jewish writing in America to a standard of factuality that seems wholly factitious. In "Sentimentalizing the Jews," Alter is undoubtedly right to satirize bogus Jewishness, injected like matzo ball soup into supposedly Jewish fictions, but his "double sentimental myth" seems patently wrong:

> Ironically, what most American Jewish writers are outsiders to is that very body of Jewish experience with which other Americans expect them to be completely at home. . . . That is, the American writer of Jewish descent finds himself utilizing Jewish experience of which he is largely ignorant, and so the Jewish skeletons of his characters are fleshed with American fantasies about Jews. The result is a kind of double sentimental myth: the Jew emerges from this fiction as an imaginary creature embodying both what Americans would like to think about Jews and what American Jewish intellectuals would like to think about themselves.[7]

Alter's definition of "Jewish experience" in this polemical statement is too narrow and literal. Kazin's notion of "constructed folklore" is much more suitable for fiction because it concerns itself with the Jewish-American writer's self-consciousness of his own Jewish experience, especially in relation to other childhood fantasies and creative reconstructions of what the world of our fathers is imagined to be. It is just those mythic distortions of the Jewish experience that make it available as a literary subject.

In the broader definition of Jewish black humor as "constructed folklore," Elkin's latest novel, *George Mills* (1982), an historical extravanganza of the unheroic ordinary man, is very Jewish in feeling even though most of the characters are clearly not Jewish. The one thoroughly Jewish character, Moses Magaziner (later in the guise of the merchant, Guzo Sanbanna), the unlikely British Ambassador to the Court of Mahmad II, is really a grotesque parody of a Jew, including an absurdly Yiddish, Bronx peddler's accent. We don't really need Magaziner to authenticate the Jewishness of the novel. In fact, his presence is rather jarring and intrusive.

Elkin's Jews tend to be grotesquely clownish figures, as if the need to declare one's Jewish identity were in itself an act of alienation from American middle-class values. Even among other Jews, the Jew who insists on his Jewishness tends to be a bizarre, comic-strip character, more a caricature than a rounded human being. There is a curious passage in the tragicomic story, "The Condominium," in which Preminger, the *schlemiel*-like hero, feels with acute anxiety his separateness from the tightly organized Jewish community of his friends and neighbors in the apartment complex. He feels tentative, uncertain, disestablished, a stand-in for his father:

> "I've lived provisionally here," he said. "Like someone under military government, martial law, an occupied life. This isn't going as I meant it to. I'm a stranger—that's something of what I'm driving at. My life is a little like being in a foreign country. There's displaced person in me. I feel—listen—I feel—*Jewish.* I mean even here, among Jews, where everyone's Jewish, I feel Jewish."[8]

To feel Jewish even among Jews is one of the crisis signs of Preminger's nervous breakdown that eventually leads him to jump off his balcony.

Elkin's first published novel, *Boswell: A Modern Comedy*

(1964), in which the hero, like Johnson's Boswell, lives by proxy in the lives of acknowledged celebrities, curiously anticipates the chameleon-like comic passivity of Woody Allen's movie, *Zelig.* In this novel the Nobel Prize-winning anthropologist, Morty Perlmutter (who will reappear later in "Perlmutter at the East Pole," a story in *Criers and Kibitzers, Kibitzers and Criers*) defines the Jewish God for Boswell in hippy terms:

> "Now, though I was a Communist in those days I believed in God. The God I believed in was a Jewish-Brahmin-Zen Buddhist mystic who wore a *yarmulke* and squatted in a room filled with art treasures, telling his beads. You prayed to this God and he turned a deaf ear. He was supposed to, you understand. Acceptance of fucking suffering was what he taught. He bled in four colors over the art treasures and posed crazy riddles. He answered all questions with questions. Revelation was when he said, 'The meaning of life is as follows,' and he'd pick his nose with his little finger. Profound? Bullcrap, my young friends who still believe in such a God, a tongue-tied God who is not so much indifferent as bewildered by life."9

The God who picks his nose, answers questions with questions, and is bewildered by life is Elkin's grotesque, Old Testament Jehovah, who still maintains an authority he cannot himself understand. The leering, insatiable Perlmutter, all-wise and all-foolish, ritual clown and shaman, trickster and seer, is himself like the obscene and terrifying gods in Bellow's novel, *Henderson the Rain King.*

Religious awe and reverence are linked in Elkin's mind with vaudeville. God in *The Living End* (1979), a comic Jewish version of Dante's *Divine Comedy,* speaks like John Osborne's Entertainer, and in a final, grotesquely apocalyptic scene, he wills the destruction of the world "because I never found my audience."10 In *The Franchiser* (1976), a panegyric of American business, Ben Flesh's godfather is a theatrical costumer for the great Broadway musicals. The mythical capital in the novel derives from profits made in the theater, and Ben conceives his franchises as stage sets for the American dream. Although Ben Flesh is only partially Jewish in origin, his turgid and tawdry dreams of America have the peculiar grandiosity of a first-generation immigrant. He is so archetypically and histrionically American that, by the very magnitude of his effort to belong, he is immediately alienated. Beginning with the hundreds of used color television sets that Ben buys as distressed merchandise for his franchise motel, the Travel Inn in Ringgold, Georgia, everything that Ben touches is overwrought and unreal. This endows *The Franchiser* with a peculiarly hallucinatory and theatrical quality.

Although Elkin resists being categorized as a Jewish-American writer, the experience of his novels and stories is peculiarly Jewish. He is, willy nilly, a Jewish black humorist, if not by conscious design then by an inevitable expression of point of view. In other words, aside from the sardonic, mocking, unstable, and treacherous world of his fictions, there is no alternative reality, and we see the existential absurdity of modern man in Elkin as essentially a "Jewish" condition. Suffering is never heroic but always trivialized; tragedy is rendered in its black comedy equivalent. Since we see the fictions through the author's consciousness, specific points of Jewish doctrine, ritual, speech, and identity hardly matter. There is, in fact, surprisingly little Jewish detail and local color in Elkin's works, especially when compared with other Jewish writers such as Bruce Jay Friedman, Philip Roth, Wallace Markfield, Mordecai Richler, and even Saul Bellow (especially in *The Adventures of Augie March* and *Herzog*). Yet Elkin creates a world that is convincingly Jewish, just as Faulkner's Yoknapatawpha County is convincingly southern. It is Jewish in its spontaneous assumptions, its feeling that triumph is inexplicably mixed with catastrophe, its manic urge for the small man, through cunning, slyness, and whimsy, to conquer the world. Its protagonists speak with prophetic fervor tinged with neurotic insufficiency. The large effects always fall short and the leading characters always turn out to be con men and vaudevillians. The pervasive irony undercuts pretension in favor of flights of fancy, arrant self-aggrandizement, and blatant wish fulfillment.

One large division in Elkin's world is that between criers and kibitzers, as in the title story of his first collection of short fiction, *Criers and Kibitzers, Kibitzers and Criers* (1965). All of reality seems to be divided between criers and kibitzers, as if there were no place for any other type of Jew. Greenspahn, the small supermarket owner now in mourning for his son, looks through the window of "The Cookery," the neighborhood restaurant where he eats lunch, and surveys his fellow merchants:

> Even without going inside he knew what it would be like. The criers and the kibitzers. The criers, earnest, complaining with a peculiar vigor about their businesses, their gas mileage, their health; their despair articulate, dependably lamenting their lives, vaguely mourn-

ing conditions, their sorrow something they could expect no one to understand. The kibitzers, deaf to grief, winking confidentially at the others, their voices high-pitched in kidding or lowered in conspiracy to tell of triumphs, of men they knew downtown, of tickets fixed, or languishing goods moved suddenly and unexpectedly, of the windfall that was life; their fingers sticky, smeared with sugar from their rolls.[11]

The kibitzers and the criers can mysteriously exchange roles, but Greenspahn's grief is defined by his looking through the window and not being able to assume either role.

The criers are the *kvetchers* and *schreiers,* the professional complainers who take pleasure from telling you how bad it is and how much worse it could have been. This is not masochism at all, but a kind of *Schadenfreude* and gallows humor because the *kvetchers* compete with each other in negative hyperboles of disaster. One *schreier*'s troubles are intended to top the *tsuris* that has just been related, so that the atmosphere is always that of a contest to see who is the biggest and most thoroughly cast-down victim of God's injustice. It is as if there were a whole table of Jobs all trying to outdo each other in affliction. Elkin's *schreiers* are distinctly related to the *schreier* types found in many of the Jewish jokes in Freud's *Jokes and Their Relation to the Unconscious* (1905), in which seemingly downcast Jews arrogantly complain of their misfortune, all the while boasting of the magnitude and special status of their troubles—as if God had chosen them from among multitudes to bear witness to his capricious tyranny.

The kibitzers are in symbiotic relation to the criers; one could not exist without the other. A kibitzer is an ironic commentator, a non-participant, who typically observes card games, checkers, and chess and offers free and unsought advice about the card you should have played or the piece you ought to have moved. The kibitzer is always very knowing about why you lost. In his own eyes, the kibitzer is always a being of superior intelligence and discernment, but cold and detached. He is the archetypal artist/observer, always ready with a comment and a wry joke (or, in the noun form, a kibitz). The kibitzer's favorite mode is sarcasm. Both kibitzer and crier are programmed into defined roles that have their own fixed rules and rituals. Despite all appearances to the contrary, the crier's personal grief and the kibitzer's detached amusement are exaggerations for effect—both equally histrionic.

Both types have their origins in the profound ambiguities of Jewish ghetto humor. On the one hand, the Jew feels excluded from the larger world around him (the *goyim*); on the other, he feels intensely superior to that world, which he not only doesn't understand but also doesn't feel the need to understand. Humor is an ironic and covert defense against the aggression that is perceived as coming from without; it is also an expression of aggression against a hostile Christian society.[12] Kibitzing and crying are mechanisms of survival.

When Greenspahn finally enters "The Cookery" and hears "the babble of the lunchers, the sound rushing to his ears like the noise of a suddenly unmuted trumpet" (p. 20), he has a black comedy awareness of how remote all of his fellow merchants are from his own grief. He sits on the aisle like a mock-kibitzer: "he felt peculiarly like a visitor, like one there only temporarily, as though he had rushed up to the table merely to say hello or to tell a joke" (p. 20). The death of his son has acutely separated Greenspahn from the society in which he exists, and he feels a pointlessness and meaninglessness in the atmosphere—boredom, ennui—he has never experienced before:

> Everywhere it was the same. At every table. The two kinds of people like two different sexes that had sought each other out. Sure, Greenspahn thought, would a crier listen to another man's complaints? Could a kibitzer kid a kidder? But it didn't mean anything, he thought. Not the jokes, not the grief. It didn't mean anything. They were like birds making noises in a tree. (p. 21)

By separating himself from the constructed folklore by which he lives, Greenspahn is in despair. If you are neither a kibitzer nor a crier, then you are nothing at all. You live parasitically in other peoples' lives, like the celebrity-hunter Boswell, or like the suicidal Preminger, who does not understand that all he needs is one joke to save his life, or like the dying Feldman in "In the Alley," who cannot connect with the compassionate world outside his own family. In true black comedy style, one feels great pathos in reading Elkin but never tragedy. His heroes are clowns and con men, brilliant talkers and persuasive salesmen—they sell themselves—but they lack the stature to be convincingly tragic.

Elkin loves freaks and misfits. Virtually all the characters in *Criers and Kibitzers, Kibitzers and Criers* are maladapted in one way or another; that is the source of both their vitality and their humor. Elkin has expressed great disdain for his short stories, some of which he has never bothered to collect in volume form. It is as if the long novel is a much better medium for hyperbole and extravagance. Thus in *The Franchiser,* which may be Elkin's black humor masterpiece—it is certainly his most eloquent fiction—all eighteen twins and triplets of the Finsberg clan are freaks, genetically damaged, "Human lemons, Detroit could recall them":

> LaVerne's organs lined the side of her body, her liver and lungs and kidneys outside her rib cage. Ethel's heart was in her right breast. Cole had a tendency to suffer from the same disorders as plants and had a premonition that he would be killed by Dutch elm blight.[13]

All the twins and triplets suddenly start dying one after the other from their bizarre inheritance. By cultivating such outrageously surrealistic detail, Elkin cuts off our human responses and prefers instead to disorient us with a curious mixture of tragic and comic materials. As audience, we are not allowed to follow through with our warm and sticky human responses. Both the crying and the kibitzing take the form of a stage performance, preferably the sort of heavily costumed musical on which the Finsberg fortune was made in *The Franchiser.* Life may resemble *Oklahoma,* but the converse of this comforting proposition is emphatically untrue.

The archetypal Jewish character in Elkin is the salesman. It is not surprising that the author's own father was a salesman, whom he remembers with affection and comic adulation:

> He sold costume jewelry, and I went with him once on one of his trips through the Midwest. . . . I was with him in small Indiana towns where he would take the jewelry out of the telescopes, which are salesmen's cases, and actually put the earrings on his ears, the bracelets around his wrists, and the necklaces about his throat. This wasn't drag, but the prose passionate and stage business of his spiel. The man believed in costume jewelry, in rhinestones and beads, and sang junk jewelry's meteorological condition—its Fall line and Spring.[14]

This is not *Death of a Salesman,* but more like *The Salesman Unbound* and *Paradise Regained.* The frantic, obsessive, and manic tone is entirely in keeping with Elkin's fiction, and Elkin admits that his father is the model for Feldman's father in his second novel, *A Bad Man* (1967), and even more so of Feldman

himself, the ironic "bad man" of the title, society's scapegoat
Jew, who is imprisoned and eventually martyred. It is hard to
know what Elkin means when he says: "There is little autobiography in my work."[15] He obviously means this in the literal
sense that his characters are distanced from his life, but still they
are very close. Elkin's father seems also to be the model for Ben
Flesh, the super salesman and spieler in *The Franchiser,* despite
Elkin's disclaimers that Ben Flesh is not even fully Jewish. What
difference could that detail make? He is the Word made Flesh.

In *A Bad Man,* Feldman is a very comfortable department
store owner and commercial tycoon before he becomes a con-
vict, but his father is the archetype of the Jewish peddler, a
parody of the Yankee peddler and his covered wagon—a romantic image also echoed in Miller's *Death of a Salesman.* His
selling is a dionysiac frenzy of wild excess that has little to do
with commercial activity. Feldman's father is more like a re-
vivalist preacher than a business man. His language is hyperbolical and apocalyptic. Selling is an end in itself:

> "Get what there is and turn it over quick. Dump and dump, mark
> down and close out. Have specials, my dear. The thing in life is to
> sell, but if no one will buy, listen, listen, *give* it away! Flee the
> minion. Be naked. Travel light. Because there will come catastrophe.
> Every night expect the flood, the earthquake, the fire, and think of
> the stock. Be in a position to lose nothing by it when the bombs
> fall."[16]

This is like the frantic story, "I Look Out for Ed Wolfe" (in *Criers
and Kibitzers, Kibitzers and Criers*), in which the crack salesman, out of a job, sells everything he owns with great finesse and
at a tremendous loss.

What finally lands Feldman in jail in *A Bad Man* are the
clandestine activities of his department store basement, where
Feldman the confidence man sells advice: drugs, abortions, par-
amilitary equipment. Selling is power: "It hadn't ever been profit
that had driven him, but the idea of the sale itself, his way of
bearing down on the world" (p. 266). In this formulation the
salesman is the existentialist hero, and selling is a way of con-
fronting reality. Thus Feldman's father seeks out the difficulties of
selling sleazy merchandise and "neo-junk" because only this
kind of salesmanship will testify to his art: " 'Sell seconds,' he'd
say, 'irregulars. Sell damaged and smoke-stained and fire-torn

things. Sell the marred and impaired, the defective and soiled'"
(*A Bad Man,* p. 38). As the elder Feldman scrutinizes ladies'
underwear, the young Feldman gets a lesson he will never forget
about the ethics and rhetoric of merchandising:

> He would pick up a pair of ladies' panties from the lingerie
> counter. "Look, look at the craftsmanship," he'd say distastefully,
> plunging his big hand inside and splaying his fingers in the silky seat,
> "the crotchmanship." He'd snap the elastic. "No sag, no give," he'd
> say to the startled salesgirl. "Give me give, the second-rate. Schlock,
> give me. They're doing some wonderful things in Japan."
> "*Because,*" he'd say, explaining, "where's the contest in sound
> merchandise? You sell a sound piece of merchandise, what's the big
> deal?" (p. 38)

The salesman is the artist of the beautiful, the Platonic idea of the
kibitzer, who, through his spiel, wants to bear down on the world.
To sell schlock is a way of asserting your power and declaring
your freedom from the material world.

Unlike the bereaved Greenspahn in "Criers and Kibitzers,
Kibitzers and Criers," the other merchants in the story consider
selling a sport: "Business was a kind of game with them. . . .
Not even the money made any difference" (p. 23). If selling is a
form of superiority, like kibitzing, it is also a vehicle for acting out
scenarios with all of their grand rhetoric and perfect timing. The
salesman is a performer, and selling is a proof that you are alive.
It is curious how closely Elkin's kibitzer-salesmen resemble the
hustlers of David Mamet's new play, *Glengarry Glen Ross,* in
which the item sold—worthless property lots in Florida—is
merely the jumping off place for wild flights of fancy and brilliant
comic invention. In this context, *caveat emptor* translates into its
theatrical equivalent: let the audience be on its guard because the
characters on stage will con you.

For a contemporary Jewish novelist, Elkin is surprisingly short
on fictional families. His novels and stories are dominated by
lonely, powerful, obsessed, brooding males always seeking mas-
culine goals that elude their grasp. Jewish macho is not primarily
sexual, but it seeks power, money, status, and recognition by the
world. Women play a minor role in Elkin. They are alternatively
either nurturant or sex objects, but they never really impinge on
the male world. Elkin's males are often unmarried or widowed—
Boswell, Dick Gibson, Flesh, the Bailbondsman—and, because
of their constant travel, they have no fixed abode (or they live, by

preference, in hotel rooms). They seem to incarnate the Wandering Jew, who is also cunning, resourceful, and fully able to thrive without women or family. Wives, when they exist, like Mrs. Feldman in *A Bad Man* or Mrs. Ellerbee in *The Living End,* are usually colorless and overweight housewives who are bent on the destruction of their mates. In "The Condominium," both the son and his recently deceased father suffer from an infuriatingly prissy and legalistic relation (orchestrated by long letters) with their seductive neighbor, Evelyn. The men wait for erotic trysts that will never occur.

Sex in Elkin tends to be an unsatisfactory product of lust, with a strongly voyeuristic element. It is tawdry, quick, and furtive. The women inspire a prurience they cannot possibly satisfy; Elkin confesses that he is "incapable of writing about a love affair."[17] This is a strange admission for a novelist to make. Like Alexander Portnoy, impotent in Israel in Roth's *Portnoy's Complaint,* Elkin's Jewish heroes seem to need the degradation of the sex object that Freud speaks of in his essay, "The Most Prevalent Form of Degradation in Erotic Life." The classic Jewish mother type, like Mrs. Portnoy, raises fears of incest that are too powerful to overcome.

That seems to be why the luxuriant scenes in the Sultan's harem in Elkin's *George Mills* have only a surface resemblance to the Victorian erotic classic, *The Lustful Turk.* Elkin's pornotopia is surprisingly relaxed and sensuous but only mildly titillating:

> Even the smells, he thought. Balmed, luxurious as jungle, sweet and fruity as tropic, as florid, shrubby produce. . . . The pampered, lovely smells had still insinuated themselves onto his very breath, caught on his tongue, snagged on his teeth, so that what he tasted, its flavors overriding the very food he chewed or liquids he drank, was like some perfumed, sexual manna, the gynecological liqueurs. . . . And he'd experienced, as he experienced now, as he'd experienced that first time in the harem—why did he have the impression that he had come not among women but into some vast and sensual female wardrobe?—a useless and cozy semitumescence, idle and abstracted.[18]

The scene is like Ingres's paintings of odalisques, especially "The Turkish Bath," but the feeling is one of comic detachment. The women are dehumanized by being converted into "some vast and sensual female wardrobe," and their power of arousal is reduced into "a useless and cozy semitumescence." The harem is a voyeur's paradise, a country of the mind in which real, flesh-and-blood women play very little part.

The most intense female sexuality in Elkin is that of the bear in heat in the curiously upper-class story "The Making of Ashenden" (in *Searches and Seizures,* 1973). This is as close as·Elkin ever comes to comic and hyperbolical pornography. This bear is no standoffish Jewish American Princess, and half playfully and half importunately she rapes the very proper and very WASP protagonist, Brewster Ashenden. The incident gives Ashenden a whole new perspective on women and the exciting possibilities of physical union. There is nothing like this bizarrely comic animal sexuality anywhere else in Elkin, who vigorously disclaims any debt to Faulkner's celebrated story, "The Bear."[19] There is a clear link with Smolak the bear in Bellow's *Henderson the Rain King* and the whole platoon of performing bears in the novels of John Irving.

Is there a distinctive style for Jewish black humor? Writers on Jewish themes have strongly emphasized the central voice of the *schlemiel.*[20] The downtrodden *schlemiel,* a victim of awkwardness and bad luck *(schlimazel),* establishes a perspective from which we see the world. He is the little man with grandiose visions, who is able, through ironic and defensive humor, to transcend his metaphysical condition. Elkin's *schlemiel* protagonists tend to be eloquent buffoons and tricksters who tease the most arcane reality to yield up its secrets.

Elkin avoids the heavily Yiddishized diction and syntax of *Portnoy's Complaint;* the Yiddish of Moses Magaziner in *George Mills* is self-consciously vaudeville Yiddish, a ridiculous parody of the immigrant Jew. There are relatively few Yiddish expressions in Elkin, yet his voice and tone seem distinctively Jewish—literary Jewish in the sense of "constructed folklore"—in three ways: his style is grotesque, exhibitionistic, and obsessive. Since style expresses a unique and personal organization of experience, these three characteristics—there are obviously many more—define Elkin's special way of coming to grips with the world, his assumptions, his metaphysics, and his own idiosyncratic rhetoric. Why are these characteristics especially Jewish? I think the grotesque, the exhibitionistic, and the obsessive are all part of the defensive persona of the Jewish humorist, clown, or stand-up comedian. They all represent stylistic ways of depersonalizing a hostile reality and making it more detached and dream-like. We are removed from the sphere of everyday reality and the harsh vulnerabilities of simple moral judgments. Everything is cloaked in self-conscious irony.

All black humor is grotesque, so we begin with the most general quality. The vision is deliberately distorted, blurred in some perspectives and super-clarified in others, so that certain details we had not noticed (or could not possibly have noticed) are brought into prominence. A dream-like if not actually halluci-natory feeling is created in the spectator. In *The Franchiser,* Ben Flesh throws a final, apocalyptic party for his failing Fred Astaire franchise. His wild and ranting oration is grotesque in most of the black-humor senses of the term, because Ben takes his advertising clichés literally, and he justifies and rationalizes the American Dream with crazy fervor. The tone is hysterically inappropriate for a bankrupt enterprise and for a party in which the guests have been dragooned off the streets. They are a ragged and joyless crew.

A woman in her mid-fifties dancing with a golden-ager is carrying her shopping-bag on the dance floor:

> In her dreamy mood she held the bag by only one beautiful handle and a bottle of ketchup dropped from it, making a lovely splash on the floor. Their shoes looked so vulnerable as the dancers guided each other through the sticky stuff that Ben wanted to cry. Lai-op, lai-op, lai-op. They smeared the ballroom floor with a jelly of ket-chup. It was beautiful, the pasty, tomato-y brushstrokes like single-hued rainbows . . . the music made visible. (*The Franchiser,* pp. 60–61)

This is a typical Elkin grotesque because it mixes so easily the sleazy and the grandiose, the tawdry details of the ketchup and the high-flown conceit of the dance writing itself out on the floor in the ketchup alphabet. Ben focuses on things rather than peo-ple—the flesh rather than the spirit—the people only the bearers of the symbolic paraphernalia of civilization. Ben is the prophet exhorting the masses and also at the time selling dance lessons in a defunct studio. Elkin specializes in grand soliloquies which don't involve any conversation. There is a total lack of communi-cation between Ben and the dancers. He is speaking for his own edification and amusement.

Like Elkin's use of the grotesque, he employs the exhibi-tionistic style for purposes of bravado and display. His enormous catalogues are a kind of Whitmanizing, but utterly unheroic and deflationary. What is most flamboyantly displayed is the flotsam and jetsam of ordinary life, dreck, crap, detritus, rejects, dis- cards. As Philip Stevick notes in his essay, "Prolegomena to the Study of Fictional *Dreck,*" "the junk of current fiction represents a new way of giving fictional specificity to a meaningless quality of life," which is balanced against "a sense of wit and play that makes that meaningless quality bearable and often very funny."[21] In Elkin's Jewish context the fictional dreck defies the rational order and middle-class purpose and trimness of Amer- ican life.

Old Feldman's stock, the birthright he passes along to his son in *A Bad Man,* is a celebration of shopping-bag culture and a demonic parody of American material values:

> There was a shapeless heap of dull rags, a great disreputable mound
> of the permanently soiled and scarred, of slips that might have been
> pulled from corpses in auto wrecks, of shorts that could have come
> from dying men, sheets ripped from fatal childbeds, straps pulled
> from brassieres—the mutilated and abused and dishonored. shards
> from things of the self, the rags of rage they seemed. . . . There were
> old magazines, chapters from books, broken pencils, bladders from
> ruined pens, eraser ends in small piles, cork scraped from the inside
> of bottle caps, ballistical shapes of tinfoil, the worn straps from
> watches, wires, strings, ropes, broken-glass—thing's nubbins.
> "*Splinters,*" his father said, "there's a fortune in splinters." (pp.
> 40–41)

The worthlessness of the items defines their value. This pile—all of which is for sale—represents his father's life. It is a collage, an assemblage, a merz-bild, a Cornell box. Everything that exists is also worth saving. We are flooded with a comic abundance.

Elkin's vision is so firmly anchored in the material world that it seems much more surreal than real, by the familiar optical illu- sion by which intense concentration on a material object causes that object to disappear as such and to disintegrate into new and startling combinations of its qualities. Everything is in excess, overflowing, a cornucopia, as if the characters are trying to stay alive by their ability to see and name the physical world. It is a kind of word magic, what Maurice Samuel has called "the humor of verbal retrieval, the word triumphant over the situation"[22]—a condition especially prominent in the works of Sholom Al- eichem. Despite the despair, there is an element of joyous abandon in all this, as in Ben Flesh's extravagant catalogue of Baskin-Robbins's ice-cream flavors:

> Chocolate like new shoes. Cherry like bright fingernail polish. We do a Maple Ripple it looks like fine-grained wood, a Peach like light coming through a lampshade. You should see that stuff—the ice-cream paints bright as posters, fifty Day-Glo colors. You scoop the stuff up you feel like Jackson Pollock. (*The Franchiser,* p. 277)

This is not realistic but hallucinatory. In the synesthetic conceits, the most heterogeneous images have been yoked together by violence. With his magical naming, Elkin wallows in exhibitionistic artifice and a feeling of overwrought, bursting fullness.[23]

Elkin's obsessiveness has been much noted both by himself (in interview) and by critics.[24] He says flatly that "fiction is about obsession,"[25] and that "most of the characters I write about are obsessed by death."[26] This is undoubtedly true, but it is too large a generalization to do justice to the obsessiveness of Elkin's characters. At their best, they are wonderfully energized, concentrated, self-directed on some single idea or vision. They illustrate, with great appropriateness, Bergson's theories of comedy: his ideas of professional deformation, mechanization, and comic inelasticity.[27] Elkin's characters possess a form of manic monomania, which expresses itself in a highly obsessive language of jargon, shoptalk, and professional acting-out.

Elkin singles out "The Bailbondsman" as his favorite story and its protagonist, Alexander Main, as his most representative character. Without elaborating on the autobiographical assumptions, Elkin says: "I admire him for his rhetoric. I, myself, am closer to Main than any other character."[28] Why should this be so? Main has a mad obsession with his job. Outside of being a bailbondsman in the world of courts and prisons, Main has no other identity, and he has inflamed dreams in the style of *Raiders of the Lost Ark* of pyramid thieves and mummy despoilers for whom he offers bail in unimaginable sums. He is Alexander Main, the Phoenician, the Ba'albondsman. Elkin has always been fascinated by obsessive excess and has felt only boredom for well-rounded and versatile human beings. The Bailbondsman has a Dickensian fervor and eccentricity, like some legal fiction dropped out of *Bleak House:*

> I love a contract like the devil, admire the tall paper and the small print—I mean the *print,* the lawful shapes and stately content.

Forget word games, secret clause, forget hidden meaning and ambiguity, all those dense thickets of type where the fast ones lie like lost balls. Your forest-for-the-trees crap is myth, the sucker's special pleading. I'll fuck you in letters nine feet high if I've a mind. I beat no one with loophole. Everything spelled out, all clear, aboveboard as chessmen: truth in advertising and a language even the dishonest understand.[29]

The bailbondsman has the salesman's obsessive self-love for his stock, and is in fact a kind of salesman. He is a freedom merchant. He is in love with legal paper and the power this gives him to control human destiny. Like many of Elkin's protagonists, he is a spieler and charlatan as well as a man of the highest probity. He feels a mad and unpredictable compassion for human suffering and weakness in all of its sordid manifestations.

In his avalanche of metaphors and figurative language, Alexander Main is also intensely literal. He is talking about the physical contract itself that constitutes the bail bond:

No, I'm talking the *look* of the instrument, texture, watermark, the silk flourish of the bright ribbon, the legend perfected centuries (I'll tell you in a moment about the Phoenicians), the beautiful formulas simple as pie, old-fashioned quid pro quo like a recipe in the family generations. My conditions classic and my terms terminal. Listen, I haven't much law—though what I have is on my side, binding as clay, advantage to the house—but am as at home in replevin, debenture and gage as someone on his own toilet seat with the door closed and the house empty. I have mainpernor, bottomry, caution and hypothecation the way others might have a second language. I have always lived by *casus foederis;* do the same and we'll never tangle assholes. (pp. 5–6)

The language here is both effortless and endless, and it comfortably mixes technical jargon with street slang. Elkin is wonderfully cozy with his puns, wordplay, and self-conscious verbalizing. This is the kind of tumescent rhetoric that has no relation at all to real life. It creates its own obsessively believable world.

I began by trying to define Stanley Elkin, against his own vociferous objections, as a Jewish black humorist. Yet I must conclude that if Elkin is indeed a Jewish black humorist, he is unlike any other Jewish black humorist of our era. He certainly avoids any sentimental identifications with Jewish characters, and most of his protagonists are not specifically Jewish at all. I

have invoked Kazin's concept of "constructed folklore" to explain Elkin's Jewishness, as if it were not a matter of conscious
intent and as if there were no need to inject Jewishness into one's
fictions. In other words, Elkin's imaginative evocation is Jewish
even if it is not neatly labeled in the Jewish Ghetto Exhibit. From
a stylistic perspective, Elkin writes with an extravagance, a mingling of the trivial and the grandiose, and ironic undercutting of
all pretension and mindless optimism that does not need Yiddish
diction to make it feel Jewish. Criers and kibitzers divide among
themselves the domain of Jewish black humor. As in the theories
of Sigmund Freud in *Jokes and Their Relation to the Unconscious,* comedy is a way of mastering anxiety and laughter is a
defense against imminent catastrophe. It is not surprising that
Freud's abstruse theories are so solidly based on the most obvious and corny of Jewish jokes.

When the bound and bleeding Saint Sebastian was asked
whether it hurt to be so powerless and so pierced with deadly
arrows, he is supposed to have answered: "Only when I laugh."
This is archetypal Jewish black humor. As a sick-joke parable,
the punch line indicates that we cannot have it both ways, that it
has to hurt for us to be able to laugh, and that the innocuous will
not inherit the earth. No one can accuse Stanley Elkin of being
bland. In the aggressive incisiveness of his Jewish black humor,
he seems to be saying not that the world is a good place to live in,
but that the only true man is the wise fool, and that comic
acceptance and exaltation can come only through suffering.

NOTES

1. Phyllis and Joseph Bernt, "Stanley Elkin on Fiction: An Interview,"
Prairie Schooner 50 (1976): 22.

2. Doris G. Bargen, *The Fiction of Stanley Elkin,* vol. 8 in *Studien und
Texte zur Amerikanistic* (Frankfurt: Peter D. Lang, 1980), p. 225. Bargen
includes a long interview with Elkin recorded in 1975.

3. Thomas LeClair, "Stanley Elkin: The Art of Fiction LXI," *Paris
Review* 66 (Summer 1976): 70.

4. Bargen, *The Fiction of Stanley Elkin,* p. 225.

5. Alfred Kazin, *Bright Book of Life: American Novelists and Storytellers from Hemingway to Mailer* (New York: Dell, 1974), p. 138.

6. See Robert Alter's remarks on "the persistence of a Jewish modality
of imagination even in the total absence of Jewish realia" in *Henderson the*

Rain King ("Jewish Humor and the Domestication of Myth," in *Veins of Humor,* ed. Harry Levin [Cambridge, MA: Harvard University Press, 1972], p. 257).

7. Robert Alter, "Sentimentalizing the Jews," in *After the Tradition: Essays on Modern Jewish Writing* (New York: Dutton, 1971), p. 39.

8. Stanley Elkin, "The Condominium," in *Searches and Seizures* (New York: Random House, 1973), p. 250.

9. Stanley Elkin, *Boswell: A Modern Comedy* (New York: Random House, 1964), p. 201.

10. Stanley Elkin, *The Living End* (New York: Dutton, 1979), p. 148.

11. Stanley Elkin, "Criers and Kibitzers, Kibitzers and Criers," in *Criers and Kibitzers, Kibitzers and Criers* (New York: Random House, 1965), pp. 13–14.

12. I am following the account of Jewish humor in Earl Rovit, "Jewish Humor and American Life," *The American Scholar* 36 (1967): 237–45.

13. Stanley Elkin, *The Franchiser* (New York: Farrar, Straus, and Giroux, 1976; Boston: David R. Godine, 1980), p. 87.

14. LeClair, "Stanley Elkin," p. 56.

15. LeClair, "Stanley Elkin," p. 57.

16. Stanley Elkin, *A Bad Man* (New York: Random House, 1967), p. 43.

17. Bargen, *The Fiction of Stanley Elkin,* p. 244.

18. Stanley Elkin, *George Mills* (New York: Dutton, 1982), p. 429.

19. Bargen, *The Fiction of Stanley Elkin,* pp. 236–37.

20. See Sanford Pinsker, *The Schlemiel as Metaphor* (Carbondale: Southern Illinois University Press, 1971), and Ruth R. Wisse, *The Schlemiel as Modern Hero* (Chicago: University of Chicago Press, 1971).

21. Philip Stevick, "Prolegomena to the Study of Fictional *Dreck,*" in *Comic Relief: Humor in Contemporary American Literature,* ed. Sarah Blacher Cohen (Urbana: University of Illinois Press, 1978), p. 278.

22. Quoted in Sarah Blacher Cohen, *Saul Bellow's Enigmatic Laughter* (Urbana: University of Illinois Press, 1974), p. 20.

23. William Gass, in the Foreword to the 1980 edition of *The Franchiser,* is certainly right to invoke Ben Jonson and his cultivated jargon and elaborately technical vocabularies (p. ix). Jonson delights in the magic of naming in such "big" plays as *Bartholomew Fair, Volpone,* and *The Alchemist.*

24. Thomas LeClair, "The Obsessional Fiction of Stanley Elkin," *Contemporary Literature* 16 (1975): 146–62.

25. LeClair, "Stanley Elkin," p. 67.

26. Bernt, "Stanley Elkin on Fiction," p. 15.

27. Henri Bergson, *Le Rire* (1900), tran. as *Laughter,* in *Comedy,* ed. Wylie Sypher (Garden City, N.Y.: Doubleday Anchor, 1956).

28. LeClair, "Stanley Elkin," p. 84.

29. Stanley Elkin, "The Bailbondsman," in *Searches and Seizures* (New York: Random House, 1973), p. 5.

MORDECAI RICHLER AND JEWISH-CANADIAN HUMOR

MICHAEL GREENSTEIN

Mordecai Richler would probably agree that Jewish-Canadian humor is neither Jewish, nor Canadian, nor humorous. Forever *kvetching* about the crass provincialism of Jews within the Canadian mosaic, Richler frequently casts a wistful glance south toward the American metropolis with its "ghetto cosmopolitanism":[1] "Looking down on the cultural life of New York from here, it appears to be a veritable yeshiva. I won't even go into the question of Broadway or television, but from *Commentary* by way of *Partisan Review* to the *Noble Savage,* from Knopf to Grove Press, the Jewish writers seem to call each to each, editing, praising, slamming one another's books, plays, and cultural conference appearances."[2] The absence of any Canadian equivalent to Broadway or Hollywood—those promised lands of laughter—renders the Jewish-Canadian humorist more marginal than his counterpart in the United States. Richler fills this void with his comic characters who take revenge on a society that confines them to a double marginality: as Jews, they have to fight against a peripheral position within a class-conscious Canadian mosaic that, unlike the American melting-pot, hinders assimilation and recognition; as Canadians, they are denied acceptance into a Jewish-American alliance that has achieved mainstream status. If Canada is "the No-man's-Land, the Demilitarized Zone . . . invisible from South of the Border as well as from the Other Side of the Atlantic,"[3] then Richler's highly visible, militant satire invades this buffer zone and seeks to restore hyphenated Jewish-Canadians from margins to center stage.

"To be a Jew and a Canadian," claims Richler, "is to emerge from the ghetto twice, for self-conscious Canadians, like some touchy Jews, tend to contemplate the world through a wrong-ended telescope. . . . Like Jews again, Canadians are inclined to regard with a mixture of envy and suspicion those who have forsaken the homestead (or *shtetl*) for the assimilationist flesh-pots of New York or London."[4] An astronomer of the near-at-hand, Richler brandishes that telescope, satirically surveying American and British perspectives from his vantage point in Montreal. "Decentered"[5] between New York's promised land and London's imperial control, the doubly displaced Jewish Canadian uses humor to challenge the authority of these cultural capitals. Vengefully he tracks pretenders of the faith on both sides of Montreal's invisible ghetto walls, those comic hurdles separating the Jewish immigrant from a WASP establishment. At one end of Mr. Richler's planet lies a parochial ghetto surrounded by English-Canadian and French-Canadian solitudes: at the other end, the universal influences of Anglo-American culture beckon; and in between, comic lenses invert, reverse, and distort these incompatible extremes. With his optical instrument indelicately poised between lowered brows and uplifted nostrils (inhaling ghetto odors), that suffering joker reminds us of our wrong-ended emergence from immodest origins—*inter urinam et faeces nascimur.*

In the Laurentians north of Montreal, Richler trains his telescope on a sign: THIS BEACH IS RESTRICTED TO LITVAKS. Here the revenger's comedy is at play, erasing natural boundaries that have become cultural barriers, insisting that marginality and territorial exclusion have no place in the New World, and rewriting the history of precedence with graffiti, comic inscriptions that open eyes by turning private privilege into public mockery. Sectarian Litvaks wage a holy war using wit as their weapon to proclaim their tribal chosenness, the superiority of the last laugh canceling any pretense to gentility. While the Gentiles refuse to mingle in the flesh on the beach, the Jews advertise their verbal mingling through the flesh made word. Back in Montreal, where persecuted Jews learned to read the writing on the ghetto wall, Semitic and semiotic compete humorously in capitalist advertisements such as DON'T BUY FROM THE *GOYISHE* CHIP MAN—FELDER IS YOUR FRIEND FOR LIFE. Richler's satiric revenge exposes the hypocrisy of such signs which are but a shorthand, the brief soul of wit. Confronted with these signs, his comic heroes stake out their territory, craftily cross borders, and trespass; in turn, they avenge themselves on other interlopers through a series of practical jokes that may have tragicomic or grotesque consequences.

Following from an earlier American tradition of *The Rise of David Levinsky, The Education of Hyman Kaplan,* and *The Adventures of Augie March, The Apprenticeship of Duddy Kravitz* (1959) chronicles the comic emergence of its young hero from Montreal's ghetto twice—as a Canadian and as a Jew. Born on the wrong side of the tracks with a rusty spoon in his mouth and the spark of rebellion in him, Duddy races across those tracks and rebels against all forms of silver-spooned authority. In crossing spiky tracks, he frequently has to retrace his steps, double-cross his friends and adversaries, and trip anyone who stands in his way, lest he himself be tripped by a society that blocks his path at every turn. Duddy's Uncle Benjy dislikes him because he is "a *pusherke*. A little Jew-boy on the make" (p. 244). Duddy knows that it's push or perish. He must push against time, racing around the clock ("ideas are ticking over like bombs in his head. Tick-tock, tick-tock"), trying to abandon the little Jew-boy in favor of a bigger man. He must push against space, abandoning the hostile soil of Montreal's ghetto and expanding to possess land in the Laurentians. And he must push against society, all those people who get in the way of his apprenticeship, fulfillment, and recognition as a man. Duddy answers Benjy: "You think I should be running after something else besides money? . . . And there won't be any superior *drecks* there to laugh at me or run me off." What Duddy loses sight of, and this is what makes him laughable, is that the *pusherke* is trapped between his past as pariah and his future as parvenu: "making it" translates into an apprenticeship toward becoming a comic *macher* rather than a respectable *mensch*. Fighting superior *drecks* is a messy business in which the victor ends up being just another superior *dreck*, a comic effort because ultimately self-defeating. Duddy, forever running, parodies the Wandering Jew, and Bergsonian laughter results from the mechanical nature of his acceleration.

By running compulsively, Duddy takes revenge against time, outwitting at break-neck speed both the clock and his opponents who stigmatize him as *schlemiel*. His apprenticeship must be as short-lived as possible in order to establish his role as anti-*schlemiel;* his is an apprenticeship marked by the comic transitions from boy to man, from immigrant to full citizenship, from working class to middle class, and from marginality to center of attention. At Fletcher's Field High School Duddy yearns for recognition, becomes class president, perfects his practical jokes, shaves to encourage a beard, and threatens anyone who invades his territory. He rebels against WASP authority in the person of his teacher Mr. MacPherson, a representative of British imperialism in Canadian education, by telephoning his moribund wife, thereby causing her death. An aggressive *pusherke* inevitably clashes with an outmoded colonial mentality: reversing the roles, Duddy teaches MacPherson the rules of Americanization and Yiddishization, speed and wit. MacPherson predicts that Duddy will go far, but sometimes he goes too far—and too fast. In Richler's hands, the comedy of cultural revenge transmogrifies into black humor or grotesque tragicomedy.

One of Duddy's blueprints for his emergence from the boy-man *schlemiel* dilemma comes from his Uncle Benjy's posthumous letter: "a boy can be two, three, four potential people, but a man is only one. He murders the others." To become a *mensch* rather than a *pusherke* Duddy must possess himself by destroying a multiplicity of personalities who accentuate his psychological marginality. The boy reflects a series of characters while the man establishes his individuality, the Jewish immigrant imitates established models en route to full citizenship, and the colonized Canadian apes British and American influences. According to Freud, "The comic, like the ego, is in rivalry with itself";[8] and Duddy's comic apprenticeship revolves around the *pusherke*'s rivalry with several potential people—Canadian, British, and American *machers*—all projections of his own ego. A resourceful chameleon or Jewish comedian, he demonstrates how parodic imitation is one of the highest forms of laughter. MacPherson, trudging along the scalp of glittering white ice in the heart of Montreal's Jewish ghetto, mirrors Duddy's similar actions on the Laurentian landscape. Duddy ruins MacPherson, with his Presbyterian heritage, for trespassing, and manages to exploit the anti-Semitic French-Canadian claim to Lac St. Pierre. Shrewdness knows no bounds, the sleek inherit the earth, for Duddy recognizes enemy territory surrounding St. Urbain's ghetto: to the east, French-Canadians, with their heckles of *maudit juif;* to the west, thrifty Scots with a different kind of commerce from that practiced by the crafty Kravitzes;[9] and in between, comic slogans, abbreviated wit, and a *pusherke* on the make, taking aim at adversaries but blinded to the possibility that his own ego may be his ultimate target. Slings and arrows become comic boomerangs.

A sorcerer's apprentice, Duddy inherits from his grandfather that magical American-Jewish formula, "a man without land is nobody," and he soon loses control. Obsessed with possession of land, he becomes possessed as if by a *dybbuk,* that soul not only of his uncle and grandfather, but of all his ghettoized European ancestors denied ownership of land. To exorcise the *dybbuk* that has crossed the Atlantic in steerage and caught up with the youngest Kravitz, he has to murder two or more potential people in his path, those *doppelgängers* who resemble him on his climb to first-class accommodation. Foremost among these is Jerry Dingleman, the voice of authority within the ghetto. Apprenticed to Dingleman, the Boy Wonder who has been paralyzed by polio, Duddy learns quickly how to become the "chief rabbi of Montreal's underworld." Just as Duddy dangles comically between boyhood and manhood, so his crippled model is a grotesque "dingle" between boy and man. Using Duddy for purposes of smuggling dope across the border, Dingleman introduces him to New York where he is totally disoriented as ghetto regionalism comes into contact with cosmopolitan society. Mocked by Dingleman and his American-Jewish connections, Duddy displaces him when he catches him trespassing on his property. David Kravitz fells yet another Goliath with his slingshot of guile, speed, and vengeful language; but since almost everyone in the novel is a Philistine, Duddy's shot boomerangs and murders four or more potential people who are extensions of his own boyhood. Where Joyce's artist resorts to silence, exile, and cunning, Richler's con artist uses boisterousness, acquisitive omnipresence, and comic cunning to remove obstacles.

With MacPherson and Dingleman down, Duddy seems to have removed the major gentile and Jewish obstacles on his road to recognition. But he still has to "murder" a few other minor characters before he emerges as a man who has dusted off any vestiges of the *schlemiel.* Like MacPherson and Dingleman, the epileptic Virgil attests to Uncle Benjy's maxim that experience deforms rather than teaches, for Duddy's apprenticeship turns into a lesson in *de*formation of self and others. Virgil attempts to identify himself with Duddy: "We're a persecuted minority. Like the Jews and the Negroes." But Duddy winces at this sort of identification that would drag him down; instead, Duddy reverses hierarchies and persecutes all other minorities or majorities in his bid for recognition. When Virgil proceeds to list history's greatest epileptics—Julius Caesar, Jesus Christ, Dostoievski, and Charlie Chaplin—Duddy retorts that Chaplin is a Jew, whereupon Virgil insists "a guy can be both you know." The paradigmatic *schlemiel* Charlie Chaplin can be both, but the anti-*schlemiel* or *pusherke* has to overcome at least one handicap; as Duddy interprets Uncle Benjy's tragicomic formulation, he has to murder his alter ego, destroying Virgil exactly as he had earlier killed Mrs. MacPherson. Rivalry with his alter ego rebounds: the *pusherke* ends up pushing himself, his own greatest obstacle to becoming an instant *mensch*. *Menschlechkeit* takes time, so Duddy's frenetic compression of economic history is doomed to comic failure.

More than either Dingleman or Virgil, Cuckoo Kaplan represents the Americanization of Jewish comic values on the Canadian scene. As a boy, Duddy merely echoes his mentor and stand-up comedian with phrases such as "that's show biz," clichés of frozen *shpritz;* as a man, he must transcend Cuckoo's failures and emerge as an individual instead of merely aping the comic gestures of others. Montreal's own Danny Kaye imports Jewish-American comic routines even as he exports himself to play nightclubs in the States. His measure of success may be taken as one of the characteristics of Jewish-Canadian humor; lacking a Broadway, a Borscht Belt, or a Hollywood, and confined to Rubin's Laurentian outpost in Ste Agathe, Jewish-Canadian humor defines itself in relation to the larger American stage. Like Kravitz, Kaplan remains a boy because he is fixated as a Canadian, a Jew, and a comedian—a blend that works against maturity into manhood. Like Kaplan who pursues his American Dream in New York, Kravitz fantasizes about his brother Bradley having made it on a ranch in Arizona. For both of them to become men with the stamp of individual identity, they must stop imitating influential characters and murder the comic tendency to mimic several potential people. By extension, they both serve as examples of how Jewish-Canadian humor must transcend mere parodying of external models if it is to mature as an indigenous culture, just as Richler must contend with the American-Jewish influence of Bellow, Roth, and Malamud who cast a long shadow northward.

Having pushed against the margins of a rigid society, and having outrun time, the trickster prepares to become a somebody on his own land, but his confusion between *macher* and *mensch* parallels his inability to distinguish natural beauty from real estate. Duddy's illusory expansion from boy to man is matched by his illusion of expanding from Montreal's ghetto to possession of land in the country; the adolescent's race against time complements his need to conquer rural space. But to that serious Canadian problem of survival in the wilderness, he brings a comic American-Jewish solution: the *pusherke* will push against the frontier and merely transplant St. Urbain's ghetto values to Ste Agathe's less hostile soil. Enter the pusher's machine in the garden: Duddy will fell the pine forests, peddle the trees at Christmas-time, and construct a summer camp and ski-run. In the midst of all this natural beauty he "urinated into a snow bank, writing his name" (p. 212). More accustomed to commercial banks than snow banks, he soon gets lost on his own property: "What the hell am I doing lost in a blizzard, a Jewish boy? Moses, he recalled from *Bible Comics,* died without ever reaching the Promised Land, and *I've* got my future to think of. . . . If God pulls me through, he thought, I'll give up screwing for two weeks. Smoked meats, too" (p. 212). In this divine comedy, cosmic Kravitz ranges from swearing in hell to burning his feet on Lac St. Pierre's purgatory to swearing a heavenly oath. Trained on Bible comics, this Jewish boy wants to surpass Moses and offer animal sacrifices of sex and the delicatessen's burnt offerings, provided that his period of cleanliness does not exceed a two-week eternity. Like his forefathers, Duddy bargains with a jealous God. The discrepancy between Duddy's future and his religious past, and the discrepancy between a Promised Land and his promises to regain Paradise, reduce the isolated boy on land to a common, recognizable *landsman*.

The anti-*schlemiel* who detests the song, "We are little black sheep who have gone astray," projects his anti-pastoral vision of a northern Vegas: "Round and round she goes, where she stops nobody knows. It's up to fate. Kismet, as they say. Outside, the stars don't care. They shine on and on. Midnight, the monkey-business hour. Bears prowl the woods, a wolf howls for its mate.

Somewhere a wee babe is screaming for its mommy. . . . The waiters and office girls are banging away for dear life on the beach: nature. PLUNK! The wheel stops. *Zero*" (p. 282). Kismet, fate, the roulette wheel, those circular deterministic forces grind away whatever free will the *schlemiel* possesses, but the anti-*schlemiel* or *pusherke* runs dizzying comic circles around these cosmic powers. An indifferent universe looks on as the animal in Duddy performs its financial business, show business, or monkey business. He prowls woods and ghetto pavement, howls for his mate, screams for his dead mother, and bangs away for dear life against life's oppressive forces. Ginsberg's, Portnoy's, Kravitz's primordial howl against the prime ordeal of civility may be fraught with the contradictory forces of *angst* and peals of laughter. The *schlemiel* never moves beyond zero; the anti-*schlemiel* runs circles counterclockwise, against himself, against society, only to find himself back at the starting point. The land remains fixed, the runner fixated—noboduddy in no-man's-land.

A scheming, older Duddy resurfaces in *St. Urbain's Horseman* (1972), but the novel's central focus is on his former classmate, Jake Hersh, one-time pusher turned middle-aged film director, who has trouble directing his own life in London. In the best *schlemiel* tradition, that ludicrous victim Jake finds himself on trial for a sexual offense he did not commit. But Jake is also on trial for being out of place: in crossing borders from Montreal to London, Jake emerges from narrow ghetto to broader Diaspora, from colony to capital, and from lower-class origins to middle-class middle age. Out of this twofold or multifold emergence arises Richler's humor.

During his trial at London's Old Bailey, disjointed Jake proudly recreates his Jewish and Canadian heritage as a way of comically escaping his present trials. "Jew boys and WASP Canadians, Jake knew, had a long and dishonorable association with the Number One Court of the London Assizes. He wasn't the first."[10] By placing him in the company of other questionable rogues, Richler takes the sting out of Jake's personal trial and overturns the courtly tables so that the scales of British justice now stand on trial. "In 1710, when Jonathan Wild, the Prince of Robbers, was the unquestioned *numero uno* of the London underworld, his indispensable aide was a *macher* named Abraham" (p. 42). Instead of looking back tragically like Orpheus, Richler's

comic rogues transcend their underworld to emerge into a ghettoized imprisonment at Newgate and the Old Bailey. If British
Jews were traditionally barred from the upper reaches of polite
society, they enjoyed recognition without prejudice behind bars
where they were able to keep "a kosher cell." Just as Richler
celebrates the emancipation of Jews in prison, so he admires the
achievements of Canadians in this jest society. "Among WASP
Canadian precursors, Jake, of necessity, identified most closely
with the cross-eyed sex nut, junkie, and McGill alumnus, Thomas
Niell Cream" (p. 43). Another *macher* and cream of the colonial
crop, Jake finds himself in good comic company and manages to
escape the accusing jurors' eyes by singing to himself.

> I'm not a butcher, I'm not a Yid.
> Nor yet a foreign skipper,
> But I'm your own light-hearted friend,
> Yours truly, Jake the Ripper.

The *schlemiel,* court jester, or innocent criminal, part of a Jewish-Canadian community, moves to the center of courtly
attention and through a "light-heartedness" rises above present
circumstantial evidence. Richler's humor plays both margins
against the middle and serves two purposes: it acts on behalf of
Jewish-Canadian defendants, and it acts as a plaintiff arguing
against British hierarchical pretensions.

But Jake's public trial carries over into his private life as he
frequently undergoes self-examination at a mirror that always
traps him. "Now Jake stood nude, legs spread wide apart and
back to the hall mirror, bent over with his head bobbing between
his knees, probing his ass hole for cancer nails" (p. 14). Knowing
that the unexamined life is not worth living, Richler inverts and
reverses his protagonist's morbid vision. With lowered trousers,
lowered brow, and low mimetic vision, comedy seeks the lowest
common denominator, dissects the anatomy of folly, under-
reaching instead of over-reaching, deflating the excesses of
hubris. The proud boast, "my son, the doctor," turns into the
Portnoyesque complaint, "my protagonist, the patient," with the
emphasis not on the whole man, but on the synecdochic sum of
the reductive parts—whether anal, oral, or genital. Comedy dis-
solves the boundaries between guilt and innocence, between an
entire self and its parts. In his mixed marriage, Jake, as St.
Urbain's horseman, feels guilty about "riding" his pregnant wife,

"Holy Mother, Our Lady of the Orifices," (p. 226) to a climax, fearing damage to his unborn son. "Some how-do-you-do, ramming him like a crazed billygoat. He was tormented by a vision of the boy, his *kaddish,* born with a depression in his skull, bearing into manhood the imprint of Jake's cockshead in his scalp." In this *felix culpa,* centaur exchanges roles with Pan, and the grotesque vision confuses birth and death, origin and aftermath, pagan and Jew. Ten years earlier in Spain, Jake had found himself in the midst of an orgy: "This is living, Yankel. . . . One leg, then another, locking his neck. Arms driving his head toward a churning vagina . . . and he felt very ghetto-liberated" (pp. 12–13). The outsider becomes insider, but the scene ends with hedonistic Hersh vomiting. Yankel is liberated from the ghetto only to be imprisoned by thighs, sea-sick from the passage between Montreal and Ibiza, as the transition to universalism and paganism proves to be an illusion. The battle between id and super-ego ends in a confused Yiddish ego, questioning its innocence, sanity, and involvement. Where anti-Semitism has found the Jew guilty simply because he is a Jew, the comedy of retribution in the person of a *schlemiel* looks for a scapegoat (or billygoat) in some form of crime from which he is innocent, but which he flirts with in order to displace guilt from abstract stereotype to something more concrete.

The trial also impinges on Jake's domestic life when his lawyer, Ormsby-Fletcher, invites him to his country home for dinner. Observing his own unorthodox dietary laws, Jake arrives with a salami-on-rye in his pocket. Outside the Georgian cottage, roses, hydrangeas, dahlias; inside, unappetizing food as insipid as Jake's sandwich is spicy. Intuitively he retreats to the bathroom where he can munch safely on his sandwich, inspect his hostess's laundry hamper, and infer her naughty tendencies from her laced panties. After-dinner conversation ranges from sexual jokes to artistic appreciation, but Jake's salami acts as a laxative, so he returns to the upstairs toilet. His anti-hero fails to adjust to the norms of British society even in the toilet where the foreign plumbing fails him: "the stool floated level with the toilet seat. Flood tide. Pig, Jake thought. Sensualist. Hirsute Jew" (p. 184). In this clash between nature and culture, between the organic and the mechanical, we are uncertain whether to blame the inadequate toilet which may have atrophied from British constipation (at most those polite bite-sized foods) or the Jew's salami-sized stool. In either case, Jake, his origins, and his end-product are all misfits; the toilet reveals the physical discrepancy within the horse-man, midway between Yahoo and Houyhnhnm. He carries on a talmudic debate with himself in the privacy of the privy. "Disgust for it is bourgeois. Yes, yes, but how do I pick it up? Sunshine soldier! Social democrat! Middlebrow!" (p. 185)— the questions and exclamations of the archetypal *schlemiel,* anal retentive, never fully able to rid himself of embarrassment, nor able to retrieve his whole self. But instead of resorting to the physical means of grabbing his feces, Jake relies on his quick wit and rushes to the downstairs toilet. *"Baruch ato Adonoi,* he said twice, before he pulled the chain. It flushed." Saved by a comic, Jewish *deus ex machina,* Jake emerges triumphant while Ormsby-Fletcher's child is left to take the blame. The juxtaposition of the Jewish-Canadian guest holding his jockey shorts and undergoing his ordeal of civility, and the bourgeois British hostess, whose laced black panties undercut her artistic aspirations, creates much of the situational humor. Always a guest, never fully assimilated, the diaspora Jew carries a burden which is sometimes displaced to scatological, comic regions and must be rectified, not by deferred eschatological dreams, but by his immediacy of wit and cultural revenge. The Jewish media director is neither inner nor outer-directed, but lower-directed, mediating reality and fantasy.

If the metaphor of the "horseman" in its physical manifestations points to comic baseness and bestiality, it also serves in its mythical dimensions as a prop for the hero's preservation amid his trials. Where Duddy Kravitz runs as a boy in the ghetto, Jake Hersh gallops as a horseman through the Diaspora. Jake keeps a journal of the Horseman, a kind of messianic figure who is ostensibly his cousin Joey Hersh, but also assumes several aliases. Occasionally Joey and Jake become interchangeable, as the spirit of the former intrudes on Jake's life, with Richler once again employing the doppleganger motif and its Yiddish variant, the *dybbuk.* Jake is obsessed by the avenging Horseman who seeks out the Nazi criminal, *Doktor* Josef Mengele, in Paraguay. Beside the Nazi crimes, Jake's sexual offense (of which he is innocent) appears trivial. In his revenge, the Horseman of the Diaspora crosses the borders of Galilee, Mexico, Germany, Catalonia, and Paraguay, but there is a comic tension between these heroic exploits and their mythic projections by Jake Hersh who merely records his fantasies in a diary tucked away in the attic of his highly domesticated London home. While the Horseman crosses international borders, the Hersh man has trouble squeezing between the bed and the baby in the bassinet, for his protruding stomach, a sign of affluence and indolence, interferes with his ascent to the attic. His desk is arranged as in a parody of a British spy novel so as to detect any intruders, but he himself cannot recall the measurements and angles of these snares, and in any case, they had been set against his mother. What appears to be cosmic, turns out to be comic, the *schlemiel* having to defend himself against the advances of a Jewish-Canadian mother.

The first reference in Jake's journal is to Isaac Babel: "When a Jew gets on a horse he stops being a Jew," (p. 34) presumably because Jews have been so accustomed to being the underdogs. Yet humor elevates Jake from inferior status to an equestrian of the comic cavalry in a quest for recognition. A cross-reference to F. Scott Fitzgerald's *The Last Tycoon* shows the Jews on horseback seeking cultural revenge against the history of victimization. When Jake goes to Germany to find Cousin Joey, the Horseman, he figures out that the true identity of Joey Hersh, also known as Jesse Hope and Yosef Ben Baruch, is the Golem, "a sort of Jewish Batman"—hence a comic hero or body without soul who wanders the world defending Jews. The Golem or body in search of a soul seems to be the converse of the *dybbuk* or soul in search of a body: until body and soul unite to form the whole person, until *dybbuk* meets Golem, Jewish comedy will prevail in parading the mishaps and confusions of this mythic tradition scattered around the globe. On his horse, Don Quixote sees giants in place of windmills; on his horse, Jake Hersh sees larger-than-life vaginas and stools in place of dignity and acceptance. "What if the Horseman was a distorting mirror and we each took the self-justifying image we required of him?" (p. 464) Jake answers his rhetorical question by reciting the Ten Commandments, but the answer also lies in the distorting mirror of comedy which reflects Jake's anus and justifies his self to the British public.

At the end of the novel Jake grabs a revolver in his hand. "Feh, he thought. . . . Pick it up, chicken" (p. 465). The gun recalls Jake's stool at Ormsby-Fletcher's, so we know that even when he presses the barrel to his forehead, the Jewish comedian will intervene: "*Putz,* you can hurt yourself," but the gun fires only blanks. Like comedy, his weapon misfires, making a loud noise but creating no damage; the monosyllabic *shpritz,* "Feh" or "putz," defuses a potentially dangerous situation. Even when a *pusherke* pulls the trigger, the *schlemiel* backfires and sprays himself innocently. Richler's protagonist has his day in comic court where he levels British hierarchical tradition with his Jewish-American egalitarianism and comic fraternity.

Richler's most recent novel, *Joshua Then and Now* (1980), exploits many of the comic themes first introduced in *Duddy Kravitz* and later developed in *St. Urbain's Horseman.* Indeed, the first half of the title refers to the 1940s childhood of Joshua Shapiro who, like Duddy and Jake, attended Fletcher's Field High School in Montreal's ghetto; Joshua "now" belongs to a later generation looking back at the earlier period, and most of the humor arises from the transformations that have taken place from the protagonist's childhood to his life as an adult. Where Jake Hersh is a media director and private historian of the Horseman, Josh Shapiro is a television personality and social historian who has passed through his Diaspora phase to return to his Montreal homeland. Within one generation, the outsider-turned-insider has made it up from St. Urbain's ghetto to the gilded garrison of Westmount, from immigrant marginality to Canadian centrality. This dichotomy between "then" and "now," not only in Joshua's personal history but in Canadian and Jewish history, plagues him wherever he turns. "Canadian-born, he sometimes felt as if he were condemned to lope slant-shouldered through the world that confused him. One shoulder sloping downwards, groaning under the weight of his Jewish heritage (burnings on the market square, crazed Cossacks on the rampage, gas chambers, as well as Moses, Rabbi Akiba, and Maimonides); the other thrust heavenwards, yearning for an inheritance, any inheritance, weightier than the construction of a transcontinental railway, a reputation for honest trading, good skiing conditions."[11] Loping, sloping, and interloping, this grotesque golem in search of a soul wanders through the Diaspora, laughable because lopsided, split between two legacies, one defying death, the other powerless to be born. To overcome his comically divided self—mind-body, upper-lower, Jewish-Canadian—Joshua tries to recapture a sense of wholeness and balance through revenge against anyone concealing the past. With Mai-

monides's *The Guide for the Perplexed* as his Baedeker through
the labyrinths of history, Joshua struggles against his own confusions and unmasks those characters hiding behind the superficial veneer of a present that conceals their modest roots.

Joshua has inherited a comic genetic code from both of his
parents. His bar mitzvah, a "then" episode, marks the pseudo-
transition from boy to man, as his mother ceremoniously performs a striptease to the delight and embarrassment of the boys.
Shedding her garments, Esther Shapiro simultaneously strips
away conventional decency so highly prized by the other Jewish
mothers. The more she is socially scorned, the greater her defiance in displaying her underwear on the ghetto's laundry line
where a middlebrow visual community may be readily established. Richler flaunts his Queen Esther, moving her out of the
closet and onto the clothesline, from embarrassing underworld of
taboo to front row; turning bar mitzvah into burlesque, he shows
what happens when religion becomes sociology, Judaism
changed into vulgar Jewishness.

And Josh's pugilistic father, Reuben, hands him an equally
aggressive comic tradition in which a hypertrophied body comes
to terms with its atrophied intellectual powers. A Bible in one
hand, a glass of ale in the other, Reuben Shapiro mixes high and
low brow, teaching his son "about fucking, and the Jewish tradition." The Shapiros' muscular Judaism has little patience with a
muted *mentshlechkeit,* and their attempts to integrate the two
extremes into a unified society meet with inevitably comic results. Reuben opens his Bible for a lesson in humorous hermeneutics that parallels his pugilistic instruction. "Quote, Thou
shalt have no other gods before me, unquote. You see there were
lots of contenders, other gods, mostly no-account idols, bums-
of-the-month, before our God, Jehovah, took the title outright,
and made a covenant with our forefathers who he had helped out
of Egypt. A covenant is a contract" (p. 81). Even Shapiro quotes
scripture: this heretic humor derives from the disjunction between sacred history "then," and its Reubenical exegesis "now."
Reuben inherits a comic covenant that permits him freedom of
interpretation to use his low-brow vernacular as a vehicle for
instructing his son in the ways of monotheism. Ironically his own
vulgar approach with its body language parallels his forefathers'
iconoclasm: where Abraham smashed idols, Reuben breaks the
fists of those who fail to adhere to their part of the contract,

whether in gangsterism or pretentious religious affiliation. In the examples of the Shapiros we see how the mighty of "then" have fallen into the commonplace of "now," how material progress becomes a facade for spiritual regression. Through these Jewish jokes we regain paradise, not for eternity, but for an instant of laughter that bridges "then" and "now," and retrieves historical loss. To counteract the Fall and the Expulsion, comedy raises the spirit and reintegrates the outsider into society.

Josh's comic inheritance helps bridge the distance between low brow and high brow, between ghetto poverty and the *arriviste*'s affluence, for Richler's satire exposes the gap between origins and margins of Jews who deny "then" in favor of "now." One of these is the psychiatrist in the novel. "The esteemed Dr. Jonathan Cole, author of *My Kind, Your Kind, Mankind,* a rotund man, brown eyes mournful, turned out to be Yossel Kugelman, of all people. When they had been kids together on St. Urbain Street, Yossel had already catalogued his library of Big Little Books. . . . And now, Joshua could see, Yossel was still a collector. From salvage he had graduated to art. Canadiana. A Pellan hung on one wall, a William Ronald on another" (p. 71). These transformations from then to now, from junk to art, from *kind* to man to universal mankind—Joshua exposes all of these as he assaults psychiatric authority, trying to remember whether Yossel had been the one to turn up at Bea Rosen's sweet-sixteen wearing a fedora hat. During their hostile reminiscence the distance between them shrinks, and by the end of their meeting Josh has Yossel worried about his wife Bessie and his own health. Later when the Coles are on vacation Joshua enters their home and defaces one of their paintings, a valuable A.Y. Jackson landscape, by erasing the signature and signing, "this copy by Hershl Sugarman." An interloper and a vandal, Josh rewrites history for those who seek to forget.

What Joshua enjoys most of all is seeking out old classmates to bait, "St. Urbain urchins who had struck it rich." Try as hard as they will, they cannot erase embarrassing traces of their ghetto upbringing that cling to them in their climb up the vertical mosaic to the heights of urbanity, Montreal's Westmount district. Irving Pinsky, now a dentist, lives on Summit Circle, drives a Mercedes 450SL, travels around the world, belongs to a gourmet club, and collects vintage wines. "They passed through a laundry room, with its twin tubs, into the sanctuary, its up-to-date thermostat set at 13° Celsius. And here a glowing Pinsky allowed a fulminating Joshua to fondle, warning him not to shake unduly, his cherished bottles of Chateau Mouton Rothschild '61 and Chateau Lafite '66" (p. 127). Pinsky's "now" exaggerated fastidiousness is deflated by his "then" "celebrated . . . sneakers he let rip in Room 42, FFHS," flatulence that must still be washed out in the twin laundry tubs. He remains blind to the two people he really is: the young stinker who once forced others to sniff, and the man who now sniffs the best wines. The contrast between an "up-to-date" thermostat and the historical 1961 and 1966 points to the broader comic incongruity of a "with-it" Pinsky who relies on labels alone, those outer superficial trappings of success. But beneath his air of success, his body still communicates with the world through its celebrated sneakers, the oenophile debased by the coprophile. Josh takes his revenge on Pinsky's historical amnesia by stealing into his mansion, invading the "inner sanctum," removing all the labels from his bottles, and rearranging them on the racks. Where once his father had broken dentists' fingers for the mob, Josh discovers a subtler method of retribution: Pinsky will now have to rely on his well-trained nose instead of his blind eyes to discover the truth in taste.

Even wealthier, the Montreal tycoon, Izzy Singer, finally receives the Order of Canada award, which forces Joshua to laugh aloud as he remembers him from Room 42 and his twelfth birthday, when he played violin and was betrayed by a "stream of hot piss darkening Izzy's trousers, spreading in a tell-tale puddle round his shiny new pair of shoes" (p. 317). And now he owns an empire that sprawls from Los Angeles to Nova Scotia, a more extensive puddle than that which surrounded him as a child. As Jews commit the genetic fallacy of forgetting their humble origins in their drive toward American expansion, Richler's satire serves as a reminder that the past deflates all pretensions to superiority. "Ostensibly, the perfect prosperity package. But his onyx cufflinks were just a mite too large, and the initials woven into the breast pocket of his shirt too prominent. Izzy, of St. Urbain born, was still pissing in his pants as he played." The emperor's clothes do not quite fit his body, his body does not quite fit his soul, and his present circumstances do not fit his past. For every centrifugal force of achievement and recognition, there is a comic centripetal force returning the assimilated to the provincial ghetto: Izzy's mainstream status is contradicted by a stream of hot piss accompanying him from one end of the continent to the other. The external Order of Canada award is denied by the internal disorders of his body, his past, and his make-believe world. Despite the opulence of his Westmount home, everything is in conflict—the conflicts of now and then, living room artifacts and kitchen delights, a veritable delicatessen tempting Izzy for a midnight snack that sets off his entire alarm system. Trespassing and pissing on his own property, the parvenu can never really be at home, for he is betrayed by his bodily needs and his roots. Comedy, which leaps over boundaries between ghettos and empires, and shifts margins, may be his true home: the tell-tale told by an idiot joy.

But there is a darker side to Joshua's comic revenge against history once he abandons his Montreal childhood and its demarcated ghetto. In his attempt to retrieve history in Spain at the age of twenty-one, Joshua encounters Dr. Mueller who forms part of his recurrent Ibiza nightmare evoking Nazi atrocities and uncovering his Jewish identity. While his bar mitzvah marked a ludicrous transition, his true entry into manhood occurs in his confrontation with Mueller, a menacing antagonist. "If you think you can rob me of my manhood, you're out of your mind. I'm not running, Mueller. . . . I'm a man, not a mouse" (p. 185). Conversations between Mueller and Joshua are not so much dialogue as debate with each accusing the other of weaknesses in their respective heritages or personal histories: victor and victim spar interchangeably with the German accusing the young Canadian of cowardice. The lie dice that they roll symbolize their tangled, perverse relationship to one another, to fate, and to history, with Joshua having to establish himself not merely as a Canadian or a Jew, but more importantly as a man rather than a mouse. Joshua humiliates Mueller when he steals a beautiful woman from him: "He had taken on a Nazi *mano a mano* and demonstrated to Mr. Hemingway that he did not lack for *cojones*" (p. 336). But comic revelations soon dispel these sinister events, for the opposition between working-class Jew and aristocratic German is too pat: Josh's victory proves illusory since the woman's preference was based on the size of Josh's ears, nose, and toes—parts that promise equally large sexual gratification. Josh has confused the literal meaning of testicles with the figurative sense of courage, just as he misinterprets Mueller, who turns out to be a celebrated author of westerns, Gus McCabe. And the entire episode turns into a parody of Hemingway in which a Jewish Canadian poses as a tough American challenging European civilization.

In pursuit of this comedy of errors, twenty-five years later Joshua returns to Ibiza to find out what had happened to its various inhabitants after his departure. With Mueller's death and innocence, he realizes his mistake "and laughed until he almost cried" (p. 396). Those ambivalent tragicomic tears deconstruct his labor of avenging history: since nothing can undo the tragedy of the Holocaust, Josh comes to terms with his limitations, but instead of despairing, he resorts to laughter as catharsis. He resigns himself to his fate, but rises above his own condition through a humor that bypasses the obstacles of history and its persecutions. "*You did. You didn't. Ancient history.* But *my* ancient history, damn it. He paused to set his wristwatch to Montreal time. Home time. Family time" (p. 397). The comic Jewish historian or Hemingway hero *manque,* who doesn't possess ultimate answers, overcomes the universality of ancient history and the Diaspora by a subjective gesture. Not general cosmic history, but a personalized version where time can be controlled. Like so many other wanderers in the Diaspora, Richler's comic hero domesticates Jewish humor by returning to his native ghetto, regressing from marginal manhood to original childhood. Powerless to change the grand designs of history, he can at least cultivate his Montreal garden and set his home in order through a comic spirit that triumphs over past tragedies. When the *pusherke* grows up, he continues pushing upward and outward beyond ghetto horizons toward a wider world that offers no answers. The prodigal son returns home without answers, but with the right comic questions; his St. Urbain street savvy broadens into worldly wisdom and wit, those comic weapons that slay hostile dragons of the Diaspora.

Duddy Kravitz, Jake Hersh, and Joshua Shapiro originate in Montreal's ghetto and FFHS where they precociously learn comic tactics to rebel against the authority of the right side of the tracks. Duddy traverses those tracks that lead eventually to Lac St. Pierre, but in doing do he drags behind him street values that clash with his pastoral vision. Jake Hersh moves further afield, but even in London he carries his St. Urbain apprenticeship that collides with his status as adult, as British resident, and as successful member of the bourgeoisie. Joshua Shapiro completes the cycle, returning from European margins to Montreal origins, having reconciled possession of land in the Eastern Townships with his experience in England, France, and Spain. Duddy circles round and round his land, and recalls Moses from *Bible Comics;* Jake thinks of his Laurentian past as "circles completed" and life in general as a "circle. A little *kikeleh,*" diminutive, homey, comic; Joshua seems to reach his promised land, but this proves to be an illusion, hence comic, for the Canadian Jew is decentered among Montreal, New York, Hollywood, London, Paris, Ibiza. Richler's aggressive triumvirate—dirty duty Kravitz, jakes Hersh, josher Shapiro—take comic revenge on this decentered world and all Dickensian caricatures and multiple doppelgängers who attempt to impede their progress. Mounted on their satiric hobbyhorses, these Jewish-Canadian rakes and rogues cross borders from a "then" apprenticeship to a "now" fulfillment, from a grudging smile to full-blown laughter.

NOTES

1. See Mark Shechner, "Saul Bellow and Ghetto Cosmopolitanism," *Studies in American-Jewish Literature* III:3 (1978), and Sarah Blacher Cohen, "The Comedy of Urban Low Life: From Saul Bellow to Mordecai Richler," *Thalia* 4, (Fall, Winter 1981–1982): 21–24.

2. Mordecai Richler, "Their Canada and Mine," in *The Spice Box: An Anthology of Jewish Canadian Writing,* ed. Gerri Sinclair and Morris Wolfe (Toronto: Lester & Orpen Dennys, 1981), p. 235.

3. Leslie Fiedler, "Some Notes on the Jewish Novel in English," in *Mordecai Richler,* ed. G. David Sheps (Toronto: McGraw-Hill, 1971), p. 101.

4. Mordecai Richler, *Hunting Tigers Under Glass* (London: Weidenfeld and Nicholson, 1969), p. 9.

5. See Reb Rida or Reb Derissa, the *animal ridens* in Jacques Derrida's *Writing and Difference* (Chicago: University of Chicago Press, 1978), pp. 78, 300.

6. Mordecai Richler, *The Street* (Toronto: McClelland & Stewart, 1969), p. 79.

7. Mordecai Richler, *The Apprenticeship of Duddy Kravitz* (Toronto: McClelland & Stewart, 1969), p. 11. All future references are to this edition.

8. See Jeffrey Mehlman, "How to Read Freud on Jokes: The Critic as *Schadchen,*" *New Literary History* vol. 6, no. 2 (Winter 1975): 460.

9. Leon Edel, "Marginal *Keri* and Textual *Chetiv:* The Mystic Novel of

A. M. Klein," in *The A.M. Klein Symposium,* ed. Seymour Mayne (Ottawa: University of Ottawa Press, 1975), pp. 16–18.

10. Mordecai Richler, *St. Urbain's Horseman* (Toronto: McClelland & Stewart, 1976), p. 42. All future references are to this edition.

11. Mordecai Richler, *Joshua Then and Now* (Toronto: McClelland & Stewart, 1980), pp. 190–91. All future references are to this edition.

IS THERE HUMOR IN ISRAELI LITERATURE AND IF NOT, WHY ARE WE LAUGHING?

ESTHER FUCHS

In a perceptive article entitled "Are We All Dead?" the poet Nathan Zach discusses the marked susceptibility of Israeli narrative fiction to tragic heroes who either commit suicide or die an unnatural death. While Zach admits that recent Jewish history—the mass migrations, the Holocaust, Israel's political and military predicaments and the sharp changes the state has undergone since its establishment—may have contributed to the pervasive morbidity of Israeli literature, he feels that much of it can be attributed to the artistic and psychological make-up of individual Israeli authors: "And the author who fails to get on with his world, and this includes the author who is troubled by his own personal life—first kills off his protagonists. Only then, and very rarely—also himself. Death is indeed a solution, but it is also a testimony to the protagonist's incapacity and often the author's own incapacity to choose for himself and his protagonists another way out."[1]

I am quoting Zach here, not because I am in complete agreement with his explanation of the morbidity of Israeli narrative fiction, but because he seems to be one of the few to have noted this peculiar fact. This fact may not be of concern to most Israeli critics or even readers, but it is a major problem for anyone who, like myself, wishes to discuss humor in Israeli literature. That

216

this is a problem can be seen from a most cursory glance at Haviva Shohet-Me'iri's book, *On Laughter in Israeli Literature.* In addition to the inescapable graveness which often plagues analyses of literary humor (including the present one), Shohet's study—the only one to date dedicated to the subject—only exacerbates one's original misgivings about the existence of laughter in Israeli literature.[2]

While the more explicit forms of humor may be rare commodities in Israeli *belles lettres,* they are more common in popular literature, media and folklore.[3] Israel's popular literature cannot be imagined without the best known humorists-satirists, Ephraim Kishon, Dahn Ben Amotz and Amos Kenan.[4] Israel's daily papers would not be complete without the satiric verse of Yosi Gamzu and Didi Menosi, the dry humor of Shalom Rosenfeld, the sarcastic columns of Meir Uziel, Ziva Yariv, Silvy Keshet or Jacob Lazar, the playful columns of Yonathan Geffen, the comic humor of Avshalom Kor and Ora Shem Ur, or the caustic caricatures and satires of B. Michael, Koby Niv, Ephraim Sidon and Dudu Geva, not to mention the daily political cartoons of Kariel Gardosh (known as Dosh), Yacov Farkas (known as Ze'ev), Ra'anan Lurieh, and Moshick Lin. It would be just as unthinkable to omit the above from Israel's newpapers and television, as it would be to envision Israel's popular culture without the comic routines of the three "Gashashim" (Poli, Gavri and Shaikeh), Dudu Topaz, Tuvya Tzafrir, Gadi Yagil and Rivkah Michaeli, or without director-producer Menakhem Golai, and comedians like Haim Topol, Shmuel Rudensky, Misha Segal, Shaikeh Ofir, Shoshik Shani, Ili Golitzki, the actor-director Yosi Banai, the late Bomba Tzur and the comedian Uri Zohar, whose delightful routines were forever lost to the Israeli public since his decision to make *Teshuvah,* and join a yeshiva in Jerusalem. By the same token, it would be impossible to understand Israeli folklore, without considering its thriving jokelore, particularly the serial jokes about prime ministers (Levi Eshkol, Golda Meir, Menachem Begin) and other key political figures.

It is clear that we cannot attribute the relatively low visibility of humor in Israel's *belles lettres* to the innate humorlessness of Israeli culture, or to Israel's socio-political and economic predicaments. The fact is that, in Israel like in other cultures, times of duress are the best catalysts for a thriving humor industry.[5] The famous Eshkol jokes, for example, reached epidemic popularity during the suspenseful months that preceded the outbreak of the Six Day War.

How then are we to account for the low profile of humor in Israel's *belles lettres?* Although I agree with Zach that the heavy casualties of Israeli literary protagonists are the product of the creative mind, I believe that in opting for the tragic hero and the tragic ending, the Israeli author is responding to a longstanding literary tradition in Israeli letters, rather than manifesting psychological immaturity, or artistic limitations. For if we argue with Zach that these are the main causes for the insanity and death plaguing the protagonists of, for example, Benjamin Tammuz, Jacob Shabtai, Amos Oz, A.B. Yehoshua, Haim Be'er, and Yitzhak Ben Ner, then we must offer the same diagnosis for the persuasive morbidity of Micha Yosef Berdichevsky, Yosef Haim Brenner, and Uri Nissan Gnessin, the great predecessors of the "generation of the state." A more likely explanation for the tragic vision of modern and contemporary Hebrew literature lies in the notion that the author's major role is moral rather than aesthetic. Largely influenced by Russian Romanticism and the Haskalah movement, Hebrew authors and critics of the nineteenth century saw literature as a means for social change. Entertaining their readers was as far from the minds of Ahad Ha-am or Bialik—who were themselves perceived as secular prophets—as it must have been from the minds of the ancient Hebrew prophets who considered laughter an expression of levity and ungodliness. Laughter entered the writings of *Maskilim,* like Isaac Euchel, Saul Berlin and later Yosef Pearl and the early Mendele Mocher Sforim as a satiric weapon against the provincialism of the Jewish *shtetl* and the repression of the rabbinic establishment. Even during the Renaissance age (1880s–1920s), which shed to an extent the ideological trappings of the Haskalah writers, Hebrew authors perceived their writing as a social vocation, and the central theme of their writing continued to be the problem of Jewish survival.[6]

The theme of Jewish survival was central to the writings of some Yiddish authors as well, but whereas the latter often celebrated the Jew's ability to survive against all odds, the former tended to criticize the obsequiousness and lament the price of this survival. While Sholom Aleichem presented the wandering *luftmensch* as a laughable yet heroic *schlemiel,* whose failures amount to triumphs of "psychic survival,"[7] Feierberg depicted the same character as a tragic, uprooted and alienated hero. It is not that Feierberg, Gnessin or Brenner lacked a sense of humor, but rather that the very act of writing Hebrew was a statement of protest against the social conditions of the Jewish Diaspora. To turn the Jewish *luftmensch* into a comic hero would have drenched the revolutionary charge implicit in their choosing to write in Hebrew, the ancient language of national Jewish sovereignty. Whereas the incongruity between the idea of the chosen people and Jewish political inferiority was a major source of Yiddish humor, it was anathema to the Hebrew writers who sought to put an end to this incongruity by reviving the proud Jewish past. To the extent that laughter helps sweeten the sting of economic deprivation and political oppression, it is an adaptive tool, unacceptable to those who seek change.

Humor was inimical to the early Hebrew authors, not only ideologically, but also instrumentally. Hebrew, the language of the Bible and Jewish Halacha—often referred to as the "Queen"—did not lend itself easily to the linguistic pranks and tricks of Yiddish, the specialty of the "maidservant."[8] The stylized Hebrew crystalized by Mendele was an improvement over the stultified language of the Maskilim, although what it offered the Hebrew writer was a highly stylized language, hardly amenable to humor.[9]

Hebrew language and literature have come a long way from the days of Mendele and Feierberg. Nevertheless, even in contemporary Israel, spoken Hebrew is still perceived as an unwelcome intruder into the printed page. The humorous charm of the *World Dictionary of Hebrew Slang* (1975, 1982), for example, would not be possible without the official resistance to "the happy bastards of the sacred language."[10] Similarly, despite the contemporary emphasis on literature as art, critics continue to expect "serious" (often identified as humorless) authors to at least articulate, if not to offer solutions to national predicaments. The obsessive search for allegorical meaning in Agnon's work is only one example of the continued tendency in the Israeli critical establishment to perceive the literary text as the locus of ideological cryptograms. This relentless search for national meaning may explain the critical obliviousness to Agnon's ironic genius, and to the humorous aspect of his work.[11] That humor is often perceived as levity can be seen from the recent critical reception of Aharon Megged's hilarious novel, *The Flying Camel and the Golden Hump*

(1982). The perception of literary writing as a social responsibility is not confined to Israeli critics despite the current tendency to discard ideology and emphasize the aesthetic aspect of
literary writing.[12] Many share the critics' confusion of good and
grave literature. Amos Oz for example, suggests that the essence
of *belles lettres* is an expression of sorrow, protest, complaint, or
renunciation.[13]

But if Israeli literature closed the door on the more explicit and
adaptive forms of humor, it opened a window for its more subtle
and critical forms. Ironic, satiric and grotesque humor begins to
infiltrate the poetry of Yehuda Amichai, David Avidan and Avoth
Yashurun in the early 1960s. Perhaps the most important catalyst
for the revival of these forms of humor was the increasing
awareness of the incongruity between the socialist Zionist ideal,
and the socio-political reality of the state. The incongruity between the highminded ideal of egalitarianism and the return to
productive labor envisioned by Dov Ben Borochov and A. D.
Gordon and preached by Nahman Sirkin and Yitzhak Tabenkin
clashed against the emerging capitalistic, urbanized, and bu-
reaucratized society of the 1950s. The military conflicts with the
Arabs, and the problems of Jewish immigration and integration
clashed cruelly with both Ahad Ha'am's cultural Zionism and
with Herzl's political Zionism.

That the incongruity between the Zionist ideal and the Israeli
state began to penetrate the public consciousness only in the late
1950s may explain why the Palmah literature (1940s to late 1950s)
is largely devoid of humor. The tendency of the Palmah authors
like Moshe Shamir, Nathan Shaham, and Hanoch Bartov to
glorify the courageous patriotic soldier–kibbutznik, or the highminded pacifist (e.g., in works by S. Yizhar) reflects a fundamental identification with the belief system of socialist Zionism, an
identification which does not allow for a humorous treatment of
the system. It would take a new, more skeptical consciousness to
depict the kibbutz ironically, as Amos Oz does in *Elsewhere
Perhaps* (1966). This does not mean, however, that the Pal-
mahniks lacked a sense of humor. Besides the humorless Palmah
literature, there thrived a body of humor, in Palmah folklore and
popular culture. Epitomized by the *Chizbat*—a humorous tall
tale about an eccentric personality, an ethnic/social stereotype,
or a clever practical joke—Palmah humor manifests a strong
sense of group superiority. As Elliott Oring explains in his study

of the *Chizbat:* "The Palmah considered themselves to be the elite of the Yishuv, and no one embodied, cultivated, dramatized and glorified the image of the native, more than themselves."[14]

This very sense of superiority may explain the somewhat crude and naive humor of the *Chizbat.* Despite the significant differences between them, there is much in the *Chizbat* that suggests the pre-emancipation Jewish humor, especially the Chelm tales and the stories of Hershele. Both the *Chizbat* and pre-emancipation humor imply that reality is logical and unnecessarily complicated by stupid or impractical people (the Chelmites, or the Jeckes and the Levantine Jews in the *Chizbat*), while smart people (like Hershele, or the performers of practical jokes in the *Chizbat*) are likely to overcome all difficulties and have a good laugh as a bonus. Both bodies of humor reflect the belief that there is some correlation between the group's belief system and reality. For the European Jews this belief began to be challenged in the second half of the eighteenth century, a period to which Sig Altman traces the origins of modern Jewish humor.[15] Similarly, one could trace the beginning of current Israeli jokelore, with its strong tendency toward criticizing Israeli political authorities, to the breakdown of the socialist Zionist value system and the growing consciousness of the incongruity between the ideal of the state and its actual reality.

Satiric humor aimed at this incongruity began to emerge in Israeli *belles lettres* in the late 1950s and early 1960s. Aharon Megged's *Hedva and I* (1954) and *Fortunes of a Fool* (1960), Benjamin Tammuz's *A Locked Garden* (1957), and David Shahar's *The Moon of Honey and Gold* (1959) attack, each in its own way, the betrayal of the socialist Zionism by a selfish, materialistic and immoral generation of Israelis. While Megged's heroes are idealists whose belief in dignified values turns them into social misfits, Shahar's nameless picaro moves from one love affair to the next, and from one petty crime to another, without ever so much as recognizing his depravity and vacuity.

The authors who came into prominence in the 1960s manifest a much more complex attitude vis-á-vis both Israeli society and the socialist Zionist ideal. The new perspective was introduced by the parodic treatment of certain themes, characters and plot structures prevalent in the Palmah literature.[16] The omniscient narrator is transformed into an unreliable one, the hero into a comic-pathetic character, and the casual plot into a series of coincidences, or circles leading to no resolution. This is most eloquently exemplified in the fiction of A. B. Yehoshua, the most consistently humorous among the new generation. If the average commander in the Palmah literature is an inspiring leader, who does not hesitate to sacrifice his life in his effort to win a battle against the Arabs, in A. B. Yehoshua's "The Last Commander" (1962) the much admired commander (Yignon) is busy sleeping throughout the story, permitting his soldiers to wander aimlessly about the desert. In "Missile Base 612" (1974), the nameless hero performs his reserve duty listlessly and mechanically, lecturing about the problems of Israeli society to a bored and indifferent crowd of soldiers.

Yehoshua's heroes are busy pursuing meaningless goals which have little to do with the national or social crises described in the story, and which often end up exacerbating their own psychological or marital difficulties. All but unaware of the 1967 war, which breaks out in the course of *The Lover* (1977), Adam, the protagonist engages in a mad pursuit of Gavriel Arditi, the expatriate, whom he employs as his wife's lover. Accompanied by his insomniac daughter, Dafi, and by his Arab employee, Naim, who is in effect paid for babysitting Arditi's grandmother, Adam finally finds Arditi disguised as a *Hasid,* in an ultra-orthodox neighborhood in Jerusalem. In the meantime, however, Adam becomes involved with Dafi's eccentric high school girlfriend, Dafi drops out of school and has a love affair with Naim, and Arditi's grandmother (whose birthday significantly coincides with the establishment of the Zionist movement) expires. These intersecting series of coincidences lead the characters further away from genuine solutions to their malaise. The apparently successful pursuit of Arditi cannot disguise the fact that Adam is a failure as a father, a lover, and a husband, and that his attempt to employ others to perform his responsibilities only exacerbates his alienation from his work, society, and family. The unexpected turn of events, the unlikely relationships, the inconsistencies, between the characters' points of view, and the hilarious scenes which expose these inconsistencies (e.g., Naim's attempt to swallow Asia's nauseatingly sweet gefilte fish, and to recite Bialik's national poem; Arditi's attempt to desert the army by donning *Hasidic* clothes; Arditi's listless lovemaking with Asia during their joint research projects on the French Revolution) are not merely funny. As Nilli Sadan-Loebenstein notes, the distorting angle through which Yehoshua presents his neurotic characters and madcap plots often dramatizes the nation's malaise.[17] The characterization of the native Israeli as petit-bourgeois (Adam), hedonist (Asia), idler (Dafi), expatriate and army deserter (Arditi) is a satirical critique of the incongruity between the Zionist dream and Israeli reality.

If Yehoshua questions the betrayal by native Israelis of the Zionist dream, Jacob Shabtai, who came into prominence in the late 1970s, questions the fanatic idealism of the early pioneers, and its results. In *Past Continuous* (1977), Shabtai describes the demise of the most venerated elite in Israeli society, the socialist Zionists who immigrated to the land of Israel to build and be rebuilt in it.[18] The aimless meanderings and repeated failures of the major three characters in the novel, Goldman, Tsezar and Israel—all sons of pioneers turned successful bourgeois businessmen—are funny, but the laughter their Bergsonian mechanicalness elicits is bitter. Goldman's attempt to find meaning in medieval astrology is just as laughable as Tsezar's attempt to find redemption in endless love affairs. What tempers their comicality is the fact that their suffering is genuine, and that the cause for their repeated errors and unawareness of their own needs is not altogether arbitrary: it lies in their inability to extricate themselves from their fathers' identities (Goldman commits suicide shortly after his father's death), and self-righteous idealism.

If Yehoshua is criticizing the dissolution of Israeli society, Shabtai is satirizing the oppressive relationships and stifling commitments which progressively dehumanize the Israeli individual. The interlocking networks of relationships are stylistically mirrored in the run-on sentences, expanding into one endless paragraph. In addition to creating a bustling scene filled with apparently disconnected details—which is rather typical of the satiric scene—Shabtai's interminable paragraphs (making up the entire novel) is comic in its total obliviousness to conventions of syntax and literary style. As we shall see, however, the humorous effect hides a bitter satiric critique on the inhuman fanaticism of the founding fathers of the Israeli elite—the idealistic pioneers. In the following excerpt, Israel remembers how Goldman's father killed Noi Sombra, his neighbor's dog, who, according to rumor, fed on delicacies, while Goldman and others had to put up with the severe economic recession of the late 1950s:

> "Either way, there is no doubt that Goldman's father determined Noi Sombra's fate according to what he considered weighty reasons and

he killed him after it was clear to him that it must die, and even if it were his own dog he would not have treated it differently, for, he was a Zionist and a socialist and believed in simplicity, diligence, morality, and culturedness in their most fundamental sense, and he hated revisionists, people who get rich or who waste money on luxuries and people who criticize the land of Israel, and all this as part of a whole set of clear and fixed principles, that encompassed all walks of life and all deeds and did not bear compromise, and that despite the changes and the difficulties he never doubted them and never found it necessary to deviate from them even slightly."[19]

Goldman's father mobilizes the haughty "fixed and clear principles" of socialistic Zionism in order to justify his ruthless and pointless murder of an innocent dog. The contradiction between the inhuman act and the high minded justification satirizes the self-righteous posture of this fanatic idealist, who will later violate his own principles, when growing wealthy and indifferent to others' needs.

If Yehoshua satirizes the Israeli pragmatist and Shabtai, the Israeli idealist, the playwright Hanoch Levin ridicules both; the former as a romantic loser and the latter as a ruthless carnivore. The limited empathy exhibited by Yehoshua and Shabtai toward even the most ridiculous of their characters, is nowhere to be found in Levin's grotesques, in which wives are prostitutes, daughters spoiled nymphomaniacs (or teases), lovers sexually frustrated perverts, and fathers greedy petit-bourgeois. The exaggeration of these stereotypes is so extreme that often the represented reality loses any authentic markers that may identify it as uniquely Israeli. The stereotypic characters in, for example, *Solomon Grip* (1969), *Young Vardahle* (1974), *Krum* (1975), *Shitz* (1975), and *Popper* (1976) are both the victims and the oppressors of each other. In *Shitz,* for example, Sprachtzi, the gluttonous daughter, and Tcharches, the greedy son-in-law, are planning to murder the greedy and gluttonous father, Fefechts Shitz, in order to inherit his wealth. What saves the latter is the war which, by taking Tcharches away, undermines Sprachtzi's hope for the status of a respectable married woman, and her mother's dream of eloping to Los Angeles after her husband's death and marrying a rich American professor. At the end of the play, Tcharches returns as a ghost, only to be tortured by the entire family.

Levin's dramatization of his characters' lives as endless rituals of overeating, vomiting, masturbating, copulating, and excreting exaggerates *ad absurdum* the usual emphasis of satire on the concrete and the physical in human life. This extreme exaggeration of human frailties which often erases the distinctions between the human and the bestial, is characteristic of grotesque satire which tends to elicit a frightened laughter, a terrified grimace, a confused or disgusted smile. Levin's *galgenhumor* is deeply pessimistic, which is why his critique transcends the essentially corrective and somewhat optimistic satires of Yehoshua and Shabtai.

One of Levin's plays, *The Queen of the Bathtub* (1967), became the object of a vehement attack by Israel's foremost humorist, Ephraim Kishon: "There are people amongst us, who are absolutely incapable of solving their personal problems, but as they face the debris of their destroyed lives, wish of all things to save the nation. All their personal frustration, [and] their wrath over their failures are vented on the public like sewage: 'we', they tell us with a deep voice, 'we' are worse than the Nazis. All right, we are like the Nazis, but why worse? The Devil knows. They are only well versed in questions, not answers, the Satyricons."[20] This attack on Levin should come as no surprise to those acquainted with Kishon's work. For despite the superficial resemblance his humoristic pieces may share with Levin's satiric grotesques (exaggeration, distortion, generalization, use of stereotypes, laughable names, *reductio ad absurdum*), Kishon differs from Levin not only in his political ideology and accessibility (the latter is associated with the left and his plays are usually addressed to a limited intellectual elite), but especially in his radically different use of humor. Whereas Levin uses laughter as a weapon of social critique, Kishon uses the social context in order to create laughter. Levin's satiric and grotesque humor criticizes Israeli reality and its sustaining (official) value system; Kishon's comic humor affirms both the value system *and* the social reality. Levin's humor rejects what it ridicules; Kishon's humor validates it. The defects Levin attacks seem incorrigible; the defects Kishon mocks are rendered acceptable through their laughability.

Kishon's humorous column, "Had Gadia," published regularly in the daily paper *Ma'ariv* till 1981, points up the laughable in Israel's inept diplomacy, faltering economy, ineffective taxation policy, rampant inflation, wasteful bureaucracy, shaky coalitions, and in different social and ethnic groups (e.g., immigrants, pioneers, Sabras, Jeckes and Levantine Jews, professionals and blue collar workers). The unforgettable characters of Arbinke, the wheeler-dealer, the square Shultheis, the chronic procrastinator Shtoks, the naive Mr. Pashutman, the pretentious actor Yarden Podmenitski, the narcissistic politician Amitz Dolniker, the confined housewife and nagging wife are only a few of the caricatures which populate his books: *Take it Easy,* 1956; *It All Depends,* 1958; *One of These Last Nights,* 1964; *A Bone in the Throat,* 1966; *Sorry We Won,* 1967; *Woe to the Victors,* 1968; *The Fox in the Hencoop,* 1972; *Partachia, My Love,* 1974. Despite the laughable eccentricities and outrageous mannerisms, these caricatures, like their counterparts in Kishon's plays and screenplays (e.g., *Oh, Julia, Salah Shabati, Policeman Azulai, Blaumilch Channel*), tend to elicit in the Israeli audience an empathetic laughter of recognition and relief, promoting acceptance and conducive to adaptation.

This does not mean, however, that Kishon's humor lacks teeth. But unlike the satirists and ironists who criticize Israeli reality in the name of betrayed ideals, Kishon's humor ridicules the idealistic stance as unrealistic, pretentious and false. The most frequent objects of his satiric humor are high minded ideologues, professional snobs, intellectual elitists and public speakers. The language he uses is a mock literary language, which parodies the highbrow Hebrew of Israeli *belles lettres,* the media, the normative Hebrew legislated by the Academy of the Hebrew language, and the stylized Hebrew of public parlance. But to qualify as the object of Kishon's mockery, one does not necessarily have to use a pompous Hebrew: English will suffice too. In one of his most memorable parodies of Israel's public officials, Kishon pretends to applaud Abba Eban's impeccable English, while mocking the latter's inability to communicate Israel's political needs to his colleagues in the U.N.:

> Abba opens beautifully. Already in his third sentence, he throws the words "MAUERESSE" and "GASTILICUM" that appeared at the time, only in the writings of the great King Alfred, glory to his name. Later [he throws] a perfect sentence, the epitome of linguistic architecture, including the explosive [word] "DISEXPOSTICULATION," a rare idiom that electrified the entire council. The representatives leaf through the dictionaries feverishly. . . . The translators are seen behind their windows sweating and frightened

like persecuted animals. . . . Abba feels that the audience is beginning to warm up, and he himself grows wings, moving imperceptibly to the archaic Welsh language. The representative of Belgium is still not aware of the fact, that he hears all the time, by mistake, the Chinese translation through the earphones. Hammarskjold closes the *Webster* in despair and goes out to take a break. The British delegation shows off its superiority by listening to Abba's speech without earphones and with no dictionary. Nobody believes the Swiss. Everybody knows that they later receive Abba's speech in simplified English with vowels. The speech ends with an excited address to world public opinion to learn and improve the English language. The translators are lying down in their booths exhausted, and the delegates, too, look pale and shocked from the intellectual effort. Hammarskjold returns, the delegates surround Abba and shake his hand enthusiastically for the fantastic words.[21]

The false praise (pretending that Eban is expected to perform as a linguist), the exaggeration *ad absurdum* of the situation (the description of the physically exhausted delegates), the comic distortion (Eban's call for improving the English language) and implicit paradox (Eban is cheered for his inability to explain Israel's position) are characteristic of Kishon's writing, which is aimed at exposing the betrayal of the real by the (false) ideal. For Kishon,. what is askew is not (Israeli political) reality, but the highmindedness of pretentious politicians and ideologues. Unlike most authors, who tend to lament the loss of the idealistic vision, Kishon aims his arrows at the absence of realism. If the mortal sin of his politicians is pretentiousness, the Achilles heel of the average Israeli—or rather, the Partachian (Partachia being the name of the Galician-Oriental country situated in the region of the Mugrabi theater in Tel Aviv)—is ineptness (as well as, come to think of it, pushiness, impatience and unreliability).

One can identify the average Partachian by his major attribute, that at half past three he must be in Haifa. In addition, he is (always) late. That is, he does not come at all. If you can find him, it is usually in places marked off with the sign: "No Entrance." If the little Partachian goes into a place, he immediately touches everything, to verify that it's real. Seeing a sandwich, he takes a bite. Seeing a switch, he turns it on. He likes to poke around, in pockets, in drawers, in the nose. . . . The authentic Partachian loves fresh paint. If something is dirty, he paints it. If rusty—an additional layer. For purposes of repairs needing electric soldering, he uses office glue; instead of screws he works with scotch tape. If he puts in screws, then only one, at most, two; it will hold. The Partachian eats noisily,

walks noisily, speaks noisily; complains about the noise. If his radio
screeches, he calls a technician after a year. The technician says: lift
up one side. He lifts, the noise stops. Puts a box of matches under-
neath the left side of the radio. If the noise returns—he changes a
box, or hits the radio. On the top, or from the side, flat blows. . . .
Large machines he kicks. . . . The Partachian language has a rich
vocabulary. "It will be all right" alludes to an impending disaster.
"Rely (on me)!", implies that nothing will be accomplished. "Right
away", is two hours. "A day or two"—a year; "After the holidays"—
never. . . . In a war he usually wins. The Partachian drives a tank in
the opposite direction because of a slight nap, gives the enemy a
good blow, returns, wins. . . . If there is a flat on the road, he gets
stuck in the middle of the battle. If there is no flat—he wins.[22]

Kishon's Partachia is somewhat reminiscent of Sholom Aleichem's Kasrilevke, the town of *Die Kleine Mentshelech*.
Among other things, the Kasrilevkers are funny because, disconnected from political reality, they construct it according to their
own desires. Mistaking their town for the center of the world, and
themselves for its rulers, they presume that their anger over the
Dreyfus case, for example, might change the facts reported in the
papers. Instead of becoming part of the world, they are venting
their anger at Zaidle who reports to them the disappointing news
of the Dreyfus trial. The Partachians are funny because of their
short-sighted pragmatism, the Kasrilevkers because of their unrealistic attachment to ideals. The former live in the immediate
present, the latter in eternity. Sholom Aleichem addressed the
incongruity between the traditional Jewish belief system and the
sordid reality of the *shtetl* and the world. Kishon is addressing
the discrepancy between the ideal image of the Sabra and the
average Israeli. Both differ from the satirists of their time in their
refusal to criticize or reject the reality at which they are poking
fun. The underlying vision of both is that, because reality cannot
be changed, one may as well get a good laugh out of it.

In the lecture Kishon delivered to the opening session of the
1984 International Congress of Humor (after asserting that there
is no identifiable Israeli humor), he told the participants one of
his favorite Israeli jokes: "You are walking down the street and
somebody kicks you from behind. Excuse me he says, I thought
you were somebody else. And if I were somebody else, you say,
Do you have to kick me? Sir, he says, Are you telling me whom I
am supposed to kick? Though the joke may have originated in
immigrant circles in response to their encounter with Israeli

Chutzpah, its popularity implies that native Israelis, too, are capable of laughing at their much touted aggressiveness, their impoliteness, their chronic inability to apologize properly, their inflated self-confidence and their resistance to criticism or advice. It may very well be that this joke has originated in the famous Jewish joke about Abramovitch, who, walking down a street in Minsk is suddenly slapped in the face by a stranger who shouts at him: "So much for you Rabinowitz!" To the stranger's amazement, Abramovitch bursts out laughing: "Aha," he says, "but the joke is on you—my name is not Rabinovitch!" This joke ridicules among other things the Jews' ability to rationalize out of existence, or laugh off the arbitrary pain and humiliation inflicted upon them by a hostile environment. While the stereotypical Israeli is ridiculed for the Israelis' alleged excessive aggressiveness, the stereotypical Jew is ridiculed for the Jews' alleged excessive passivity. Both jokes reflect, however, a healthy capacity for self-criticism, and I am emphasizing "healthy," because I disagree with the notion that there is anything masochistic, pathological or even unique in the self-critical Jewish joke, a notion suggested by Sigmund Freud and endorsed by many other scholars as self-evident (e.g., Martin Grotjahn and Theodore Reik). For one thing, as Dan Ben Amos points out, the Jewish joke teller usually disassociates him/herself from the butt of the joke, who may well be Jewish, but belongs to a distinct subgroup.[23] For another, the Jewish or Israeli joke teller tends to laugh at the *stereotyped weaknesses* ascribed to his/her national/religious group, not at the group *per se*.

Like Kishon's comic humor, which both criticizes and accepts Israeli reality, Israeli jokelore demonstrates a growing awareness of the discrepancy between the Zionist ideal and the Israeli state. While routines by professional stand-up comedians tend to be resoundingly affirmative in their skits on the state, Israeli folkhumor often features open-ended jokes reflecting deep skepticism toward public pieties and widely shared values. In their skit, "They Cry for You Homeland," the "Gashashim" mock those Israelis who complain about inflation, recession and taxes while stuffing their faces with expensive delicacies. In "Expatriates" they parody Israeli emigrants who pledge allegiance to Israel, promising to return soon—as soon as their three-year-old son has graduated from college. This adaptive humor implies an unreserved endorsement of the state, despite its possible short-

comings. Similarly, Dudu Topaz, in his popular show, "A Slip of
the Tongue," presents an Israeli who, minutes before his departure to Australia, decides to stay in Israel. The affirmation of
Israeli reality by professional comedians, is complemented by
their popular parodies of immigrant Jews (East European, German, Sephardic), notably of their foreign accents and *Galut*
mannerisms and mentality. It can perhaps be said that contemporary comic routines resemble the adaptive humor of the Palmah
(which also tended to mock outsiders) in its attempt to affirm the
superiority of those most devoted to Zionist ideals, and most in
line with the in-crowd of the native Sabras.

Israeli folkhumor, on the other hand, is often less defensive
and more daring in its treatment of both the Zionist ideal and the
Israeli reality. One of the most popular jokes (which may have
originated in Jewish immigrant circles, or even among Jews
outside of Israel) refers to the fateful moment which determined
that Israel became the land of the Jews: "When God asked
Moses which country he wished to choose as the Jewish homeland, Moses was going to say Canada. Being a stutterer, however,
he began with, Ca..Ca..Ca...na..na...nan.., which God mistook
for Canaan." Fortified by the bawdy implication of Moses's
"Ca..Ca," (which in Hebrew/Yiddish slang means feces), this
joke offers a rather skeptical explanation of the question which
many Israelis ask themselves in earnest: "Why were we doomed
to live in a small country, with almost no natural resources, and
precarious borders?" The presentation of Moses as a stutterer,
God as an inattentive listener, and Israel as a mistake, resembles
Jewish European jokes which offered equally skeptical explana-
tions for the incongruity between God's promise to the chosen
people, and their miserable existence in the Diaspora.[24] The
above joke gives vent to the frustration with the chosen land by
parodying a mythical moment in the Jewish past. The following
saying reflects a widely shared anxiety by dramatizing a dreaded
moment in the future: "The last one departing from Lod (Israel's
national airport), must not forget to turn off the lights." Like the
joke about the Jew who tries to flee Nazi-occupied Europe by
immigrating to the United States, and, told by the American
officer to return in 13 years, asks, "Morning or afternoon?" the
Israeli joke shifts the emphasis from the focus of national anxiety
to a trivial point. While the Jew, whose survival is threatened,
appears to be preoccupied with the bureaucratic protocol, the

Israeli, who advises the last expatriate to switch off the lights in Lod, appears to be more obsessed with saving electricity than with the impending end of the state. Both jokes ridicule social complacency and inattentiveness to potential crises, while at the same time, exorcising anxieties about national extinction. The black humor inspiring these jokes demonstrates, among other things, that Jewish European *Galgenhumor* is not quite as dead in Israel as some believed it to be.[25] This kind of humor appears to be undergoing a minor revival in Israeli folkhumor, as well as in Israeli *belles lettres*.

Israeli *belles lettres* may still be turning up its nose at more explicit and less serious forms of humor, in keeping with the commitment of Hebrew literary tradition to the solemn and the idealistic, but it is possible that, with the growing awareness of the fact that Israeli reality may never fulfill the lofty requirements of the Zionist ideal, it will become more hospitable to Israeli folkhumor and even to the comic humor of popular humorists and to Jewish European humor, which seemed subversive—and at the time for good reasons—to the pioneers of Hebrew literature.

NOTES

1. Nathan Zach, *Air Lines: Talks on Literature* (Jerusalem: Keter, 1983), p. 18. [In Hebrew.]

2. Haviva Shohet-Me'iri, *On Laughter in Israeli Literature* (Tel Aviv: Sifriat Poalim, 1972). [In Hebrew.] Shohet's disparate studies of A. B. Yehoshua, Yehuda Amichai and Nathan Zach do not offer a unified vision of humor in Israeli literature. In her specific analyses she focuses on verbal irony and the grotesque, precluding any attempt to point out or explain the "laughter" her title invokes.

3. For the purposes of this essay, I shall define humor as that which produces laughter by creating incongruities between the real and the ideal. The comic is here understood as a form of humor which affirms the real, while satire, in contrast, criticizes the real in the name of the ideal. Irony refers here to a mechanism playing up the incongruity between the real and the ideal through a pretended confusion of the two, while the grotesque refers to the humorous form which rejects both the real and the ideal through extreme distortion and exaggeration.

4. Dahn Ben Amotz and Netiva Ben Yehuda continue to thumb their noses at the restrictive conventions of literary Hebrew in their books. The former uses heavy doses of contemporary slang and bawdy language in,

among other books, *Fucking Isn't Everything* (Tel Aviv: Metzuit, 1979) and *Screwing of the Road* (Tel Aviv: Metzuit, 1981). The latter revives the spoken Hebrew and slang of the Palmah in her funny and touching *1948— Between the Calendars* (Jerusalem: Keter, 1981).

5. Sarah Blacher Cohen, "Introduction: The Variety of Humors." In *Comic Relief: Humor in Contemporary American Literature,* ed. Sarah Blacher Cohen (Urbana: University of Illinois Press, 1978), pp. 1–14.

6. Simon Halkin, *Modern Hebrew Literature* (New York: Schocken, 1970), pp. 51–110.

7. Ruth R. Wisse, *The Schlemiel as Modern Hero* (Chicago: University of Chicago Press, 1971), pp. 25–40.

8. Irving Howe and Eliezer Greenberg, eds., *A Treasury of Yiddish Stories* (New York: Schocken, 1973), pp. 19–27.

9. Gershon Shaked, *Hebrew Narrative Fiction 1880–1970,* Vol. 1 (Jerusalem and Tel Aviv: Keter and Hakibbutz Hameuchad, 1977), pp. 83–88. [In Hebrew.]

10. Dahn Ben Amotz and Nevita Ben Yehuda, *The World Dictionary of Hebrew Slang* (Tel Aviv: Zmora Bitan, 1982). [In Hebrew.]

11. For a detailed critique of allegorical approaches to Agnon and an analysis of Agnon's irony see Esther Fuchs, *S.Y. Agnon's Irony: Form and Meaning* (Tel Aviv: Tel Aviv University Press, 1986). [In Hebrew.] See also Esther Fuchs, " 'Edo and Enam': The Ironic Perspective," *Modern Languages Studies* 13, no. 1 (Winter 1982): 85–100; Esther Fuchs, "*Ad Olam:* Pathos or Irony," *Jerusalem Studies in Hebrew Literature* (1983): 199–221; Esther Fuchs, "Ironic Characterization in the Works of S.Y. Agnon," *AJS Review* 7-8 (1982–1983): 101–28.

12. Esther Fuchs, *Encounters with Israeli Authors* (Marblehead: Micah, 1982).

13. Amos Oz, *Under This Blazing Light: Essays (Be'or hatekhelet ha'aza,* 1979), p. 64.

14. Elliot Oring and Ofra Nevo also emphasize, each in his/her own way, the distinctions between Jewish and Israeli jokes. Nevo argues, for example, that the self-critical edge of the Jewish European joke is in fact less popular among Jews than among Arabs living in Israel. See Nevo, *Humorist Reactions as Expressive of Aggressiveness Among Jews and Arabs in Israel: An Emphasis on Different Aspects of Humor* (Jerusalem: Hebrew University, 1981; unpublished), p. 123.

15. Sig Altman, *The Comic Image of the Jew: Exploration of a Pop Culture Phenomenon* (Rutherford, NJ: Fairleigh Dickinson University Press, 1971), pp. 125–45.

16. Nurith Gertz, *Generation Shift in Literary History: Hebrew Narrative Fiction in the Sixties* (Tel Aviv: Hakibbutz Hameuchad, 1983), pp. 138–76. [In Hebrew.]

17. Nilli Lobenstein, *A. B. Yehoshua* (Tel Aviv: Sifriat Poalim, 1981), pp. 23–26. [In Hebrew.]

18. Jacob Shabtai, *Past Continuous* (Tel Aviv: Siman Kriah, 1977).

19. Ibid., p. 17.

20. Ephraim Kishon, "The Satyricons," *Ma'ariv* (1976): 150–51.

21. Ephraim Kishon, "On Abba Eban," *Ma'ariv* (1973): 21–22.

22. Ephraim Kishon, "The Partachian," *Ma'ariv* (1976): 13–15.

23. Dan Ben Amos, "The 'Myth' of Jewish Humor," *Western Folklore* 32, no. 2 (April 1973): 112–31.

24. Ruth R. Wisse, *The Schlemiel as Modern Hero* (Chicago: University of Chicago Press, 1971), pp. 47–49.

25. Elliott Oring, *Israeli Humor: The Content and Structure of the Chizbat of the Palmah* (Albany: State University of New York Press, 1981); Amos Elon, *The Israelis: Founders and Sons* (New York: Holt, Rinehart and Winston, 1971), p. 146.

A SELECTED CHECKLIST ON
JEWISH HUMOR

Adams, Joey, with Henry Tobias. *The Borscht Belt*. New York: Bentley Publishing Co., 1966.

Adler, Bill, ed. *Jewish Wit and Wisdom*. New York: Dell Publishing Co., 1969.

Adler, Bill, and Jeffrey Feinman. *Woody Allen: Clown Prince of American Humor*. New York: Pinnacle Books, 1975.

Adler, Hermann. "Jewish Wit and Humor." *The Nineteenth Century* 33 (1893): 457–69.

Adler, Jerry, with Pamela Abramson and Susan Agrest. "Joan Rivers Gets Even with Laughs." *Newsweek* (October 10, 1983): 59.

Allen, Steve. *The Funny Men*. New York: Simon and Schuster, 1956.

———. *Mark It and Strike It, An Autobiography*. New York: Holt, Rinehart and Winston, 1960.

Allen, Woody. *Getting Even*. New York: Random House, 1971.

———. *Side Effects*. New York: Random House, 1980.

———. *Without Feathers*. New York: Random House, 1972.

Altman, Sig. *The Comic Image of the Jew: Explorations of a Pop Culture Phenomenon*. Rutherford, NJ: Fairleigh Dickinson University Press, 1971.

"Analyzing Jewish Comics." *Time* 112 (October 2, 1978): 76.

Appel, John J. "Jews in American Caricature: 1820–1914." *American Jewish History* 71 (September 1981): 103–18.

Ausubel, Nathan, ed. *A Treasury of Jewish Folklore*. New York: Crown Publishers, 1948.

———. *A Treasury of Jewish Humor*. New York: Doubleday and Co., 1951.

Ben-Amos, Dan. "The 'Myth' of Jewish Humor." *Western Folklore* 32, no. 2 (1973): 112–31.

Benny, Mary Livingstone. *Jack Benny*. New York: Doubleday and Co., Inc., 1978.

Berger, Phil. *The Last Laugh: The World of the Stand-up Comics*. New York: Ballantine Books, 1975.

Berle, Milton, with Haskel Frankel. *Milton Berle, An Autobiography*. New York: Delacorte Press, 1974.

Bermant, Chaim. *What's the Joke: A Study of Jewish Humor through the Ages*. London: Weidenfeld and Nicolson, 1986.

Blumenfeld, Gerry. *Some of My Best Jokes Are Jewish.* New York: Paperback Library, 1969.

Brandes, Stanley. "Jewish-American Dialect Jokes and Jewish-American Identity." *Jewish Social Studies* 45 (Summer–Fall 1983): 233–40.

Brode, Douglas. *The Films of Woody Allen.* Secaucus, NJ: Citadel Press, 1985.

Caesar, Sid, and Bill Davidson. *Where Have I Been? An Autobiography.* New York: Crown Publishers, Inc., 1982.

Cahn, William. *The Laugh Makers: A Pictorial History of American Comedians.* New York: G. P. Putnam's Sons, 1957.

Chandler, Charlotte. *Hello, I Must Be Going: Groucho and His Friends.* New York: Doubleday and Co., Inc., 1978.

Chotzner, J. *Hebrew Humor and Other Essays.* London: Luzac and Co., 1905.

Cohen, John, ed. *The Essential Lenny Bruce.* New York: Ballantine Books, 1968.

Cohen, Sarah Blacher. "Introduction: The Variety of Humors." In *Comic Relief: Humor in Contemporary American Literature,* edited by Sarah Blacher Cohen, 1–13. Urbana: University of Illinois Press, 1978.

———. "The Jewish Literary Comediennes." In *Comic Relief: Humor in Contemporary American Literature,* edited by Sarah Blacher Cohen, 172–86. Urbana: University of Illinois Press, 1978.

———. *Saul Bellow's Enigmatic Laughter.* Urbana: University of Illinois Press, 1974.

———. "Sex: Saul Bellow's Hedonistic Joke." *Studies in American Fiction* 2 (Autumn 1974): 223–29.

Cowan, Lore and Maurice Cowan. *The Wit of the Jews.* Nashville: Aurora Publishers, Inc., 1970.

Cray, Ed. "The Rabbi Trickster." *Journal of American Folklore* 77 (1964): 331–45.

Dickstein, Morris. "Urban Comedy and Modernity: From Chaplin to Woody Allen." *Partisan Review* 52, no. 3 (1985): 271–81.

Distler, Paul Antonie. "Ethnic Comedy in Vaudeville and Burlesque." In *American Popular Entertainment,* edited by Myron Matlaw, 90–98. Westport, CT: Greenwood Press, 1979.

Dorinson, Joseph. "Jewish Humor: Mechanism for Defense, Weapon for Cultural Affirmation." *Journal of Psychohistory* 8, no. 4 (Spring 1981): 447–64.

———. "Lenny Bruce, A Jewish Humorist in Babylon." *Jewish Currents* 35, no. 2 (February 1981): 14–19, 31–32.

Dorson, Richard M. "Jewish-American Dialect Stories on Tape." In *Studies in Biblical and Jewish Folklore,* edited by Raphael Patai, Francis L. Utley, and Dov Noy, 111–74. Bloomington: Indiana University Press, 1960.

———. "More Jewish Dialect Stories." *Midwest Folklore* 10 (1960): 133–46.

Druyanow, A. *Sefer ha-Bedihah ve-ha-Hidud* (The Book of Jokes and Wit). 3 vols. Tel Aviv: Dvir, 1963. [In Hebrew.]

Dundes, Alan. "The J.A.P. and J.A.M. in American Folklore." *Journal of American Folklore* 98 (1985): 456–75.

———. "A Study of Ethnic Slurs: The Jew and the Polack in the United States." *Journal of American Folklore* 84 (1971): 186–203.

Dundes, Alan, and Thomas Hauschild. "Auschwitz Jokes." *Western Folklore* 42, no. 4 (October 1983): 249–60.

Ehrlich, Howard J. "Observations on Ethnic and Intergroup Humor." *Ethnicity* 6 (1979): 393–98.

Fowler, Douglas. *S. J. Perelman.* Boston: Twayne Publishers, 1983.

Freud, Sigmund. *Jokes and Their Relation to the Unconscious,* translated by James Strachey. New York: W. W. Norton, 1960.

———. "On Humour." In *Character and Culture,* Sigmund Freud. New York: Coffier Books, 1963.

Fuchs, Esther. *S. Y. Agnon's Irony: Form and Meaning.* Tel Aviv: Tel Aviv University, 1986. [In Hebrew.]

Gilliatt, Penelope. "Woody Allen." In *Unholy Fools, Wits, Comics, Disturbers of the Peace,* 35–44. New York: Viking Press, 1973.

Glanz, Rudolph. *The Jew in Early American Wit and Graphic Humor.* New York: Ktav Publishing House, 1973.

Gleick, James. "Survival: The New York Joke." *New York Times Magazine* (April 28, 1985): 49, 66, 68, 70.

Gold, Herbert. "Funny Is Money." *New York Times Magazine* (March 30, 1975): 16–31.

Golden, Harry. *The Golden Book of Jewish Humor.* New York: Putnam, 1972.

Goldman, Albert. "Boy-man, *Schlemiel:* The Jewish Element in American Humour." In *Explorations,* edited by Murray Mindlin and Chaim Bermant, 3–17. London: Barrie and Rockliff, 1967.

———. "The Comedy of Lenny Bruce." *Commentary* 36 (October 1963): 312–17.

———. "The Comic Prison." *Nation* 200 (February 8, 1965): 142–44.

———. *Ladies and Gentlemen—Lenny Bruce!* New York: Random House, 1974.

———. "Mel Brooks Zaps the Movie *Schmendricks.*" In *Freakshow,* edited by Albert Goldman, 243–51. New York: Atheneum, 1971.

———. "Shaking Hands with Philip Roth." In *Freakshow,* edited by Albert Goldman, 229–42. New York: Atheneum, 1971.

———. "Sick Jew, Black Humor." In *Freakshow,* edited by Albert Goldman, 187–221. New York: Atheneum, 1971.

Goldman, Mark. "Bernard Malamud's Comic Vision and the Theme of Identity." *Critique* 7 (Winter 1964–1965): 92–109.

Grebstein, Sheldon. "The Comic Anatomy of *Portnoy's Complaint.*" In *Comic Relief: Humor in Contemporary American Literature,* edited by Sarah Blacher Cohen, 152–71. Urbana: University of Illinois Press, 1978.

Grotjahn, Martin. *Beyond Laughter.* New York: McGraw-Hill, 1957.

———. "Jewish Jokes and Their Relation to Masochism." In *A Celebra-*

tion of Laughter, edited by W. Mendel. Los Angeles: Mara Books, 1970.

Guttmann, Allen. "Jewish Humor." In *The Comic Imagination in American Literature,* edited by Louis D. Rubin, Jr., 329–38. New Brunswick, NJ: Rutgers University Press, 1973.

———. "Saul Bellow's Humane Comedy." In *Comic Relief: Humor in Contemporary American Literature,* edited by Sarah Blacher Cohen, 127–51. Urbana: University of Illinois Press, 1978.

Hentoff, Nat. "Yiddish Survivals in the New Comedy." In *Jewish-American Literature: An Anthology of Fiction, Poetry, Autobiography, and Criticism,* edited by Abraham Chapman, 690–93. New York: New American Library, 1974.

Hirsch, Foster. *Love, Sex, Death, and the Meaning of Life: Woody Allen's Comedy.* New York: McGraw-Hill, 1981.

Hoffman, Frederick J. "The Fool of Experience: Saul Bellow's Fiction." In *Contemporary American Novelists,* edited by Harry T. Moore, 80–94. Carbondale: Southern Illinois University Press, 1964.

Howe, Irving. "Entertainers and Popular Artists." In *World of Our Fathers,* 556–73. New York: Harcourt Brace Jovanovich, 1976.

Hurvitz, Nathan. "Blacks and Jews in American Folklore." *Western Folklore* 33, no. 4 (October 1974): 301–25.

Israel, Lee. "Joan Rivers and How She Got That Way." *Ms. Magazine* 13, no. 4 (October 1984): 108–14.

Jacobs, Diane. *But We Need the Eggs: Magic of Woody Allen.* New York: St. Martin's Press, 1982.

Jahr, Cliff. "No Kidding, Joan Rivers is the Queen of Comedy." *Ladies Home Journal* (November 1983): 86–90.

Janus, Samuel S. "The Great Jewish-American Comedians' Identity Crisis." *The American Journal of Psychoanalysis* 40, no. 3 (Fall 1980): 259–65.

Janus, Samuel S., Barbara E. Bess, and Beth R. Janus. "The Great Comediennes: Personality and Other Factors." *American Journal of Psychoanalysis* 38 (1978): 367–72.

Jason, Heda. "The Jewish Joke: The Problem of Definition." *Southern Folklore Quarterly* 31 (1967): 48–54.

Johnson, Robert. *Neil Simon.* Boston: G. K. Hall, 1983.

Josefsberg, Milt. *Jack Benny Show.* New Rochelle, NY: Arlington House, 1977.

Katz, Naomi, and Eli Katz. "Tradition and Adaptation in American Jewish Humor." *Journal of American Folklore* 84 (April 1971): 215–20.

Kishon, Ephraim. *New York Ain't America.* New York: Bantam Books, 1982.

Knox, Israel. "The Traditional Roots of Jewish Humor." *Judaism* 12 (1964–1965): 327–33.

———. "The Wise Men of Helm." *Judaism* 29 (Spring 1980): 187–93.

Kofsky, Frank. *Lenny Bruce: Comedian As Social Critic and Secular Moralist.* New York: Monad Press, 1974.

Kohn, J. P. and L. Davidsohn. "Jewish Wit and Humor." In *The Universal Jewish Encyclopedia,* Vol. 10, 545–47. New York: The Universal Jewish Encyclopedia, Inc., 1943.

Kristol, Irving. "Is Jewish Humor Dead?" In *Mid-Century,* edited by Harold U. Ribalow, 428–32. New York: Beechhurst Press, 1955.

Lahr, John. *Notes on a Cowardly Lion.* New York: Limelight Editions, 1984.

Landman, Salicia. "On Jewish Humour." *The Jewish Journal of Sociology* 4 (1962): 193–204.

Lang, Berel. "On the Biblical Comic." *Judaism* 11, no. 3 (Summer 1962): 249–54.

Larner, Jeremy. "The New *Schlemiel.*" *Partisan Review* 30 (Summer 1963): 273–76.

Lax, Eric. *On Being Funny: Woody Allen and Company.* New York: Woodhill Press, Inc., 1979.

Learsi, Rufus (Israel Goldberg). *The Book of Jewish Humor: Stories of Jewish Wit and Wisdom.* New York: Bloch, 1941.

Levenson, Sam. "The Dialect Comedian Should Vanish." *Commentary* 14, no. 2 (August 1952): 168–70.

———. *Meet the Folks: A Session of American-Jewish Humor.* New York: The Citadel Press, 1958.

Lewis, Anthony. "The Jew in Stand-up Comedy." In *From Hester Street to Hollywood: The Jewish-American Stage and Screen,* edited by Sarah Blacher Cohen, 58–70. Bloomington: Indiana University Press, 1983.

Macaree, D. "Study of Humorous Fiction and *The Education of H*Y*M*A*N K*A*P*L*A*N.*" *English Journal* 57 (March 1968): 334–38.

McGovern, Edyth M. *Neil Simon: A Critical Study.* New York: Frederick Ungar Publishing Co., Inc., 1979.

———. *Not-So-Simple Neil Simon.* Van Nuys, CA: Perivale Press, 1978.

McKnight, Gerald. *Woody Allen: Joking Aside.* New York: W. H. Allen, 1983.

Markfield, Wallace. "Yiddishization of American Humor." *Esquire* 64 (October 1965): 114, 115, 136.

Marx, Groucho. *Groucho and Me.* New York: Woodhill Press, Inc., 1978.

———. *The Groucho Letters.* New York: Woodhill Press, Inc., 1978.

———. *Memoirs of a Mangy Lover.* New York: Woodhill Press, Inc., 1978.

Marx, Maxine. *Growing Up With Chico.* Englewood Cliffs, NJ: Prentice-Hall, 1980.

Mehlman, Jeffrey. "How to Read Freud on Jokes: The Critic as *Schadchen.*" *New Literary History* 6, no. 2 (Winter 1975): 439–61.

Memmi, Albert. "The Humor of the Jew." In *The Liberation of the Jew,* edited by Albert Memmi, 43–54. New York: Orion Press, 1966.

Mendelsohn, Samuel Felix. *The Jew Laughs: Humorous Stories and Anecdotes.* Chicago: L. M. Stein, 1935.

Meryman, Richard. "Can We Talk? Why Joan Rivers Can't Stop." *McCalls* 110 (September 1983): 61–62.

Mikes, George. *Laughing Matter.* New York: Library Press, 1971.

Mindess, Harvey. "Introduction: So Here It Is—Who Needs It?" In *The Chosen People?*, edited by Harvey Mindess. Los Angeles: Nash Publishing, 1972.

Mintz, Lawrence E. "Jewish Humor: A Continuum of Sources, Motives, and Functions." *American Humor* 4 (Spring 1977): 4–6.

———. "Stand-Up Comedy as Social and Cultural Mediation," *American Quarterly* 37, no. 1 (Spring 1985): 71–80.

Niger, Shmuel. "The Humor of Sholom Aleichem." In *Voices from the Yiddish,* edited by Irving Howe and Eliezer Greenberg, 41–50. Ann Arbor: University of Michigan Press, 1972.

Novak, William, and Moshe Waldoks, eds. *The Big Book of Jewish Humor.* New York: Harper and Row, 1981.

Olsvanger, Immanuel, ed. *Röyte Pomerantsen or How to Laugh in Yiddish.* New York: Schocken Books, 1947.

Opdahl, Keith. "The 'Mental Comedies' of Saul Bellow." In *From Hester Street to Hollywood: The Jewish-American Stage and Screen,* edited by Sarah Blacher Cohen, 183–96. Bloomington: Indiana University Press, 1983.

Oring, Elliott. *Israeli Humor: The Content and Structure of the Chizbat of the Palmah.* Albany: State University of New York Press, 1981.

———. *The Jokes of Sigmund Freud: A Study in Humor and Jewish Identity.* Philadelphia: University of Pennsylvania Press, 1984.

———. "The People of the Joke: On the Conceptualization of a Jewish Humor." *Western Folklore* 42 (1983): 261–71.

Palmer, Myles. *Woody Allen: An Illustrated Biography.* New York: Charles Scribner's Sons, 1980.

Perelman, S. J. *The Best of S. J. Perelman,* with a critical introduction by Sidney Namlerep. New York: Modern Library, 1947.

———. *The Most of S. J. Perelman.* New York: Simon and Schuster, 1963.

Pinsker, Sanford. "Bernard Malamud's Ironic Heroes." In *Bernard Malamud: A Collection of Critical Essays,* edited by Leslie A. Field and Joyce W. Field, 45–71. Englewood Cliffs, NJ: Prentice-Hall, 1975.

———. *The Comedy That "Hoits": An Essay on the Fiction of Philip Roth.* Columbia: University of Missouri Press, 1975.

———. "Mel Brooks and the Cinema of Exhaustion." In *From Hester Street to Hollywood: The Jewish-American Stage and Screen,* edited by Sarah Blacher Cohen, 245–56. Bloomington: Indiana University Press, 1983.

———. *The Schlemiel as Metaphor: Studies in the Yiddish and American Jewish Novel.* Carbondale: Southern Illinois University Press, 1971.

Pollack, Simon R. *Jewish Wit for All Occasions.* New York: A. & W. Visual Library, 1979.

Prawer, S. S. *Heine's Jewish Comedy.* Oxford: Oxford University Press, 1983.

Rader, Dotson. "The Jewish Comedian." *Esquire* 84 (December 1975): 106–9, 192–99.

Reik, Theodor. "Freud and Jewish Wit." *Psychoanalysis* 2 (1954): 12–20.
———. *Jewish Wit.* New York: Gamut Press, 1962.
Richman, Jacob. *Laughs from Jewish Lore.* New York: Hebrew Publishing Co., 1926.
Rivers, Joan. *The Life and Times of Heidi Abromowitz.* New York: Delacorte Press, 1984.
Roback, A. A. "Sarcasm and Repartée in Yiddish Speech." *Jewish Frontier* 18 (April 1951): 19–25.
———. "Sholom Aleichem's Humor." *Congress Bi-Weekly* 26, no. 6 (March 16, 1959).
Rosenberg, Bernard, and Gilbert Shapiro. "Marginality and Jewish Humor." *Midstream* 4, no. 2 (Spring 1958): 70–80.
Rosten, Leo. *The Joys of Yiddish.* New York: McGraw-Hill, 1972.
———. *Treasury of Jewish Quotations.* New York: McGraw-Hill, 1972.
Rovit, Earl. "Jewish Humor and American Life." *The American Scholar* 36 (Spring 1967): 237–45.
Samuel, Maurice. *The World of Sholom Aleichem.* New York: Schocken Books, 1943.
Sandrow, Nahma. "A Little Letter to Mama: Traditions in Yiddish Vaudeville." In *American Popular Entertainment,* edited by Myron Matlaw, 90–98. Westport, CT: Greenwood Press, 1979.
Schlesinger, Kurt. "Jewish Humour as Jewish Identity." *International Review of Psycho-Analysis* (1979): 1–14.
Shechner, Mark. "Philip Roth." *Partisan Review* 41, no. 3 (1974): 410–27.
———. "Woody Allen: The Failure of the Therapeutic." In *From Hester Street to Hollywood: The Jewish-American Stage and Screen,* edited by Sarah Blacher Cohen, 231–44. Bloomington: Indiana University Press, 1983.
Sheffer, Isaiah. "You Don't Have to be Jewish." *Midstream* 13 (February 1967): 58–62.
Shohet-Me'iri, Haviva. *On Laughter in Israeli Literature.* Tel Aviv: Sifriat Poalim, 1972. [In Hebrew.]
Shulman, Robert. "The Style of Bellow's Comedy." *PMLA* 83 (March 1968): 109–17.
Siegel, Ben. "Saul Bellow and Mr. Sammler: Absurd Seekers of High Qualities." In *Saul Bellow: A Collection of Critical Essays,* edited by Earl Rovit, 122–34. Englewood Cliffs, NJ: Prentice-Hall, 1975.
———. "Victims in Motion: Bernard Malamud's Sad and Bitter Clowns." In *Recent American Fiction: Some Critical Views,* edited by Joseph J. Waldmeir, 203–14. Boston: Houghton Mifflin, 1963.
Simmons, Donald C. "Protest Humor: Folkloristic Reaction to Prejudice." *American Journal of Psychiatry* 120 (1963): 567–69.
Simon, Ernst. "Notes on Jewish Wit." *Jewish Frontier* 15 (1948): 41–44.
Smith, Joe. "Dr. Kronkhite Revisited." In *American Popular Entertainment,* edited by Myron Matlaw, 127–31. Westport, CT: Greenwood Press, 1979.
Sochen, June. "Fanny Brice and Sophie Tucker: Blending the Particular with the Universal." In *From Hester Street to Hollywood: The Jewish-

American Stage and Screen, edited by Sarah Blacher Cohen, 44–57. Bloomington: Indiana University Press, 1983.

Spalding, Henry D. *Jewish Laffs.* New York: Jonathan David Publishers, Inc., 1982.

———. *The Treasure-Trove of American Jewish Humor.* New York: Jonathan David Publishers, Inc., 1976.

———. *Encyclopedia of Jewish Humor.* New York: Jonathan David Publishers, Inc., 1969.

Walden, Daniel. "Neil Simon's Jewish-style Comedies." In *From Hester Street to Hollywood: The Jewish-American Stage and Screen,* edited by Sarah Blacher Cohen, 152–66. Bloomington: Indiana University Press, 1983.

Ward, J. A. "The Hollywood Metaphor: The Marx Brothers, S. J. Perelman, and Nathaniel West." *The Southern Review* 12 (July 1976): 659–72.

Weisberger, Ron. "Where Have All the *Schlemiels* Gone?" *Cultural Correspondence* 8 (Fall/Winter 1978): 22–27.

Whitfield, Stephen J. "Jules Feiffer and the Comedy of Disenchantment." In *From Hester Street to Hollywood: The Jewish-American Stage and Screen,* edited by Sarah Blacher Cohen, 167–82. Bloomington: Indiana University Press, 1983.

———. "Laughter in the Dark: Notes on American-Jewish Humor." *Midstream* (February 1978): 48–58.

Wilde, Larry. *The Last Official Jewish Joke Book.* New York: Pinnacle Books, 1980.

———. *More of The Official Jewish/Irish Joke Book.* New York: Pinnacle Books, 1979.

———. *The Official Jewish/Irish Joke Book.* New York: Pinnacle Books, 1974.

Williams, M. "Comedy of Lenny Bruce." *Saturday Review* 45 (November 24, 1962): 60–61.

Wisse, Ruth R. *The Schlemiel as Modern Hero.* Chicago: University of Chicago Press, 1971.

Yacowar, Maurice. *In Method Madness: The Comic Art of Mel Brooks.* New York: St. Martin's Press, 1981.

———. *Loser Takes All: The Comic Art of Woody Allen.* New York: Frederick Ungar Publishing Co., Inc., 1979.

Ziv, Avner, ed. *Jewish Humor.* Tel-Aviv: Papyrus Publishing House at Tel-Aviv University, 1986.

NOTES ON CONTRIBUTORS

ROBERT ALTER is Professor of Hebrew and Comparative Literature at the University of California at Berkeley. He is the author of two volumes of essays on modern Jewish writing, *After the Tradition* and *Defenses of the Imagination*. He has also written books on Stendhal, Fielding, and the European novel, and two studies of biblical literature, *The Art of Biblical Narrative* and *The Art of Biblical Poetry*.

JOSEPH BOSKIN, Professor of History at Boston University, is an expert on racial humor. He is the author of *Humor and Social Change in 20th Century America* and the co-author of the article "Ethnic Humor: Subversion and Survival." He has also written a book on humor stereotyping, *Sambo: The Rise and Demise of an American Jester*.

MAURICE CHARNEY is Distinguished Professor of English at Rutgers University. He is the author of *Comedy High and Low* and editor of *Comedy: New Perspectives*. In other areas he has published *Shakespeare's Roman Plays, Style in "Hamlet", How to Read Shakespeare, Sexual Fiction,* and a critical study of Joe Orton.

SARAH BLACHER COHEN, Professor of English at the State University of New York at Albany, is the author of *Saul Bellow's Enigmatic Laughter*. She is the editor of *Comic Relief: Humor in Contemporary American Literature* and *From Hester Street to Hollywood: The Jewish-American Stage and Screen*. Currently, she is the General Editor of the SUNY Press Series, Modern Jewish Literature and Culture.

ALAN COOPER chairs the Department of English at York College, CUNY, where he is the founder and co-director of "Rewrite," a national grammar hotline. His articles on contemporary Jewish literature and Victorian literature have appeared in

242

The New York Times, Newsday, The New Leader, Commentary, and *Library Journal.*

ESTHER FUCHS is Associate Professor of Hebrew Literature and Coordinator of the Hebrew Program at the University of Arizona at Tucson. She is the author of *Encounters with Israeli Authors, No License to Die: Fiction and Poetry* (in Hebrew), and *Cunning Innocence: On S.Y. Agnon's Irony* (in Hebrew). Her forthcoming books are, *Israeli Mythogynies: Women in Contemporary Hebrew Literature, Sexual Politics in the Biblical Narrative: Towards a Feminist Hermeneutics of the Hebrew Bible,* and *Hidden Laughter: The Comic Aspects of S. Y. Agnon's Writings* (in Hebrew).

ALBERT GOLDMAN has written two best-selling biographies, *Elvis* and *Ladies and Gentlemen, Lenny Bruce.* His other books include *The Mine and the Mint: Sources for the Writings of Thomas DeQuincey, Freakshow,* and *Gig and Other Scenes from the Counter-Culture.*

MICHAEL GREENSTEIN is Associate Professor of English at the University of Sherbrooke, Quebec. His many articles on Canadian literature have been published in *Mosaic, Essays on Canadian Writing, Canadian Literature,* and other journals. He has recently completed a book-length study of Canadian-Jewish literature.

IRVING HOWE is Distinguished Professor of English at the Graduate Center of the City University of New York and at Hunter College. His books include *The Critical Point, Decline of the New, Steady Work, Thomas Hardy, Politics and the Novel, William Faulkner, Sherwood Anderson,* and *World of Our Fathers.* He is the Editor of *Dissent.*

GERALD MAST is Professor of English and General Studies in the Humanities at the University of Chicago. His books on film include *A Short History of the Movies, The Comic Mind: Comedy and the Movies, Film/Cinema/Movie,* and *Howard Hawks, Story-Teller.*

SANFORD PINSKER is Professor of English and Chairman of the Department at Franklin and Marshall College. A critic and poet, his books include *The Schlemiel as Metaphor, Between Two Worlds: The American Novel in the 1960's, The Comedy That "Hoits": An Essay on the Fiction of Philip Roth, Still Life and Other Poems,* and *Conversations with Contemporary American Writers.*

MARK SHECHNER, Professor of English at the State University of New York at Buffalo, is the author of *Joyce in Nighttown: A Psychoanalytic Inquiry into Ulysses.* His essays and reviews appear regularly in *Partisan Review, Salmagundi,* and *The Nation.* One of his recent books is *After the Revolution: Studies in the Contemporary Jewish Imagination.*

MEYER WIENER (1893–1941) held the chair of Yiddish Language and Literature in the Jewish sector of the Kiev Pedagogic Institute from 1928 to 1931. Besides writing novels and short stories in Yiddish on historical themes, Wiener's major achievement is his two-volume study, *Toward the History of Yiddish Literature in the Nineteenth Century.*